A Book Of

RESEARCH METHODOLOGY

For
MPM Semester - I
As Per Pune University's New Syllabus
Effective from June 2013

Dr. Kirti Gupta
M. Sc. (Statistics), M.P.M.
Ph.D. (Management)
Professor, Head Ph.D Research Centre
Bharati Vidyapeeth Deemed University's
Institute of Management & Entrepreneurship Development
Pune.

Advancement of knowledge

RESEARCH METHODOLOGY – MPM : (Sem. - I) ISBN 978-93-83525-54-6
First Edition : September 2013
© : **Author**

The text of this publication, or any part thereof, should not be reproduced or transmitted in any form or stored in any computer storage system or device for distribution including photocopy, recording, taping or information retrieval system or reproduced on any disc, tape, perforated media or other information storage device etc., without the written permission of Author with whom the rights are reserved. Breach of this condition is liable for legal action.

Every effort has been made to avoid errors or omissions in this publication. In spite of this, errors may have crept in. Any mistake, error or discrepancy so noted and shall be brought to our notice shall be taken care of in the next edition. It is notified that neither the publisher nor the author or seller shall be responsible for any damage or loss of action to any one, of any kind, in any manner, therefrom.

Published By :	Printed By :
NIRALI PRAKASHAN Abhyudaya Pragati, 1312, Shivaji Nagar, Off J.M. Road, PUNE – 411005 Tel - (020) 25512336/37/39, Fax - (020) 25511379 Email : niralipune@pragationline.com	Repro Knowledgecast Limited, Thane

DISTRIBUTION CENTRES
PUNE

Nirali Prakashan
119, Budhwar Peth, Jogeshwari Mandir Lane
Pune 411002, Maharashtra
Tel : (020) 2445 2044, 66022708, Fax : (020) 2445 1538
Email : niralilocal@pragationline.com

Nirali Prakashan
S. No. 28/27, Dhyari,
Near Pari Company, Pune 411041
Tel : (020) 24690204, Fax : (020) 24690316
Email : bookorder@pragationline.com

MUMBAI
Nirali Prakashan
385, S.V.P. Road, Rasdhara Co-op. Hsg. Society Ltd.,
Girgaum, Mumbai 400004, Maharashtra
Tel : (022) 2385 6339 / 2386 9976, Fax : (022) 2386 9976
Email : niralimumbai@pragationline.com

DISTRIBUTION BRANCHES

NAGPUR
Pratibha Book Distributors
Above Maratha Mandir, Shop No. 3, First Floor,
Rani Jhanshi Square, Sitabuldi, Nagpur 440012,
Maharashtra, Tel : (0712) 254 7129

JALGAON
Nirali Prakashan
34, V. V. Golani Market, Navi Peth, Jalgaon 425001,
Maharashtra, Tel : (0257) 222 0395
Mob : 94234 91860

BENGALURU
Pragati Book House
House No. 1, Sanjeevappa Lane, Avenue Road Cross,
Opp. Rice Church, Bengaluru – 560002.
Tel : (080) 64513344, 64513355,
Mob : 9880582331, 9845021552
Email:bharatsavla@yahoo.com

KOLHAPUR
Nirali Prakashan
New Mahadvar Road,
Kedar Plaza, 1st Floor Opp. IDBI Bank
Kolhapur 416 012, Maharashtra. Mob : 9855046155

CHENNAI
Pragati Books
9/1, Montieth Road, Behind Taas Mahal, Egmore,
Chennai 600008 Tamil Nadu, Tel : (044) 6518 3535,
Mob : 94440 01782 / 98450 21552 / 98805 82331, Email : bharatsavla@yahoo.com

RETAIL OUTLETS
PUNE

Pragati Book Centre
157, Budhwar Peth, Opp. Ratan Talkies,
Pune 411002, Maharashtra
Tel : (020) 2445 8887 / 6602 2707, Fax : (020) 2445 8887

Pragati Book Centre
676/B, Budhwar Peth, Opp. Jogeshwari Mandir,
Pune 411002, Maharashtra
Tel : (020) 6601 7784 / 6602 0855

Pragati Book Centre
Amber Chamber, 28/A, Budhwar Peth,
Appa Balwant Chowk, Pune : 411002, Maharashtra,
Tel : (020) 20240335 / 66281669
Email : pbcpune@pragationline.com

PBC Book Sellers & Stationers
152, Budhwar Peth, Pune 411002, Maharashtra
Tel : (020) 2445 2254 / 6609 2463

MUMBAI
Pragati Book Corner
Indira Niwas, 111 - A, Bhavani Shankar Road, Dadar (W), Mumbai 400028, Maharashtra
Tel : (022) 2422 3526 / 6662 5254, Email : pbcmumbai@pragationline.com

www.pragationline.com info@pragationline.com

Preface ...

The subject of **Research** is of relevance and importance for businesses and managers alike. Knowledge of research methodology and business research helps a business researcher in decision making.

This book **Research Methodology** has been written as per the revised syllabus of University of Pune effective from June 2013. The book covers topics on foundations of research, problem identification and formulation, research design, qualitative and quantitative research, measurement and attitude scaling techniques, types of data, sampling and analysis of data. A unique feature of the book is the simple language and structured organisation of the matter. It has been written keeping in mind the direct approach to learning of the concepts. As per the requirements of the new pattern of evaluation, students will find this book extremely useful for brief and to the point explanations.

I take this opportunity to earnestly thank the Hon'ble Chancellor Dr. Patangraoji Kadam, Vice Chancellor, Prof. Dr. Shivajirao Kadam and Secretary, Hon'ble Vishwajeet Kadam of Bharati Vidyapeeth Deemed University for their motivation and encouragement.

I place on record my sincere thanks to the Shri Dinesh Bhai Furia and Mr. Jignesh Furia of Nirali Prakashan for giving me this valuable opportunity.

I would also like to thank the production team of Nirali Prakashan namely Nirja Sharma, Prachi Mantri, Ilyas Shaikh, Chaitali Takale and Ravindra Walodare and all other staff members for their valuable efforts and support in the completion of this book.

Any suggestions for improvement are most welcome.

Kirti Gupta

Syllabus ...

1. Foundations of Research
Meaning, Objectives and Concept of theory - Deductive and Inductive theory. Characteristics of scientific method - Understanding the language of research - Concept, Construct, Definition, Variable. Research Process

2. Problem Identification and Formulation
Management Question - Research Question - Investigation Question - Measurement Issues. Hypothesis – Qualities of a good hypothesis - Null hypothesis and Alternative hypothesis. Hypothesis testing - Logic and importance.

3. Research Design, Qualitative and Quantitative Research
Concept and importance in research - Features of a good research design - Exploratory Research Design - Concept, types and uses, Descriptive Research Designs - Concept, types and uses. Experimental Design - Causal relationships, Concept of independent and dependent variables, concomitant variable, extraneous variable, treatment, control group, Qualitative research - Quantitative research - Concept of measurement, causality, generalisation and replication. Merging the two approaches.

4. Measurement and Attitude Scaling Techniques
Concept of measurement - What is measured? Problems in measurement in management research - Validity and Reliability. Levels of measurement - Nominal, Ordinal, Interval, Ratio. Attitude Scaling Techniques: Concept of Scale - Rating Scales viz. Likert Scales, Semantic Differential Scales, Constant Sum Scales, Graphic Rating Scales - Ranking Scales - Paired Comparison and Forced Ranking.

5. Types of Data Sampling and Analysis of Data
Secondary Data - Definition, Sources, Characteristics, Primary Data - Definition, Advantages and disadvantages over secondary data, Observation method, Questionnaire construction, Personal interviews, Telephonic interview, Mail survey, Email/Internet survey.
Sampling: Concepts of Statistical Population, Sample, Sampling frame, Sampling error, Sample size, Non-response. Characteristics of a good sample. Probability sample - Simple random sample, Systematic sample, Stratified random sample and Multi-stage sampling. Non probability sample - Judgment, Convenience, Quota and Snowballing methods. Determining size of the sample - Practical considerations in sampling and sample size.
Data Analysis: Data preparation - Univariate analysis (frequency tables, barcharts, pie charts, percentages), Bivariate analysis - Cross tabulations and Chi-square test including testing hypothesis of association.

Contents ...

1. Foundations of Research	1.1 – 1.28
2. Problem Identification and Formulation	2.1 – 2.16
3. Research Design, Qualitative and Quantitative Research	3.1 – 3.34
4. Measurement and Attitude Scaling Techniques	4.1 – 4.26
5. Types of Data, Sampling and Analysis of Data	5.1 – 5.100
Multiple Choice Questions	M.1 – M.6
Case Studies	C.1 – C.6
Projects/Tasks/Activities	P.1 – P.4

Chapter 1...

Foundations of Research

Contents ...

Introduction
1.1 Research
    1.1.1 Definition
    1.1.2 Why Study Business Research?
    1.1.3 What is Good Research?
1.2 Concept of Theory – Deductive and Inductive Theory
    1.2.1 Deductive Research Theory
    1.2.2 Inductive Research Theory
1.3 Concept of Scientific Enquiry
    1.3.1 Research and the Scientific Method
    1.3.2 Characteristics of Scientific Method
1.4 Understanding the Language of Research - Concepts, Constructs, Definitions, Variables and Measurement
1.5 Research Process
    1.5.1 Steps in Research Process
    1.5.2 Research Applications in Functional Areas of Business
    Points to Remember
    Questions for Discussion

Learning Objectives

- To understand the concept of research
- To grasp the significance of research in various aspects of business, trade and government
- To know the concept of scientific enquiry
- To comprehend the key elements involved in drafting a research proposal

Introduction

In the present century, the business environment is characterised by complex nature of operations. Decision makers are faced with a challenge of taking decisions against various constraints and hence require a reliable supply of information and tools for arriving at optimal feasible solutions. It is in this context that the study of research assumes great importance to a manager. This chapter discusses the concept of research as applicable to the business environment. It guides the reader through the basics of business research and its applications to functional areas of business and management. Concepts of Scientific enquiry, the research process and the research proposals are also dealt with in detail.

> Mr. Narang plans to start a fast food joint in a posh and busy locality of a city. This locality is marked with presence of many educational institutes and corporate offices. He is faced with many questions in his mind:
> - Who would be the potential customers?
> - What would be their tastes and preferences for various food items?
> - Who are the competitors for this business?
> - How should the implementation be done?
> - What are the anticipated challenges? etc.

> Mr. Joshi is the manager of a bank at Tilaknagar branch. Of late, he is faced with irate customers most of the times approaching him with difficulties and complaints. In spite of resolving the issues as and when they arise, he wants to find out the cause of such situations and the solutions thereof. He approaches a consultant Mr. Jason and asks for assistance in this matter. How should Mr. Jason proceed?

> Aspi Haveliwala, the manager of the newly opened Ozone Mall is interested in finding out the feedback from the visitors to the mall regarding the different facilities and outlets at the mall. He is interested in ensuring the maximum enjoyment and satisfaction for the visitors to the mall. But the problem is that he is in need of a proper plan to carry out the exercise and derive proper and important inputs for improvement.

To answer such, and many other questions arising out of the above contexts Mr. Narang, Mr. Joshi and Mr. Aspi have to carry out an exercise of conducting a thorough study on the above situations. The knowledge of research, business research methods and process would certainly help to understand and tackle issues in business and management.

1.1 Research

The world today is experiencing tremendous advancements in all walks of life. To keep pace with the resultant dynamic changes and challenges, the advanced nations are increasingly earmarking huge amounts of money and resources for undertaking research activities. Competitive business environment and the increasing cost of poor decisions drive the need for research to provide sound information. The objective of a given research may be either to gain new insights or for adding to existing knowledge and/or for problem solving.

Pure research enables contribution to frontiers of knowledge; whereas applied research aims at the use of this knowledge for solving different social, economic or other problems faced by individuals, business houses or any other entity.

1.1.1 Definition

The term 'research' pertains to a 'search for facts'. It refers to a careful and exhaustive investigation of a given phenomenon/subject with a definite objective of attaining or enhancing one's knowledge level. In other words, it conveys a sense of deep and purposeful study through scientific and scholarly investigation. It may be accomplished with the help of study, observation, comparison, and experiments. In short, research is a process whereby, one gains knowledge about any phenomenon – natural or human.

Some definitions of the term 'Research'

- "Research is the systematic and objective analysis and recording of controlled observations that may lead to development of generalisation, principles, or theories resulting in prediction and perhaps ultimate control of events". — **John W Best**
- "Research is a method of studying, analysing, and conceptualising social life in order to extend, modify, correct or verify knowledge, whether that knowledge aids in construction of theory or in practice of an art." — **P. V. Young**
- "Research is the process which includes defining and refining problems, formulating hypothesis or suggested solutions; collecting, organising and evaluating data; making deductions and reaching conclusions, and at last, carefully testing the conclusions to determine whether they fit the formulating hypothesis". — **Clifford Woody**
- "Research is a careful, patient, systematic, diligent enquiry or examination in some field of knowledge undertaken to establish facts or principles."
  — **Webster's Twentieth Century Dictionary**
- "Research is a systematic controlled, commercial and critical investigation of hypothetical propositions about the presumed relations among natural phenomenon."
  — **Kerlinger**
- Over the Internet, 'Research' means Scholarly or scientific investigation or inquiry or close, careful study.

  Or

  "To study (something) thoroughly so as to present in a detailed, accurate manner".
- "Research is an attempt to increase the sum of what is known, usually referred to as 'a body of knowledge', by the discovery of new facts or relationships through a process of systematic inquiry, the research process".
  — **Macleod Clark and Hockey 1989 as cited by Cormack 1991 p4**

- *"It is a systematic and objective attempt to study a problem for deriving general principles."*
- *"Research is a systematic investigation to find solutions to a problem".* – **Robert Burns**

In other words, research refers to any original and systematic investigation undertaken in order to increase knowledge and to establish facts and principles. It is an organised and systematic activity and may lead to new and improved insights, development of new products and processes. Thus, research is an 'organised' and 'systematic' way of finding answers to questions or finding solutions to problems. Research is said to be systematic because, it involves the following of definite set of steps in order to arrive at some conclusion. Also, it is said to be organised, as it is a planned procedure which is focused and having a well-defined scope, i.e., it has a structure and method. Research is aimed at finding answers – maybe to simple questions or for some hypothesis. It is said to be successful when answers are found. Lastly, questions constitute the main component of research because if there is no question, then, it follows that there can be no research. This is so, since the dynamics of research invariably involves the process of focusing on relevant, useful and important questions. The questions for the same may originate from management dilemma.

To sum up, research may be termed as "systematic, controlled, empirical and critical investigation of hypothetical proposition". It is a scientific undertaking, which, by means of a logical and systematic techniques aims to:

- To discover new facts or verify and test old ones.
- To analyse their sequences, inter-relationships and causal explanations.
- To develop new scientific tools, concepts and theories which would facilitate reliable and valid study of human behaviour.

Purpose of Research

Research may be undertaken with the following purposes; to describe, to explain, understand, foresee, criticise, and/or analyse already existing knowledge or phenomenon in social sciences.

- To minimise risks.
- To save time and money during start-up.
- To learn where and how to sell the product and/or service.
- To learn where and how to produce and distribute the product and/or service.
- To determine what it will cost to run the business and how to plan to cover costs.

Motivations in Research

It would be worthwhile to note what motivates a person to undertake a research activity? Some of the factors that lead to research are:

(i) **Curiosity of the Unknown**: Curiosity is a common trait of a human being right from one's childhood. It applies equally insofar as unearthing new facts or embarking on a quest for knowledge goes. In short, the aforesaid curiosity factor inspires a researcher to undertake research activity.

(ii) **Intellectual Delight:** At times, people carry out research to satisfy one's own attainment of intellectual joy or satisfaction.

(iii) **Requirement of Curriculum:** A person desiring to acquire a research degree carries out research in his/her chosen field. Also, students of different courses are required to undergo training in carrying out research projects as part of their degree curriculum requirements.

(iv) **Sudden or Unusual Developments:** At times, sudden changes in the environment, namely, social or business motivate a person to take up the research activity to find answers to situations, such as, sudden crisis occasioned due to the global depression etc.

(v) **Search for Cause and Effect Relationship:** Scientific investigations aimed at discovering cause and effect relationships between variables also leads to research activity.

(vi) **Research for Service to Society or for Gaining Respectability in Society:** The pursuit of research may be undertaken for serving the society by addressing social issues as also to gain respectability in society.

(vii) **Research as Part of Research Organisations:** As part of a research team of any research organisation, one may be involved in research projects undertaken by the organisation to address various issues.

Business research is the systematic gathering, recording, and analysis of information regarding issues concerning business. It is undertaken in the areas of business operations so as to aid in better managerial decision making. Business research includes the analysis and evaluation of important areas of business. Business research is very important for a number of people like businessmen, students studying business, business researchers, entrepreneurs and investors.

Business Research refers to the process of planning, obtaining, and recording, analysing and disseminating relevant data, information and insights to decision makers so as to enable organisations to take appropriate actions and thereby enhance their business performance.

Business research is an important management activity that helps companies determine which products will be most profitable for companies to produce. It helps the management to gain important, accurate, and current information and hence aid in decision making. Business research refers to study carried out when starting or running any kind of business and aims at confirming the competitors or identifying target customers.

For example, starting any type of business would invariably require one to carry out research into not only one's target customer base but also *vis-à-vis* one's competition in order to come up with an effective business plan. The process of conducting research into existing businesses helps one to stay tuned to the latest consumer demand. Small business research begins with researching an idea and a name and continues with research based on customer demand and other businesses offering similar products or services. All business research is done with an objective to gather cutting edge information – information that could play a decisive role in a given company's success.

Alternatively, customer research may involve the finding out of both the customer's feelings and experiences on using a given company's product or service. The methods used to gauge customer satisfaction may, include, questionnaires, interviews or seminars. Also, business research comes in handy insofar as providing useful information for investors. In this regard, the tools of research and statistics help identify where an investment is likely to pay off. Large or small business research can also help a given company to analyse its strengths and weaknesses by learning what customers are looking for in terms of products or services it is offering. Then, a company can use the business research information to adjust itself to better serve its customers, gain a competitive edge over competition and thereby ensure its success. Thus, Business research is used to identify, potential markets and the needs of each and how these needs can be met.

Every viable business is born from some form of business research. Why? Because you can't start something without figuring out whether it is first possible and second probable. Conducting business research provides the opportunity to take a step back and really look at the idea from all angles. Something such as checking whether or not a trademark or patent exists on an idea can be conducted in less than five minutes over the Internet. Even during times when the economy is struggling, businesses understand that a good research and development strategy is vital to the continued success of the operation.

Business research needs to be done in order to gain enough knowledge about a particular subject so that the right decision can be made about it and a better strategy can be formulated. Business research may arise from a collaborative project or individual project or by an external agency (industry, government, semi-government body, commercial organisation etc.) or may follow on from a specific request from an external agency for a research project to be undertaken. Business research has identified aims and objectives as well as project milestones, and often involves commercial outcomes. Like all research, it involves potential innovation and risk.

For example, if a marketer is facing decline in the sales of the product and conducts business research on "Impact of packaging and shelf positioning on impulse buying behaviour of consumers". This research will show that why consumers go for impulse buying and how marketers can get benefit by offering attractive packaging and locating products on the front shelves. A research on business ethics may be "Business ethics and sales risks" or for the new start ups the topic can be "How to write a business plan".

Business research methods vary depending on the size of the company and the type of information needed. For instance, customer research may involve finding out both a customer's feelings about and experiences using a product or service. The methods used to gauge customer satisfaction may be questionnaires, interviews or seminars. Researching public data can provide businesses with statistics on financial and educational information in regards to customer demographics and product usage, such as the hours of television viewed per week by people in a certain geographic area. Business research used for advertising purposes is common because marketing dollars must be carefully spent to increase sales and brand recognition from ads.

Some of the areas of conducting business research are shown in Fig. 1.1.

Fig. 1.1: Business Research Areas

1.1.2 Why Study Business Research?

Business research serves a number of purposes. Entrepreneurs use research to make decisions about whether or not to enter a particular business or to refine a business idea. Established businesses employ research on aspects such as whether they can succeed in a new geographic region, to assess competitors or select a marketing approach for a product.

Whether a business is just starting out or has been well established over an extended period of time, doing business research helps executives to make proper decisions on running the company. Research allows the potential business the knowledge if the proposed business is too narrow or wide in scope. It also offers feedback regarding what product or services might be in the highest demand, thus raising the possibility of a successful business venture.

Research helps to answer various questions like:
- From who are your competitors to where they are located, their region of influence, their products and prices, their manufacturers, distributors, partners and customers.
- Business research creates an intricate picture of the world of your competition that will enable you to identify opportunities and gaps in the market, potential partnerships and the international playing field that you are entering.
- Understanding the quality and price of your competitors' products and learning how they portray and promote themselves is vital information that will help you to develop more effective strategies for the growth of your business in India.
- Business research can go even deeper and identify key players - why they buy, sell, distribute or manufacture what they do, and in doing so provide you with all the information one needs to maximise your prospects in the marketplace.

The two main types of Business Research is basic research which is the fundamental research drive by scientist curiosity. The motivation behind it, is to expand his knowledge and the second one is applied research which is designed to solve practical problems, rather than to gain knowledge.

1.1.3 What is Good Research?

Every research must adhere to certain characteristics so as to be recognised as good research. A good research study must possess the following characteristics:

(i) **Have a Clearly Stated Purpose:** The study must have a clearly stated purpose in the form of objectives stated, along with precise definition of the scope and domain of the study. The variables and constructs being investigated should be clearly and precisely defined. Only relevant details need be covered and studied.

(ii) **It should be Systematic:** A good research is a structured process which entails a series of steps to be followed. There should be a systematic and detailed plan specifying clearly the sources of data, sample representativeness, etc. along with the sequentially linked research plan.

(iii) **Logical:** A good research is based on logical treatment of the principles of induction and deduction. The techniques of data collection, sampling plans and data analysis tools must be supported by logical justification.

(iv) **Objectivity:** The results of the study must be presented in an unbiased and objective manner. The researchers own judgements, biases and feelings should not be revealed or stressed upon, while making recommendations from findings.

(v) **Ethical:** The research study must conform to the highest ethical standards at every stage.

(vi) **Empirical:** Good research is based on real data that provides validity to the research results.

(vii) **Replicable:** A good research is characterised by the fact that the study may be replicated so as to build firm conclusions. This means that the study carried out in a structured, ethical, logical and objective manner must be so reliable that if a similar study is carried out under similar constraints and conditions, then it should be able to reveal similar results.

(viii) **Controlled:** In a good research activity, the variables are identified and controlled in order to achieve best results.

Components of Research

In every research activity, there are four components, each having its own sphere of interest. These components are, namely,

(a) the researcher: one who conducts the research,
(b) research sponsor: one who pays for the research,
(c) research participant(s): one who replies to questions and, finally the,
(d) research consumer: one who uses the findings of the research.

Objectives of Research

Every research study is undertaken with certain aims which guide the entire study. It may be undertaken with the following objectives:

(i) To extend knowledge of human beings, social life and environment.
(ii) To bring out useful information.
(iii) To establish generalisations.
(iv) To verify and test existing facts and theory.

(v) To make reliable predictions of events yet to happen.
(vi) To analyse inter-relationships between variables.
(vii) To develop new tools, concepts and theories for better study of unknown phenomenon.
(viii) To aid planning and hence help national development.

To summarise, good research is systematic, logical, empirical and replicable.

1.2 Concept of Theory – Deductive and Inductive Theory

While pursuing any research study it is important to identify the appropriate nature of research approach to be used. There are mainly two types of research approaches/theories which allow to explain, interpret, defend, challenge, and explore - deductive and inductive or Deduction and Induction. The inductive deductive theory refers to reasoning efforts, abilities or logic by humans in testing hypothesis.

1.2.1 Deductive Research Theory

This approach allows a researcher to establish a hypothesis based on theory. Then appropriate data is collected to confirm or reject the hypothesis. Hence the steps of using deductive approach are development of theory, hypothesis, observation through data and information and confirmation. It is a basic form of valid reasoning. In deductive reasoning, if something is true of a class of things in general, it is also true for all members of that class. For example, "All men are mortal. Ramesh is a man. Thus, Ramesh is mortal." For deductive reasoning to be sound, the hypothesis must be correct and logical. Deductive theory works from the more general to the more specific. At times it is informally called a "*top-down*" approach. This theory is more narrow in nature and concerned with testing or confirming hypothesis.

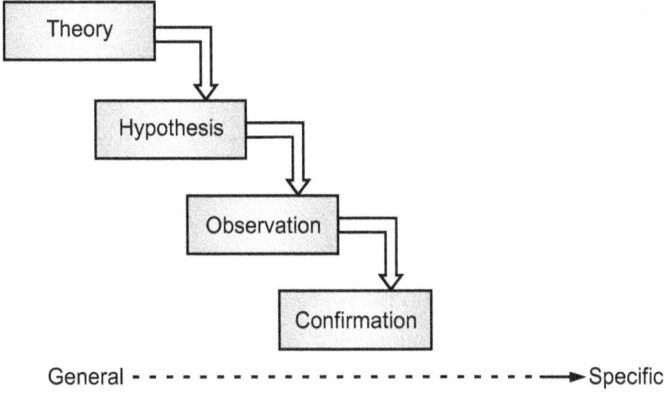

Fig. 1.2 : Deductive Approach (Trochim 2011)

Another example of deductive approach may be seen from these set of statements:

Hari leaves for work in his car at eight o'clock every day. Every day, the drive to work takes 45 minutes and he arrives to work on time. Therefore, if Hari leaves for work at eight o'clock today, he will be on time.

The deductive statement above is a perfect logical statement that relies on the initial premise being correct.

1.2.2 Inductive Research Theory

Inductive approach is the opposite of deductive approach. It makes broad generalizations from specific observations. In this approach, the researcher begins with specific observations and measures, attempts to detect patterns and regularities, formulates tentative hypotheses, and finally ends with some general conclusions or theories.

Even if all of the premises are true in a statement, inductive reasoning allows for the conclusion to be false. For example "Ramesh is a grandfather. Ramesh is weak. Therefore all grandfathers are weak". The conclusion does not follow logically from the statements. Inductive reasoning, by its very nature, is more open-ended and exploratory, especially at the beginning, it works in moving from specific observations to broader generalisation and theories. It is often referred to as *"bottom up"* approach.

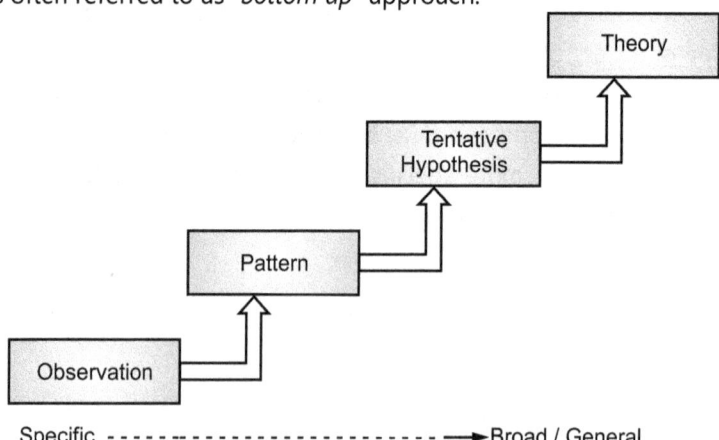

Fig. 1.3 : Inductive Approach (Trochim 2011)

An example of inductive reasoning can be seen in this set of statements: Today, Hari left for work at eight o'clock and arrived on time. Therefore, every day that Hari leaves the house at eight o'clock, he will arrive to work on time.

Inductive reasoning is not always logically valid because it is not always accurate to assume that a general principle is correct. In the above example, perhaps 'today' is a weekend with less traffic, so if you left the house at eight o'clock on a Monday, it would take longer and Hari would be late for work. Hence, it is illogical to assume an entire premise just because one specific data set seems to suggest it.

Deductive Research Theory vs Inductive Research Theory

Deductive	Inductive
Allows to establish theory – hypothesis - data – confirm hypothesis.	Begins with specific observations and measures - detect patterns /regularities tentative hypotheses ends with some general conclusions or theories.
Works from more general to specific.	Moves from specific to broader generalisations/theories.
Narrow in nature as concerned with testing or confirming hypothesis.	More open ended and exploratory.
Often referred as "Top Down" approach.	Often referred as "Bottom Up" approach.

1.3 Concept of Scientific Enquiry

Scientific enquiry is the act of systematically observing, inducing, deducing, testing and finally evaluating a science based testing procedure. It is then compared to previous findings and documented for later research works. Scientific enquiry is considered to have no biased conclusions.

Scientific Enquiry is a systematic method researchers use to obtain sufficient relevant information that can then be analysed and utilised to answer a question or solve a problem. This step-by-step process is a universally recognised and adhered to investigative approach that ensures consistency of implementation across fields of study and objects of inquiry. Inevitably, every question will lead to new questions because the material that has been accumulated builds upon previous material obtained and developed, thus resulting in progress occurring in an incremental fashion.

> **Formulation of Research Problem**
> **Management Question**
> **Research Question**
> **Investigation Question**

These guidelines for scientific inquiry may also be applied in a business, where data must be interpreted and then serve as a basis for decision making by managers. Having a structured formal protocol to follow in order to arrive at answers to questions helps control and thereby minimises the effects of emotional gut feelings and cognitive biases that may not accurately reflect the situation. Managers that consistently apply these steps can more confidently expect to arrive at correct conclusions over the long-term because they can more effectively analyse arguments for and against decisions.

1.3.1 Research and the Scientific Method

Research using the scientific method is a process that moves an idea from hypothesis to theory. The scientific method is the backbone of all rigorous scientific inquiry and consists of a set of techniques and principles designed to advance scientific inquiry and further the accumulation of knowledge.

The **scientific method** is a body of techniques for investigating phenomena, acquiring new knowledge, or correcting and integrating previous knowledge wherein the method of inquiry must be based on empirical and measurable evidence subject to specific principles of reasoning.

The **Oxford English Dictionary** defines the scientific method as: "*a method or procedure that has characterised natural science since the 17th century, consisting in systematic observation, measurement, and experiment, and the formulation, testing, and modification of hypotheses.*"

Scientific enquiry is generally intended to be as objective as possible in order to reduce biased interpretations of results. Another basic expectation is to document, archive and share all data and methodology so they are available for careful scrutiny by other scientists, giving them the opportunity to verify results by attempting to reproduce them.

The steps of the scientific method are to:
- Ask a Question
- Do Background Research
- Construct a Hypothesis
- Test Your Hypothesis by Doing an Experiment
- Analyse Your Data and Draw a Conclusion
- Communicate Your Results

1.3.2 Characteristics of Scientific Method

(i) **It is a systematic and critical investigation into a phenomenon:** Research is a systematic investigation since it is carried out in an organised manner for critically viewing all the dimensions of a given phenomenon so as to unravel the hitherto unknown useful facts. All this calls for great amount of planned activity. In other words, reproducing something that is already found or stated cannot be termed as research.

(ii) **It adopts scientific method:** Research requires to be carried out scientifically, meaning that it has to be based on systematic inter-relation of facts. The terms of research and scientific method are closely related. The scientific method refers to pursuit of truth as determined by logical considerations that may be achieved through experimentation, observation, logical arguments or a combination of all the above.

(iii) **Well-defined:** A research has to start off with a clearly defined problem with objectives and research design in place.

(iv) **It is objective and logical:** A research is carried out in an objective manner without any biases or prejudices of whoever is involved in the entire process. A research needs to be free from all biases; otherwise it will not be relevant and useful. This is so, since only logically drawn conclusions can give meaningful insights into the phenomenon under study.

(v) **It is based on experience and evidence:** Good research calls for expert and accurate investigation for which the researcher needs to be well versed with the required tools of research methodology. A researcher should be experienced enough to differentiate and thereby identify what is known and unknown from the mass of data available in his chosen field of work.

(vi) **Research aims to find answers to questions and solutions to problems:** A good research always aims to find answers to significant questions and solutions to key problems which may aid in formulating further policies or decision making or, for understanding something in more detail.

(vii) **Research is based on factual observations, quantified and recorded data:** A good research requires that actual information and observations be properly collected, quantified and recorded. No speculations must be made to ensure unbiased work.

Research Methods and Research Methodology

Just as method refers to the technique used to collect data on empirical results, research methods are all those methods / techniques that are used to conduct the process of research. On the other hand, methodology refers to the logic of scientific investigation. It denotes describing, explaining and justifying the methods of research and not the methods themselves. Research methodology can be perceived as a science of studying how research is done scientifically or pick out the rules for reasoning, i.e., a specific logic to acquire insights. Research methodology has many dimensions and research methods constitute a part of research methodology. Examples: survey method, experimental method, case study method, statistical method, and so on.

The scope of research methodology is wider than that of research methods. It is an important tool in a researcher's tool bag. Hence, research methodology, refers not only to the research methods but also to the logic behind the methods used in a given research study. In short, research is closely related to finding, selecting, structuring and solving problems.

1.4 Understanding the Language of Research - Concepts, Constructs, Definitions, Variables and Measurement

Measurement is at the core of any research activity. It involves conceptualisation and operationalisation of concepts and constructs. The challenge is to convert the concepts into concrete terms that can be measured.

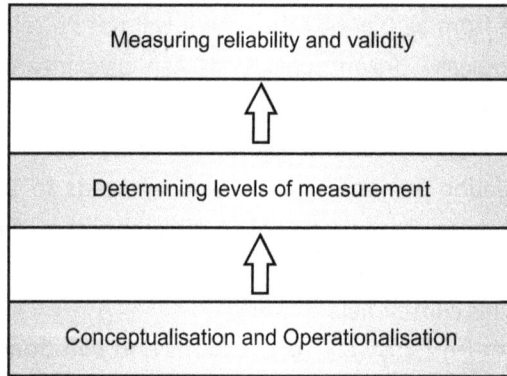

Fig. 1.4: Steps in Measurement

Concepts and Constructs
Concepts

Defining concepts is very important in research. Concepts are the mental representations and based on experience. Concepts vary from abstract to concrete and need to be defined carefully. If the concept is more abstract, then it is less obvious and needs to be defined more carefully. Whereas, when a concept is more concrete then it is easier to communicate the meaning.

Considerations while defining the concepts
1. Keep clear definitions: use simple words to give clear definitions.
2. Define appropriately and consistently. At times researchers define a concept just for the sake of giving a new definition when one may already be existent.
3. Base definitions after a thorough literature review.
4. Avoid circular definitions

Constructs

A researcher may come across situations to measure things which may be directly observable (height, weight etc), indirectly observable (questionnaire of gender, age etc) or in the form of constructs. Constructs are theoretical creations based on observations but cannot be seen directly or indirectly, for example IQ, satisfaction etc. Constructs are developed through logical combination of a number of observable concepts.

Measurement

Measurement refers to assigning symbols or numbers to observable facts or occurrences. These may be of two kinds: constants and variables. Also, while measuring counting, ordering or classifying may be used.

Variables

Concepts or constructs that are free to vary are variables, otherwise they are constant.

Definitions of Variables: In order to enable measurement of variables, they need to be defined. Definitions of Variables may be of two types:
- **Theoretical Definition:** Dictionary or common usage words used in theory.
- **Operational Definition:** Explaining how the variable is to be measured. This involves giving more meaning to a concept or variable by stating the operations needed to measure it. Operational definitions may be those that can be directly measured i.e. weight, IQ etc. or those that need to be measured through experiments like frustration in children, behavior of children etc.

Independent and Dependent Variables

Every research except for descriptive research must have at least two variables. Variables may be independent or dependent. Independent variables allow for examining the cause-effect relationship and also allow more control and better inference about their impact.

Levels of Measurement of Variables

Nominal (qualitative)	- Naming / Classifying - Only counting operation possible
Ordinal	- Ordered on some dimension - Boolean operations possible
Interval (quantitative)	- Equal interval - Addition, subtraction and Boolean operations
Ratio (Quantitative)	- Ordered - Equal intervals - Absolute and meaningful zero - All mathematical operations possible

1.5 Research Process

Training in research methodology imparts to the learner the necessary skills required to gathering materials, conducting field work, using statistical tools etc., and instil confidence to even take up research as a career in any field where research is required. Also, it enables intelligent decision making and analysis of situations in daily life, thereby enabling a person to have the ability to look at life objectively. Hence, it is helpful in personal as well as professional development of a person.

1.5.1 Steps in Research Process

The research process or methodology is the approach to the entire study, it is the master plan. Irrespective of the research being conducted, there are several fundamental stages one has to go through. Since research is a scientific process it can be carried out systematically in a sequence of steps as described below.

A typical research process includes:

1. Selection of problem.
2. Review of existing research and theory (when relevant).
3. Development of hypotheses or research questions.
4. Determination of appropriate methodology/research design.
5. Collection of relevant data.
6. Analysis and interpretation of the results.
7. Presentation of the results in appropriate form.
8. Replication of the study (when necessary).

The Process of Research

Generally, research is understood to follow a certain structural process. Though the step order may vary depending on the subject matter and researcher, the following steps are part of most formal research, both basic and applied:

1. Defining the Research Problem

Every research begins with a question. Intellectual curiosity is often the foundation for scholarly inquiry. For embarking on research study, the problem under study needs to be clearly specified. A well defined problem goes a long way in ensuring the success of the research.

Therefore, a research problem must be identified and defined without any ambiguity. If a researcher proceeds with ill-defined problems, the researcher may end up with misleading conclusions or aborting the research project in between due to improper knowledge about the study.

For defining the research problem, the researcher should study the present literature like books and journals, available in the field with an interdisciplinary perspective to base his research topic on some reliable background. It should also concentrate on the relevance of the present research with the past works. In short, a research problem may be arrived at by one or more of the following:

- Critical evaluation of current literature
- Shortlisting topics of new research
- Extending and generalising results
- For improvement of Process, Operational, Management etc.

The features of a good research problem are:

(i)   Significance
(ii) Originality
(iii) Feasibility

A research problem must cover the following aspects clearly:

(a) The specification of the unit of analysis for the study.
(b) The identification of particular units within the scope of study.
(c) The specification of the kind of information sought concerning those units.
(d) The time dimension for the study.

Defining a research problem provides a format for further investigation. Since, there are a wide variety of techniques for the researcher to choose from, a well-defined problem points to a method of investigation.

What topics interest me? What about this topic interests me most?

Specifically, what do I want to know? What is the purpose of asking this question? What will the answer tell me? Can this question be answered through research? (Can I describe how I might answer it?)

2. Statement of Research Objectives

Defining the goals and objectives of a research project is one of the most important steps in the research process.

Objectives explain what the researcher aims to achieve through the research. The objectives should also explain the extent to which the research work is related to the specific field. Clearly stated goals keep a research project focused. The process of goal definition usually begins by writing down the broad and general goals of the study. As the process continues, the goals become more clearly defined and the research issues are narrowed.

In the process of identifying objectives of the research, the researcher must finalise the research questions, hypotheses and boundary or scope of the study.

3. Review of Literature

It is important for the researcher to review existing literature so as to understand the basis of research. This may be through:
- Reviewing the research work in the field.
- Surveying the existing books available in the field.
- Reviewing other published literature like articles, journals, reports, conference proceedings etc.

By reviewing the earlier works, the researcher is in a position to finalise the focus of his research study.

The literature review is especially important because it prevents the need to reinvent the wheel for every new research question. More importantly, it gives researchers the opportunity to build on each others' work.

4. Formulation of Hypothesis

A hypothesis is simply the investigator's belief about a problem. Typically, a researcher formulates an opinion during the literature review process. The process of reviewing other scholar's work often clarifies the theoretical issues associated with the research question. It also can help to elucidate the significance of the issues to the research community.

The hypothesis is converted into a null hypothesis in order to make it testable. "The only way to test a hypothesis is to eliminate alternatives of the hypothesis." (Anderson, 1966, p.9).

5. Research Design

Once the objectives of the research are identified and defined clearly, the next stage is to prepare the research design – a blueprint for the research. Research design can be thought of as the structure of research, rather, research design provides the 'glue' that holds the research project together.

The research design provides a complete guideline for data collection, selection of research approach, determining the sample design and design of experiment. It is used to structure the research, to show how all of the major parts of the research project the samples or groups, measures, treatments or programs, and methods of assignment work together to try to address the central research questions.

A research design should cover:

(a) Which method of research should be adopted?

(b) How many observations should be made on each study and when?

(c) What method of sampling is to be used?

6. Sampling

For a researcher, it is very important to clearly define the target population i.e., the sample. So, the next step is to decide about the sampling procedure to be used for selection of sample from the population. There are a wide variety of sampling methods available and the appropriate one is to be chosen as per the requirement of the study.

7. Collection of Data

Data are the basic inputs to any decision making process in a business. Basic concepts such as environment in which data is to be collected, designing of instruments for data collection and recording should be defined. Data may originate from two sources – namely, primary and secondary. Primary data can be collected through experiment or through survey. In the case of surveys, however, the researcher can adopt one or more of the following ways to collect data:

- By observation.
- Through personal interview.
- Through telephonic interview.
- By mailing of questionnaires.
- Through schedules.

The collection phase must also consider the ways of increasing responses, proper training of personnel etc. This phase needs to be well planned and supervised. Decision is to be made regarding what the type of questions would be like, whether open-ended or checks responses? The number of alternatives given, and out of these how many could be selected single or multiple, etc. Careful wording of questions is necessary, like:

- Do you use brand X?
- Do you regularly use brand X?
- Have you ever used brand X?
- Is brand X your favourite brand?

The data collection plan i.e., questions, instruments and procedures must be appropriate. The data collection plan must be properly implemented.

Also, possibility of using secondary data should be considered because it would lead to an immediate availability and saving in cost terms. But secondary data if used must be carefully scrutinised for errors and relevancy before use. The secondary data are collected from sources which have already been created for the purpose of first-time use and future use. The secondary data can be obtained from internal sources and external sources. The internal sources of secondary data for marketing applications are sales records, marketing activity, cost information, distributor reports, feedback and customer feedback. The different external sources of secondary data are government publications, foreign government publications, journals, publications of trade associations, books, magazines, newspapers, annual reports, research reports in universities etc.

Data collected needs to be analysed and the various analytical techniques should be decided beforehand and data should be collected keeping in mind these techniques.

8. Analysis of Data and Testing of Hypothesis

After data are collected, proper tools and techniques should be used for classification and analysis of data. For this, the data collected are processed in order to analyse and summarise the results. Also, special care should be taken to avoid understatement or overstatement of various characteristics.

First the data should be processed to make it suitable for analysis. The bulk data should be compressed into a few manageable groups and tables for further analysis. This can be done using:

- Editing
- Coding
- Classification
- Tabulation

The researcher can analyse the collected data by using various statistical measures through:

- Univariate analysis
- Bivariate analysis
- Multivariate analysis

Hypothesis Testing: After analysing the data, the researcher should test the hypothesis, if any. He should check if the facts support the hypothesis or happen to be contrary. The analysis of data after data collection yields a set of results either in the form of statistics, regression equations, identification of significant factors or in the form of acceptance or rejection of different hypothesis.

9. Interpretation of Results

In interpretation, the researcher presents an explanation in a systematic manner. This is the "so what?" of results. Research results must have relevance for the decision to be made. Results must be interpreted also recommendations be given. Results should be in as simple a manner as possible.

The real value of any research work lies in its ability to arrive at certain generalisations. In the generalisations process, the researcher draws inferences or generally accepted conclusions from the data collected.

10. Report Writing

This is the concluding or last step of research, where the researcher has to prepare the report of what study has been done by him.

The research process may be summarised as follows:

Selection of Problem Area
↓
Acquaintance with Current Theory and Knowledge in the Area
↓
Definition of the Problem
↓
Statement of Objectives
↓
Review of Literature
↓
Development of Hypothesis
↓
Development of Formal Argument
↓
RESEARCH DESIGN
↓
Definition of the Resources of Data
↓
Creation of Instruments (Questionnaires, Scales, Recording devices)
↓
Writing a Dummy Argument
↓
Pre-test of the Instruments and Possible Revision
↓
Formal / Systematic Acquisition of Data
↓
Processing of Data
↓
Analysis of Data
↓
REPORT WRITING
↓
Formal Write-up of Conclusions reached

1.5.2 Research Applications in Functional Areas of Business

Importance of Research in Business and Management

The attributes of practical problem solving and decision making are becoming more and more common to research. Both economic and marketing researches are amongst the commonly undertaken activities in medium and large-scale companies as most of the decision making here is based on research. Research in business studies is not much different from practical problem solving. The managers need to have some knowledge and evaluation capabilities to understand the consequences of their decisions. Hence, more and more firms and managers are using research as a tool to gain competitive edge over others.

Research in Functional Areas of Management

With each passing day, research is gaining more and more importance in the field of management. In almost all the areas of management, a deeper understanding of the problems and sound decision making is required. Here, research plays a decisive role in enabling the process of decision making. For example, in the field of financial management, research plays a very important role.

Financial Management

It is one of the most pivotal functional areas of management, as the effectiveness of a business enterprise significantly depends on the efficient utilisation of its financial resource. The shareholders provide capital to a company with the expectation of earning a competitive rate of return from their investment and if this expectation is not fulfilled, they may have to sell their shares which may push down the market price of the company's stock, thus jeopardising its ability to raise additional financial resources in the capital market. Hence, it is of utmost importance to efficiently manage the finances of the company concerned. These and other such questions that are often faced by the managers in their day-to-day activities make it an imperative for them to be well-versed with the potentials of research in management functions and areas.

Production and Materials

The research carried out for the production department and processes has, as its objective, namely, to help enable the production manager in taking various decisions. It helps to determine - what to produce, when to produce, how much to produce, besides ensuring quality control and optimum inventory level. That apart, it aims to frame suitable policies as regards - where to buy, how much to buy, when to buy and at what price to buy?

Banking and Insurance

The banking sector carries out extensive research activities to study the different aspects of banking so as to help them introduce newer products in the market, increase the customer satisfaction towards the banks etc. That apart, it aims to make in-depth studies on economic conditions of business, planning and management reporting activities.

Also, the insurance sector is a growing sector of the economy and needs various studies to indicate the performance of the different plans introduced in the market, to study the future products which can attract more customers etc.

Human Resource Development

The aim of research in the field of HRM is to aid in Human Resource Planning and to understand the relationships between personnel variables. It may involve the study of wage rates, incentive schemes, cost of living, employee turnover rates, employment trends, performance appraisal etc. The purpose may be to find solutions to questions, such as:
- What increases employee performance the most; punishment for poor performance, or rewards for good performance?
- What are the traits that distinguish good managers from bad managers?
- What psychological/personality characteristics are most compatible with a sales job?
- How can we predict whether a prospective employee will steal from the company?
- Why is there so much turnover/attrition in the information technology sector?
- Why is morale of employees so low?
- Collecting basic information about employees, such as, what are their outside interests?
- Analysing data already available in the organisation, such as, salaries, in order to identify and correct inequalities (e.g., male employees making more money than female employees in similar positions; or salespeople in one division making more than salespeople in another division with comparable performance).

The ultimate goal of basic personnel research is to provide a complete understanding of human behaviour in the context of organisations so that employees would be happier and more productive, and the organisation more successful.

Government Sectors

Research forms the foundation of all government policies, insofar as the formulation of namely, annual union finance budget, railway budget, economic planning, besides ensuring optimum allocation of resources, and for collecting relevant and important information. Research serves as a major instrument for supporting policy formulation and planning in the different government sectors.

Marketing

Marketing research is the research that companies do to study the consumers and other companies. Marketing research seeks to understand the best ways to connect a consumer and a product, with the hopes that the consumer will buy. Marketing research involves the process of systematic data collection, compilation, analysis, interpretation of data for marketing research about issues related to marketing products and services. It involves evaluating the current marketing already being done for a product, or similar products that are created by the same company, and determining how well the marketing campaigns are working. This also involves studying the marketing techniques of other companies.

Examples: Demand forecasting, consumer buying preferences, measuring advertising effectiveness, media selection, test marketing, product positioning, new product potential etc. Market research is concerned specifically with markets whereas marketing research deals with the entire marketing process.

Marketing research may be divided into two categories, namely:
- Consumer marketing research, and
- Business-to-business (B2B) marketing research.

The goal of marketing research is to provide the facts and direction that managers need to make important marketing decisions. Some areas of marketing research are:

Advertising Research	Product Research	Consumer research	Sales Research	Corporate Research
Advertisement effectiveness studies	Competitive product studies	Panel research	Sales analysis tests	Trend analysis
Media research	Product testing	Diary research	Marketing distribution channel studies	Forecasting
Readership surveys	Concept testing	Consumer profile	Market analysis	Pricing studies
Motivation surveys	Positioning studies	Consumer Behaviour	Market potential	Product mix studies
	Packaging research	Prospecting	Sales research	Environmental analysis
	Brand profile			Consumer studies
				Corporate image

Research in Marketing may be useful for:

Marketing Decision regarding	Research on
Target Markets	Sales, market size; demand for product, customer characteristics, purchase behaviour, customer satisfaction, website traffic.
Product	Product development; package protection, packaging awareness; brand name selection; brand recognition, brand preference, product positioning.
Distribution	Distributor interest; assessing shipping options; online shopping, retail store site selection.
Promotion	Advertising recall; advertising copy testing, sales promotion response rates, sales force compensation, traffic studies (outdoor advertising), and public relations media placement.
Pricing	Price elasticity analysis, optimal price setting, discount options.
External Factors	Competitive analysis, legal environment; social and cultural trends.
Other	Company image, test marketing.

Research Approaches

Research is a very challenging task especially so since it involves voluminous data and dynamic situations. The researcher has to be very judicious in deciding where to begin? What is the next step? What are the sources of information?

Research may be considered as addressing the following broad areas of business research questions:

General Questions to consider:
- What is the issue?
- Who does it impact?
- What are the challenges?
- Is there another solution?
- What are the country's size, location, population, capital, and natural resources?
- Are its political climate and regulatory environment favourable toward business?
- What about the country's major economic drivers?
- What are the most important investment trends in the country?

Research on Companies and Organisations
- How does the company compare with others of its size and industry?
- How is the company managing critical issues and trends? Is its strategy sound?
- How does the company communicate with all of its stakeholders? (customers, investors, employees, the media)
- How does its future look? Are you optimistic about its future?

Research on Industries and Products
- What does the industry do/produce?
- What are the most critical issues and emerging trends currently driving this industry?
- Who are the major players in this industry?
- How have technology, globalisation and competition affected this industry?

Research on Economic and Financial Data
- Production and trade of goods and services
- GNP (Gross National Product) and GDP (Gross Domestic Product)
- Imports and exports
- Financial and equity markets
- Money supply
- Interest rates for saving or lending
- Foreign exchange rate
- Stock market indexes
- Price indexes and consumption patterns
- Consumer and wholesale price indexes
- General consumption of products and services
- Housing market
- Labour and employment

- Labour force characteristics
- Employment and unemployment
- Trade union membership
- Income and wages
- Income levels and poverty rates
- Wages and compensation

Research on Demographics and Consumers
- Who are my potential customers? (Age, gender, income, marital or family status, race or ethnicity).
- Where are my potential customers? (Geography, industry, supply chain).
- What are the current consumption patterns? (Expenditures, frequency, brands, distribution channels).
- What new products or services might be suggested by demographic changes?

Research in Decision making

Research is an important part of a business' decision making process, especially when it comes to major structural changes or new product lines. This is because it's often less difficult for a business to replicate past successes than it is to develop an entirely untested approach. Even highly innovative companies rely on extensive information about consumer needs, market trends and management practices when developing a business strategy. In some cases, an effective business manager must also be able to recognise some of the weaknesses of research and rely on her own experience or intuition to guide decisions.

Shortcomings of Research

While research is highly useful to guide business decisions, managers should use it with an awareness of potential weaknesses. Many errors can arise in the research process. For example, if a problem is inaccurately stated in a particular study, the questions researchers ask may not be relevant to the business' actual challenges. In another situation, the variables researchers are able to examine may not actually be useful for making conclusions. It is important to remember that research is often only as good as the data available, and that it must sometimes be used with caution.

Points to Remember
- The term 'research' pertains to a 'search for facts'.
- It refers to a careful and exhaustive investigation of a given phenomenon/subject with a definite objective of attaining or enhancing one's knowledge level.
- Research is the systematic and objective analysis and recording of controlled observations that may lead to development of generalisation, principles, or theories resulting in prediction and perhaps ultimate control of events.
- A research may be undertaken with the following purposes; to describe, to explain, understand, foresee, criticise, and/or analyse already existing knowledge or phenomenon in social sciences.

- While pursuing any research study it is important to identify the appropriate nature of research approach to be used. There are mainly two types of research approaches/theories which allow to explain, interpret, defend, challenge, and explore - deductive and inductive or Deduction and Induction.
- Research using the scientific method is a process that moves an idea from hypothesis to theory. The scientific method is the backbone of all rigorous scientific inquiry and consists of a set of techniques and principles designed to advance scientific inquiry and further the accumulation of knowledge.
- **A typical research process includes:**
  1. Selection of a problem.
  2. Review of existing research and theory (when relevant).
  3. Development of hypotheses or research questions.
  4. Determination of appropriate methodology/research design.
  5. Collection of relevant data.
  6. Analysis and interpretation of the results.
  7. Presentation of the results in appropriate form.
  8. Replication of the study (when necessary).
- The attributes of practical problem solving and decision making are becoming more and more common to research. Both economic and marketing researches are amongst the commonly undertaken activities in medium and large-scale companies as most of the decision making here is based on research.
- Research in business studies is not much different from practical problem solving. The managers need to have some knowledge and evaluation capabilities to understand the consequences of their decisions. Hence, more and more firms and managers are using research as a tool to gain competitive edge over others.

Questions for Discussion

1. Define Research and discuss its applications to managerial decision making.
2. State the objectives and characteristics of research.
3. Discuss the role of research in functional areas of business.
4. Name and briefly discuss the steps of research process.
5. Define scientific method and state its characteristics.
6. What do you understand by 'objectivity' and 'reproducibility' in research?
7. Discuss Deductive and Inductive theory.
8. Explain the terms 'construct' and 'concept' giving suitable examples.
9. Discuss the variables and attributes in research.

Chapter 2...

Problem Identification and Formulation

Contents ...
Introduction
2.1 Identification of Research Problem
    2.1.1 Sources of the Research Problem
    2.1.2 Formulation of Research Problem
    2.1.3 Requisites of a Good Research Problem
    2.1.4 Statement of the Research Problem
2.2 Management Questions – Research Questions – Investigation Questions
    2.2.1 Management Questions
    2.2.2 Research Questions
    2.2.3 Investigative Questions
2.3 Measurement Questions
2.4 Hypothesis and its Testing
Points to Remember
Questions for Discussion

Learning Objectives
- To understand the critical issues involved in identifying and formulating a research problem
- To know the importance of hypothesis and the method of stating a research hypothesis

Introduction

For solving any managerial dilemma or conducting research into a business problem, it is very important to understand the different dimensions of the problem so as to clearly define it. A well defined research problem is just like saying "Well begun is half done". Also, statement of the research hypothesis plays a very key role in giving directions to the research study. This chapter deals with these two important aspects viz problem formulation and hypothesis statement and testing.

2.1 Identification of Research Problem

Identification of a research problem is the first and foremost step in scientific method for conducting research.

Defining and formulating a research problem is an important and basic function of the researcher. The whole building of research work is based on the "Research Problem". It is observed that many research activities fail only because of not selecting and formulating the research problem systematically and logically. If the research problem is not well defined, subsequent inquiries will prove to be irrelevant and the researcher will be left groping in the dark.

2.1.1 Sources of the Research Problem

A research problem may originate from various sources, such as:
1. Daily problems / personal experiences
2. Technological changes
3. Theory of one's own interest
4. Unexplored (Unknown) Area
5. Discussion with supervisor or Research Guide
6. Literature

1. Daily Problems: A research problem may be selected on the basis of the daily experiences of the researcher. The intelligence of the researcher is important in identifying and translating his daily experiences and challenges into an appropriate research problem.

2. Technological Changes: Technological changes impact the society and are constantly bringing up new problems and new opportunities for the research. The impact of a changed technology on the existing socio-economic setup always interests the researcher and inspires him to undertake such studies which reveal the impact of new technology on the existing system.

3. Theory of One's Own Interest: A researcher may select a problem for investigation from an area of his interest. In such situations the researcher must have thorough knowledge of that theory and should be sufficiently inquisitive to explore some unexplained aspects or assumptions of that theory.

4. Unexplored Areas: A research problem can also be selected from those areas which have not been explored so far. Such areas may be theoretical or empirical in nature.

5. Discussion with the Research Guide: The research guide must provide all resources, needed at the time and the student should be directed to proceed along on proper lines wherever necessary. The research guide is expected to advise and encourage the students to successfully pursue the research.

6. **Literature:** During the literature review, one often comes across summaries and reviews that help to narrow down the research problem, but some studies have suggestions regarding next-step studies that can be conducted and involve a logical extension of the present study. As per the interest of the researcher, these may be considered for further formulation.

Identifying the research problem is indicating a specific area for answering some research questions. The selection and formulation of a research problem is one of the primary steps and also the most important step in the research planning process. Selection of an appropriate research problem helps the researcher to proceed methodically in his work. A properly selected research problem solves half the problems of research. The proper selection of a topic has various advantages and boosts the morale of the researcher.

2.1.2 Formulation of Research Problem

Although the problem is identified in a broader perspective, it needs to be defined specifically in terms of what is to be researched. It is important to define the problem in a precise manner. A well-defined problem gives the researcher a proper direction for carrying out investigation. It also helps in utilising the resources provided for the research effectively. A researcher can focus his efforts on collecting relevant information, if the problem is defined properly. Some research problems such as conducting a survey on the newspaper, reading habits of a given sample of the population can be clearly defined. But if a company wants to define a research problem such as declining sales, it is needed to define the research problem further through exploratory research. At the end of this process the researchers should be clear about what type of information needs to be gathered and how the research process should proceed. Once the research problem is identified and clearly defined, a formal statement containing the research objectives must be developed. In the social sciences, the research problem establishes the means by which you must answer the "So What?" question. The "So What?" question refers to a research problem surviving the relevancy test (the quality of a measurement procedure that provides repeatability and accuracy). Note that the "So What" is question requires a commitment on your part to not only show that you have researched the material, but that you have thought about its significance.

To survive the "So What" question, problem statements should possess the following attributes:

- Clarity and precision identification of what would be studied, while avoiding the use of value-laden words and terms,
- Identification of overarching an or comprehensive question and key factors or variables,

- Identification of key concepts and terms,
- Articulation of the study's boundaries or parameters,
- Some generalisability,
- Conveyance of the study's importance, benefits, and justification [regardless of the type of research, it is important to address the "so what" question and to demonstrate that the research is not trivial],
- No use of unnecessary jargon and,
- Conveyance of more than the mere gathering of descriptive data providing a snapshot.

Research Problem Formulation

The selection of a suitable topic for research is in many ways the most difficult task. The selection of a topic for research requires commitment of the researcher's time and efforts in a particular direction. There should be no hurry in deciding on the topic, or in defining its scope.

After having selected the problem carefully, the researcher must state the problem clearly. The problem to be investigated must be defined unambiguously so that the researcher will remain on the right track. Defining a research problem requires systematic handling. The purpose is to understand how and why things happen. Research relates to questions to be answered, such as 'what is the size of the market?' and 'what is the effect (if any) of our advertising effort?' The research problem must be defined unambiguously and requires intelligence on the part of the researcher.

To answer a research problem one must be able to answer the following two questions:
- What is the problem?
- How should I proceed in order to solve the problem?

The general mistake most researchers make is to go ahead with the 'data collection' activities and other 'practical' activities before perceiving the problem.

Steps in defining a research problem

The following steps may be followed in defining a problem properly:

1. Statement of the problem in a general way: First, the research problem may be stated in a broad way and general way regarding a practical concern or some scientific or intellectual interest. For this, the researcher must thoroughly understand the area of study and also undertake a pilot survey at this stage. He may define the problem in a general way only and seek opinion of some guide or expert person in the field who will help him to focus on a particular aspect or narrow down the scope so as to rephrase the problem in operational terms. While stating the problem the feasibility aspect should also be kept in mind.

2. Understanding the nature of the problem: Next, one needs to understand the origin and nature of the problem clearly in terms of the general environment within which the problem is to be studied and understood. This may be done by discussing with someone who has earlier worked on similar lines and have a good knowledge of the nature of problem involved.

3. Surveying the available literature: All available literature on the topic must be surveyed and examined before the final formulation of the problem. This requires that the researcher must be aware and well versed with the relevant development in the field of research. He must spend enough time on studying the recent works carried out in the area of his research and extensive literature review will help him identify the gaps, if any, in the study which can be further pursued.

The main purpose of the literature review is to structure the research problem and to position the study. It helps to frame the problem under scrutiny properly. Hence, literature review is important because it helps:

- To frame the problem under scrutiny.
- To identify relevant concepts, methods / techniques and facts.
- To position and study.
- To suggest useful lines of approach.
- To identify the relevant analytical shortcomings.

4. Developing the ideas through discussions: Whatever insights the researcher has gathered till now, he can discuss with his colleagues and others who have relevant experience or are working on similar problems. They can enlighten the researcher on different aspects of the proposed study. Discussing the problem with colleagues and experts helps the researcher to view the research problem from different angles and helps him to focus attention on the problem. This is also termed as experience survey. Experience survey helps to sharpen the focus of the study.

5. Rephrasing the research problem into a working proposition: Once the nature of the problem has been clearly understood, the environment has been defined, literature and experience survey conducted, then the problem should be rephrased in specific terms so that it becomes operationally viable. The time and scope dimensions should also be clearly specified. Now the researcher must state the problem in specific terms so that it becomes operationally viable and also helps in the development of a working hypothesis.

At the end of the problem formulation stage the researcher now has a clear idea about the specific problem along with the scope of the study. The environment of study and limits within which the study will be conducted will also be clear now.

In addition to the clear definition and formulation of the research problem, the following points must also be borne in mind:
- Technical terms and phrases used in the statement of the problem must be clearly defined.
- Basic assumptions (if any) relating to the research problem must be clearly indicated.
- Also the criteria for selection of the problem should be clearly indicated.
- The scope of the research study and limitations, of the study if any, must also be clearly mentioned while formulating the research problem.

2.1.3 Requisites of a Good Research Problem

Once the field of interest is narrowed down and several problems/areas for possible investigation are identified, then the following questions should be asked about the topic as to its feasibility. To ensure that the research problem is perfect to be worked upon, the following points may be ensured:
- Is it **interesting**? One must check whether the research problem is interesting enough to keep up the interest of the researcher throughout the research process.
- Is it **researchable**? Next, it needs to be verified whether the research problem can be investigated through appropriate collection and analysis of data.
- Is the problem **feasible**? It must be ensured whether it is feasible to carry out the research study on the problem specified objectives and scope.
- Is the research problem **significant**? Any research is expected to contribute to the improvement and understanding of theory and practice, hence it would be desirable to ensure whether the problem under study will make significant contributions to the body of knowledge or not.
- Is it **manageable**? Also, it should be confirmed whether the chosen research problem fits the researcher's level of research skills, needed resources, and time restrictions.
- Is it **ethical**? Very importantly, any research problem chosen for study must not embarrass or harm participants of the study.
- Is it **clear**? The very basic question one needs to ask while defining a research problem is to make sure that there is enough clarity regarding the problem definition.
- Is it **safe**? A research problem must be free of unknown hazards and dangers which may arise during the course of study.
- Hence the research problem should be a good one from the researcher point of view in terms of his level of research skills, available resources, time and resources etc.

2.1.4 Statement of the Research Problem

Many a times, the research is being funded by an interested organisation or researcher seeks to get funding for his research. Funding agencies would like to fund research problems having direct implications. No agency would like to fund a proposal that has no value. So, it is the duty of the researcher to convey to the stakeholders about the research problem in detail so that its importance is realised. Following points should be considered while designing research problem:

- A brief introduction of the problem and few relevant statistics describing the context of the problem
- Nature of the problem in terms of size, distribution and severity.
- Factors affecting the problem and proving that available knowledge is insufficient to solve it
- A brief description of solutions that have been tried, and why further research is needed
- A list of definitions of crucial concepts used in the statement of the problems

Rationale of Research Problem: He needs to justify the research problem on the following grounds:

- Is the problem current and timely? How?
- Is it critical? Does the problem have serious implications?
- Does the problem affect a large number of people?
- Does the problem have broad social, economic, political or health implications?
- Is it viewed as a concern by different people of the society?
- How many studies have already addressed the problem?

Research problems may be categorised into the following types in general:

1. **Casuist Research Problem:** Problem relating to the determination of right and wrong in questions of conduct or conscience by analysing moral dilemmas through the application of general rules and the careful distinction of special cases.
2. **Difference Research Problem:** This type of problem statement is used when the researcher compares or contrasts two or more phenomena.
3. **Descriptive Research Problem :** Underlying purpose to describe a situation, state, or existence of a specific phenomenon, typically asks the question, "what is...?"
4. **Relational Research Problem:** The underlying purpose is to investigate qualities/characteristics that are connected in some way. Suggests a relationship of some sort between two or more variables to be investigated.

2.2 Management Questions – Research Questions – Investigation Questions

Once the research problem has been identified, the researcher's job moves to the stage of thinking about the investigative questions.

2.2.1 Management Questions

The management dilemma is translated into management questions. These questions are general in nature and may be narrowed down further into specific questions. Management questions give directions to the research and are useful in exploring the system to find solutions to the problems. Management questions generally explore all the possibilities for finding solutions to the problem some of which may not be relevant to the study.

Example:

Management Dilemma – Declining sales at a retail outlet

Management questions could be –
- *Why are the profits declining?*
- *What should be done to improve sales?*
- *What should be done to increase customer satisfaction?*
- *What should be done to increase footfall in the retail outlet?*

Further the management question "What should be done to improve sales?" may be narrowed down to
- *How to improve efficiencies to reduce cost?*
- *How to increase sales to increase profit?*

2.2.2 Research Questions

- After having a clear understanding about the objectives and the management questions the researcher translates the management questions into research questions. Out of the several management questions, few are selected by the researcher for further analysis. The questions chosen should address the management dilemma and achieve the objective. Research questions are more specific than management questions. The selected management questions are examined in-depth for further investigation.
- In the above example, for the management question: "How to increase efficiency by reducing costs?" The research questions could be:
  o How can we reduce the employee cost without affecting the output?
  o How can we reduce the logistic cost without affecting the functioning of the outlet?
  o How can we reduce the infrastructure cost?

2.2.3 Investigative Questions

A general research question translated into a more specific question related to gathering information is known as an investigative question. Investigative questions are questions, the researcher must answer to satisfy and arrive at a conclusion about the research questions. Investigative questions are more specific in making a systematic inquiry or examination. Investigative questions observe the problem and inquire in detail. These need to be answered satisfactorily to arrive at conclusions and also lead to selections of proper research design. In the development of the research design, investigative questions should be included in the research proposal. In short, investigative questions are important in the research process. The researcher must answer these questions satisfactorily, because these questions are ultimately related to the findings of the research work.

- In the above research question, "How can we reduce the employee cost without affecting the output?" this can be reduced to investigative questions as,
  - *How to have appropriate balance of permanent and temporary / casual employees to improve efficiencies?*
  - *Which is the best compensation policy?*
  - *How to improve output without paying overtime/bonus?*

These questions will play an important role in building the hypothesis.

2.3 Measurement Questions

Measurement questions enable the researcher to collect specific information required for the study and help in designing the questionnaire.

For above example, the measurement questions could be,

- *How to measure the efficiency of the employee?*
- *How to measure the output of the employee?*
- *How to measure productivity?*
- *What information about the employees is required?*

Hence to trace the origin of investigative questions it is found that 'Management dilemma' generate 'Management questions'. Management questions are translated in "Research questions" and these research questions generate "Investigate questions". The skill of the researcher lies in defining and refining the problem in such a way that there is no ambiguity and all the relevant fields are clearly indicated such that further progress may not be hindered.

Research Methodology
Problem Identification and Formulation

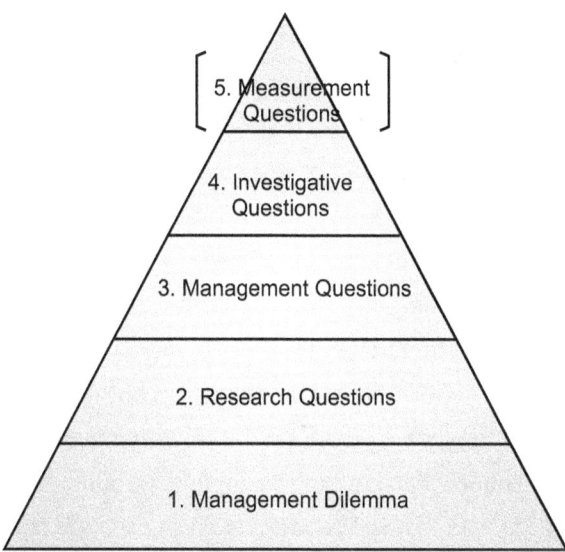

Fig. 2.1

Defining a research problem involves interrelated steps like:
1. Ascertain the decision maker's objective.
2. Understand the background of the problem.
3. Isolate and identify the problem rather than its symptoms.
4. Determine the unit of analysis.
5. Determine the relevant variables.
6. State the research questions (hypotheses) and research objectives.

2.4 Hypothesis and its Testing

Statement of the research problem provides a general direction to the study. It also includes a hypothesis. Direct knowledge about the population parameters is rare. Test of hypotheses enables us to make probable statements about the population parameters based on the sample statistics. Tests of hypotheses are used for deciding whether a sample data supports a particular hypothesis so that generalisations can be made.

Hypothesis
- A hypothesis is a proposition or probable solution to a problem, relations of two or more variables or nature of some phenomenon. It is an educated guess based on available fact.
- A predictive statement capable of being tested by scientific methods that relates an independent variable to some dependent variable. It may be understood as a mere assumption or supposition or a formal question to be resolved.
  e.g., Product A is performing as well as Product B.

Hypotheses are essential to all research studies with the possible exception of some descriptive studies whose purpose is to answer certain specific questions. The hypothesis is formulated following the review of related literature as it is based on the implications of previous research. The related literature leads one to expect a certain relationship.

A hypothesis is a tentative explanation for certain behaviours, phenomena, or events that have occurred or will occur. It is the most specific statement of the problem and states the researcher's expectations concerning the relationship between the variables in the research problem. It states what the researcher thinks the outcome of the study will be. The researcher never attempts to "prove" his or her hypothesis but rather collects data that either support the hypothesis or do not support it. Formal statements of hypotheses help the researchers to be clear about what he expects to find through the study and also gives crucial questions about the data that will be required in the analysis stage.

Thus, a hypothesis is an unproven proposition or possible solution to a problem or simply a educated guess. Hypothetical statements assert probable answers to research questions. A manager may assume that salespersons who show the highest job satisfaction will be the most productive salespersons. A purchase manager may want to decide if the proportion of defective bulbs in a shipment exceeds 3% (the manufacturer's specification).

An organisational researcher may believe that if workers' attitudes toward an organisational climate are changed in a positive direction, there will be an increase in organisational effectiveness among these workers.

Characteristics of the Hypothesis

Any hypothesis should be based on a sound rationale such that it should be a bridge between the past and future research. There are some desirable characteristics to be confirmed in a hypothesis:

1. It should be clear and precise.
2. It should be based on theory or evidence
3. It should be capable of being tested.
4. It should be stated in declarative form.
5. It should state expected relationship between two or more variables if it is a relational hypothesis.
6. It should be specific and stated in simple terms.
7. It should be consistent with known facts and previous research.
8. It must explain what it claims to explain.

Types of Hypotheses

Inductive Hypotheses: It is a generalisation based on observation and has limited scientific value.

Deductive Hypotheses: These are derived from theory and contribute to the field through evidence.

Research Hypotheses: A declarative statement of an expected relationship or difference between two variables

Statistical Hypotheses or Null Hypothesis assumes no relationship (or difference) between variables.

While a research hypothesis may be a null hypothesis, this is not very often the case. Statistical, or null, hypotheses are usually used because they suit statistical techniques that determine whether an observed relationship is probably a change relationship or probably a true relationship.

Testing of Hypothesis

Testing of hypothesis is the core of scientific research. In order to test a hypothesis, the researcher determines the sample, measuring instruments, design, and procedure that will enable her or him to collect the necessary data. Once the data is tabulated it needs to be analysed, i.e., the hypothesis stated in the problem should be verified. If the manager of a shopping mall wants to find out if customer satisfaction is at least 85 percent, we can test the validity of this hypothetical parameter by the use of hypothesis testing. Hypotheses testing enable the researcher to decide on the basis of the sample results if the deviation between the observed sample statistic and the hypothetical parameter value (or) statistic is significant (or) might be attributed to chance (or) the fluctuations of sampling.

Definitions of Hypothesis

(i) **Hypothesis:** It is a statement or assertion about the statistical distributor or parameter of statistical distribution. Alternatively hypothesis is a claim to be tested.

(ii) **Null Hypothesis (H_0) :** A hypothesis of 'no difference' is called null hypothesis. It is a statement of no change / difference / relationship. It is specifically formulated for possible rejection or nullification.

(iii) **Alternative Hypothesis (H_a or H_1):** It is a hypothesis to be accepted in case null hypothesis is rejected. In other words, a complementary hypothesis to null hypothesis is called alternative hypothesis. It is a regular hypothesis which is logical opposite of the null hypothesis.

Both null and alternate hypothesis are expressed in terms of population parameters and not sample statistics. During testing of hypothesis, sample results are likely to vary leading to sampling error. A decision rule is needed to enable to accept or reject a hypothesis.

Statistical Significance

Every sample will vary from population to population to some extent. To accept that a population parameter to be equivalent to the sample statistic, we should be sure that the difference between these two is only due to random fluctuations. The difference has statistical significance only if there is good reason to believe that the difference does not represent random sampling fluctuations. A test of significance is to verify if the deviation of a statistic is statistically significant or not.

Significance Level (Level of Confidence)

The levels of probability at which the null hypothesis can be rejected with confidence. It is denoted by α and generally fixed at 5% or 1 %.

Decision Rule

It is a rule for accepting or rejecting the null hypothesis. It is specified in terms of the specific level of significance, i.e. if sample results fall within the specified region of rejection then we say that the null hypothesis is rejected at that level of significance.

One – Tailed Test

In this type of tests the rejection region is located on one end. Either left or right tail.

Two – Tailed Test

In this type of tests the rejection region is located on both the ends.

Type I and Type II Errors

- **Type I Error:** It is the probability of rejecting the null hypothesis when it is true.
  i.e. Type I error = P[Reject H_0 / H_0 is true]
- **Type II Error:** It is the probability of accepting the null hypothesis when it is false.
  i.e. Type I error = P[Accept H_0 / H_0 is false]
  or   = P[reject H_1 / H_1 is true]

Null Hypothesis \ Action	Accept H_0	Reject H_0
True	✓	Type I error
False	Type II error	✓

Parametric and Non-parametric Tests

There are two types of tests of significance used for hypothesis testing.

Parametric tests: These tests depend on the parameters of the population. In this type of tests, the population from which the samples are drawn are assumed to be normally distributed and the data collected are of interval level. These tests are very powerful in nature.

Non-Parametric tests: These tests are also known as distribution-free tests as they are not based on the characteristics of the parent population. No assumption of normality is there.

Procedure for Testing of Hypothesis
1. Make a formal statement. i.e. State the null and alternate hypothesis. H_0 and H_1.
2. Select a significance level - $\propto$. (1% or 5%)
3. Decide the proper type of probability distribution to be used and state the decision rule.
4. Draw the critical region.
5. Select a random sample and compute the appropriate value of the test statistic.
6. Obtain critical test value.
7. Make a decision. Accept or reject the null hypothesis.
8. State the Conclusion in non-technical language.

Logic and Importance of Testing of Hypothesis

The logic behind hypothesis testing is similar to the trial by the jury where defendant is 'assumed innocent until proven guilty'.

A research hypothesis is formulated after the review of related literature and prior to the execution of the study. It is based on the implications of previous research and suggests one to expect a certain relationship. Every aspect of the research is affected by the hypothesis, including subjects (the sample), measuring instruments, design, procedures, data-analysis techniques, and conclusions. So in the light of the previous studies, whatever assumption the researcher makes about the population parameter needs to be tested and verified scientifically. Therefore the scientific procedure of testing of hypothesis assumes great importance. Unless the results of the research display something different, the assumption is taken to be true. If the hypothesis gets rejected then action needs to be taken, which will make certain contribution to the field of research. It is important to test a hypothesis to establish or verify the cause and effect relationships as well as to find patterns.

Points to Remember

- Identification of a research problem is the first and foremost step in scientific method for conducting research. Defining and formulating a research problem is an important and basic function of the researcher. The whole building of research work is based on the "Research Problem". It is observed that many research activities fail only because of not selecting and formulating the research problem systematically and logically.
- A research problem may originate from various sources, such as: Daily problems / personal experiences, Technological changes, Theory of one's own interest, Unexplored (Unknown) Area, Discussion with supervisor or Research Guide, Literature.

- The selection of a suitable topic for research is in many ways the most difficult task. The selection of a topic for research requires commitment of the researcher's time and efforts in a particular direction. There should be no hurry in deciding on the topic, or in defining its scope.
- Many a times, the research is being funded by an interested organisation or researcher seeks to get funding for his research. Funding agencies would like to fund research problems having direct implications. No agency would like to fund a proposal that has no value. So, it is the duty of the researcher to convey to the stakeholders about the research problem in detail so that its importance is realised.
- Once the research problem has been identified, the researcher's job moves to the stage of thinking about the investigative questions.
- The management dilemma is translated into management questions. These questions are general in nature and may be narrowed down further into specific questions. Management questions give directions to the research and are useful in exploring the system to find solutions to the problems.
- After having a clear understanding about the objectives and the management questions the researcher translates the management questions into research questions. Out of the several management questions, few are selected by the researcher for further analysis. Research questions are more specific than management questions.
- A general research question translated into a more specific question related to gathering information is known as an investigative question. Investigative questions are questions, the researcher must answer to satisfy and arrive at a conclusion about the research questions. Investigative questions are more specific in making a systematic inquiry or examination.
- Measurement questions enable the researcher to collect specific information required for the study and help in designing the questionnaire.
- A hypothesis is a proposition or probable solution to a problem, relations of two or more variables or nature of some phenomenon. It is an educated guess based on available fact.
- Test of hypotheses enables us to make probable statements about the population parameters based on the sample statistics. Tests of hypotheses are used for deciding whether a sample data supports a particular hypothesis so that generalisations can be made.
- A hypothesis is a tentative explanation for certain behaviours, phenomena, or events that have occurred or will occur.
- Types of Hypotheses are Inductive Hypotheses, Deductive Hypotheses, Research Hypotheses, Statistical Hypotheses or Null Hypothesis.

- Null hypothesis (H_0) is a hypothesis of 'no difference' is called null hypothesis. Alternative Hypothesis (H_a or H_1) is a hypothesis to be accepted in case null hypothesis is rejected. In other words, a complementary hypothesis to null hypothesis is called alternative hypothesis. It is a regular hypothesis which is logical opposite of the null hypothesis.
- There are two types of tests of significance used for hypothesis testing, parametric tests and non-parametric tests.
- The logic behind hypothesis testing is similar to the trial by the jury where defendant is 'assumed innocent until proven guilty'.
- A research hypothesis is formulated after the review of related literature and prior to the execution of the study. It is based on the implications of previous research and suggests one to expect a certain relationship. Every aspect of the research is affected by the hypothesis, including subjects (the sample), measuring instruments, design, procedures, data-analysis techniques, and conclusions.

Questions for Discussion

1. What is the necessity of defining a research problem?
2. How does a research problem originate? What are the considerations for formulation of a research problem?
3. "An academic research problem is based on academic interest, while a management research problem is based on management practice." Explain with suitable examples.
4. What are the characteristics of a hypothesis?
5. Explain the procedure to test a research hypothesis?
6. What is testing of hypotheses? Explain Null, Alternate, Errors involved, Level of significance.
7. Discuss the parametric and non-parametric tests of significance?
8. Describe in detail the various steps involved in testing of hypotheses?
9. Explain in brief, what you understand by 'management questions', 'research questions', and 'investigative questions'.

Chapter 3...

Research Design, Qualitative and Quantitative Research

Contents ...
Introduction
3.1 Concept and Features of a Good Research Design
3.2 Types of Research Design
3.3 Exploratory Research Design
3.4 Descriptive Research Design
3.5 Causal Research – Experimental Design
3.6 Qualitative Research and Quantitative Research Approaches
    3.6.1 Qualitative Research
    3.6.2 Quantitative Research
    3.6.3 Concept of Measurement, Causality, Generalisation and Replication
    3.6.4 Merging Quantitative and Qualitative Approaches
3.7 Research Proposal
    3.7.1 Elements of a Research Proposal
    3.7.2 Drafting a Research Proposal
    3.7.3 Evaluating a Research Proposal
    Points to Remember
    Questions for Discussion

Learning Objectives
➢ To understand the fundamentals and significance of a good research design
➢ To comprehend the various types of research designs and steps needed to formulate a good research design

Introduction

Once the research problem has been identified and stated appropriately, the next crucial step is formulating the research design for the same. The research design depends on the purpose and nature of the research problem. A good design is one that yields maximum information with minimum experimental error, minimises bias and maximises the reliability of the data. It involves decisions regarding what, where, when, how much etc., concerning the research inquiry. The starting point for the research design is, in fact, the research questions and hypotheses that have been so carefully developed. In essence, the research design answers the question: How are we going to get answers to these research questions and test these hypotheses?

The research design is a plan of action indicating the specific steps that are necessary to provide answers to those questions, test the hypotheses, and thereby achieve the research purpose that helps choose among the decision alternatives to solve the management problem or capitalise on the market opportunity.

Meaning of Research Design

Research design is an overall plan or scheme prepared by the researcher for executing the research study. It is an important stage in the process of conducting research as it facilitates systematic and smooth conduct of the research project. It acts as a guide for the researcher to work step by step on his research study.

Definitions of Research Design

(i) "Research design is the logical and systematic planning and directing of a piece of research". – **P. V. Young**

(ii) "A research design is the arrangement of conditions for collection and analysis of data in a manner that aims to combine relevance to the research purpose with economy in procedure."

(iii) "A research design is the determination and statement of the general research approach or strategy adopted for the particular project. It is the heart of planning. If the design adheres to the research objective, it will ensure that the client's needs will be served." – **David J. Luck and Ronald S. Rubin**

(iv) "Research design is the plan, structure and strategy of investigation conceived so as to obtain answers to research questions and to control variance." – **Kerlinger**

(v) "A research design is the specification of methods and procedures for acquiring the information needed. It is the over-all operational pattern or framework of the project that stipulates what information is to be collected from which source by what procedures." – **Green and Tull**

The fourth definition includes three important terms - ***plan, structure and strategy***. The plan is the outline of the research scheme on which the researcher is to work. The structure of the research work is a more specific scheme and the strategy suggests how the research will be carried out i.e., methods to be used for the collection and analysis of data. In brief, research design is the blueprint of research. It is the specification of methods and procedures for acquiring the information needed for solving the problem. Questionnaires, forms and samples for investigation are decided while framing research design. Finally, the research design enables the researcher to arrive at certain meaningful conclusions at the end of the proposed study.

A Research Design

- Refers to a conceptual structure within which research would be conducted.
- A plan which specifies the sources and types of information relevant to the research problem.
- Strategy specifying which approach will be used for gathering and analysing data.
- Includes time and cost budgets.
- It facilitates the collection of relevant evidence with minimal expenditure of time, effort and money.
- A blueprint for collection, measurement and analysis of data.

3.1 Concept and Features of a Good Research Design

Components of a Research Design

A research design refers to the preparation of sampling design, observational design, statistical design and the operational design which means,

(a) The **sampling design** which deals with the method of selecting items to be observed for the given study;

(b) The **observational design** which relates to the conditions under which the observations are to be made;

(c) The **statistical design** which relates to the conditions under which the observations are to be made;

(d) The **operational design** which deals with the techniques by which the procedures specified in the sampling, statistical and observational designs can be carried out.

Importance of Research Design

A researcher who does not understand the importance of research design starts collecting and processing data without preparing a 'Research design'. But this may result in falling into trouble later. Research design is important as it prepares a proper framework within which the research work/activity will be actually carried out. It introduces efficiency in investigation and generates confidence in the final outcome of the study. A research design gives proper direction and time-table to the research activity. It keeps adequate check on the research work and ensures its completion within a certain time limit. It keeps the whole research project on the right track.

Research design avoids possible errors as regards research problem, information requirement and so on. It gives practical orientation to the whole research work and makes it relevant to the marketing problems faced by the sponsoring organisation. Finally, it makes the whole research process compact and result-oriented. A researcher should not go ahead with his research project unless the research design is framed properly.

A well framed research design is helpful in answering the following questions:
- What is the study about, i.e. problem of the research?
- Why is the study undertaken, i.e. the rationale behind the research?
- What are the time and scope considerations for the study?
- Which research method should be adopted?
- What are the time and money estimates?
- What information is required? Which data is relevant and which is irrelevant?
- What is the universe or population?
- How to select the sample? What should be the sample size?
- What methods of sampling may be used?
- How much data should be collected?
- How to analyse the data obtained?

Need for Research Design

Research design is necessary because it facilitates the smooth execution of the various research activities thereby bringing efficiency and effectiveness to the study. The research design may be compared to the blueprint developed by an expert architect before construction of a building so as to incorporate the best of plans for the building. Research without a pre-drawn plan is like an ocean voyage without a mariner's compass. The preparation of a research plan for a study, aids in establishing *direction* to the study and in knowing exactly what has to be done and how and when it has to be done at every stage.

A research plan prescribes the *boundaries* of research activities and enables the researcher to channelise his energies in the right direction. With clear research objectives in view, a researcher can proceed systematically towards his goal. The design also enables the researcher to anticipate potential problems of data gathering, operationalisation of concepts, measurements etc.

A research design proves to be effective in yielding the required information within the constraints of time, money and energy. Research design helps the researcher to organise his ideas and improve upon any flaws or deviations from the right path.

Uses or Goals of Research Design

According to social scientists like **Black** and **Champion**, **Berger**, **Mannheim**, the goals or functions of research design are as mentioned below.

1. **Provides blueprint:** Just as an architect's plan guides him about the location of the various parts of the construction, like where the doors will be or passage etc. and various other details about a construction, so also a research design helps the researcher about the minute details regarding the research title, rationale of research, scope of investigation, objectives of study, hypothesis, sample design, methods of data collection and processing etc.
2. **Limits boundaries of research activity:** Research design helps to narrow down the research problem so as to conduct a focused study on the problem without being swayed away.
3. **Predicts potential problem:** Research design anticipates the probable problems the researcher may face during the research and makes provision for the same.
4. **Helps to attain research goals economically:** Research design leads the project so that the research objects are attained at minimum cost and time by avoiding duplication, irrelevant work and other wastages. It helps to use the resources very effectively by avoiding errors and bias.
5. **Simplifies research work:** Research design works as an effective tool to co-ordinate the various research activities.

Advantages of Preparing a Research Design

The advantages of research design can be stated as under:
1. **Time Saving:** Preparation of research design saves a lot of time of the researcher.
2. **Resource Planning:** Research design enables resource planning and procurement at the right time.
3. **Systematic Execution:** Research design directs the researcher for the correct and timely execution of various tasks and activities of research in the most systematic manner.
4. **Better Documentation:** It enables better documentation of the work while the project is in progress.
5. **Increases Confidence and Satisfaction:** It provides satisfaction and a sense of success from the beginning to the end of the research project at every stage.

Phases Involved in Research Design

Research design can be thought of as the **structure of research,** it is the "glue" that holds all of the elements in a research project together. There are certain broad steps involved in planning the research design as explained below.

1. **Selection of Problem:** A researcher before, getting on to the job of planning a research design for the proposed study, should select and define the problem clearly and in operational terms. He should be clear about the following aspects:
   - What to observe?
   - Whom to observe?
   - How to observe?
   - Why to observe?
   - How to record the observations?
   - How to analyse the observations?
   - What inferences can be drawn?

Once the researcher has perfect understanding about these aspects he can take up the job of planning a research design in the following steps.

2. **Title of the Research:** The title of the research project should be spelled out in clear words. It should be brief, precise and highlight the scope of the research problem in generalised terms.

3. **Purpose of the Research:** The rationale of the research work undertaken should be presented in an effective manner. How the present research will contribute to the general fund of knowledge and help in solving complex problems facing the society or business should be stated. The worth of research should be proved and theoretical and practical justification of investigation should be given.

4. **Critical Appraisal of Previous Studies:** The critical appraisal of previous research studies should be given categorically. This enables the researcher to get acquainted with the previous research work in the field of his investigation, to know the meaning of different concepts involved in those studies, to identify the loopholes in existing research, to avoid duplication of work and to cover up the shortcomings of past research in the current research design.

5. **Statement of the Problem:** After critical review of previous research, the researcher will be able to state his problem in unambiguous and precise terms. Generally, the problem of investigation is stated in the form of statements or questions.

6. **Scope of Investigation:** In view of the time, money and other resources at the disposal of the researcher, he has to specify the geographical limits of the design and the time-span covered by the current research.

Once the scope of the investigation is delimited, the investigator will report the scope in clear terms while giving out the limitations of his research.

7. Objectives of the Study: The investigator should clearly state the objectives of his research in the form of statements. The objectives depend on whether the research is descriptive, exploratory, explanatory or experimental. Statement of objectives delineates the type of information that needs to be collected. It determines the scope of the research. The investigator should ensure that the objectives mentioned are well within the scope of investigation undertaken by him.

8. Definition of Concepts and Terms: The researcher should define clearly every term and concept he uses in the investigation. This will help him to communicate his research to the audience without ambiguity. For example, in some researches, the concepts needing clear operational definition could be 'development', 'Black money', 'marginal farmers', 'sick units', 'small industries', 'marketing strategy', 'operational cost', 'solvency', 'liquidity' and so on. Such terms need proper explanation.

9. Identification of Variables: A variable refers to an event or process or feature that can be changed or can change on its own accord. The researcher should identify the various variables involved in his investigation say cost, sales, price, profit, debt, education level, family structure, production, labour hours, capacity, turnover etc. The variables are classified as quantitative variables (i.e. continuous) or qualitative (i.e. discrete) independent variables (which can be manipulated by the experimenter) and dependent variables (i.e. response variables).

10. Formulation of Hypothesis: Framing of hypothesis makes the objectives of study as well as many other aspects of the research comprehensible. The hypothesis is a testable statement of potential relationship between two or more variables.

11. Selection of Sample: Majority of investigations make use of sampling. For this the investigator should define the population or universe of study, determine the appropriate size of sample and use the proper method of selecting a sample which is a true representative of population.

12. Data Collection: The empirical phase of research design includes the collection and processing of data. The primary data may be collected through observation, interview, and questionnaire schedules. The secondary data may be collected through records, reports, periodicals, journals and books.

13. Data Processing and Tabulation: The data collected through different sources by using different methods should be edited, compiled, codified and classified. Finally, it should be presented in the form of tables with suitable headings; and should also be presented in the form of charts, graphs and diagrams, wherever necessary.

14. Analysis of Data: Depending upon the nature of data, objectives of research and relationship of variables expressed in hypothesis, the investigator should subject the data to appropriate statistical analysis. The researcher may make use of computers for accurate processing of data within a short span of time.

15. Interpretation of the Results: The results of statistical and accounting analysis should be interpreted. The investigator can generalise his findings, draw the inferences and form the hypothesis.

16. Suggestions for further Research: The investigator while concluding his research should also explore the areas of further research in the field of his investigation on the basis of insights he has gained in the course of his research.

17. Bibliography: There are different ways of reporting the bibliography. However, a large number of researchers while reporting the references use the following order:
   (i)   Name of author
   (ii) Year of publication
   (iii) Title of book or article
   (iv) Page numbers referred
   (v)   Publisher's address.

18. Summary of Report: The researcher should report his research to the audience by briefly highlighting the findings of his research.

19. Chapter Scheme: Research design should also give a scheme of chapterisation indicating the serial number, title of each chapter and the theme of each chapter.

20. Time Schedule and Budget: A clear schedule indicating time to be devoted for each stage of investigation is essential. The budget of expenses under different heads of accounting such as salaries to supervisors, travelling, computer analysis, report preparation, contingencies and other expenses should be stated.

Note also that conducting qualitative research does not exclude the use of quantitative measures. Various types of data can be collected through observation, discussion, and other techniques that could be statistically analysed.

Features of a Good Research Design

A good research design is expected to be flexible, appropriate, efficient, and economical. It should minimise the bias and maximise the reliability of the data collected and analysed, at the same time giving rise to minimum of experimental errors, if any. Consideration of the following factors would help in framing a better research design:
   (i)   Nature and scope of the research problem;
   (ii) The means of obtaining information;
   (iii) The availability and skills of the researcher and his staff, if any;
   (iv) The objective of the problem to be studied;

(v) The nature of the problem to be studied; and

(vi) The availability of time funds, and human resources i.e. enumerators, experts, technicians and money for the research work.

(vii) Practical and theoretical worth of the research.

Hence, a good research design is related to the purpose or objective of the problem and also with the nature of the problem to be studied.

If a research study is an exploratory or formulative, i.e., it focuses on discovery of ideas and insights, the research design should be flexible enough to consider different aspects of the study. Similarly, if the study focuses on accurate description or association between variables, the design should be accurate with minimum bias and maximum reliability. However, in practice, it is difficult to categorise a particular study into a particular group. A study can be categorised only on the basis of its primary function and accordingly, its design can be developed. Moreover, the above mentioned factors must be given due weightage while working on the details of the research design.

Characteristics of a Good Research Design

No ideal research design exists for all the problems because a research design varies from problem to problem. It is desirable that a research design must satisfy the following conditions:

1. **Objectivity:** Objectivity on part of the researcher ensures good quality of the data which in turn leads to reliable results.
2. **Reliability:** Reliability means consistency throughout a series of measurements. A good research design should ensure cross verification of responses from respondents.
3. **Validity:** Any measuring instrument is said to be valid when it measures what it is supposed to measure. A good research design should ensure the validity in measuring the responses of the respondents.
4. **Generalisations:** Generalisations done on the basis of a sample should be applicable to the entire universe.
5. **Economy:** A good research design should enable attaining of research objectives with minimum cost, efforts and time.
6. **Minimum errors:** A good research design which should minimise the associated errors like experimental error, sampling error, errors of measurement etc.
7. **Maximum output:** The research design should enable multi-dimensional study of the research problem and provide solutions to practical social and business problems to maximise the output.
8. **Flexibility:** A good research design should be flexible enough and not be a rigid one.

Factors affecting Research Design

1. Availability of scientific information
2. Availability of sufficient data
3. Time availability
4. Proper exposure to the data source
5. Availability of the money
6. Manpower availability
7. Magnitude of the management problem
8. Degree of Top management's support
9. Ability, knowledge, skill, technical understanding and technical background of the researcher
10. Controllable variables
11. Un – controllable variables
12. Internal variables
13. External variables

3.2 Types of Research Design

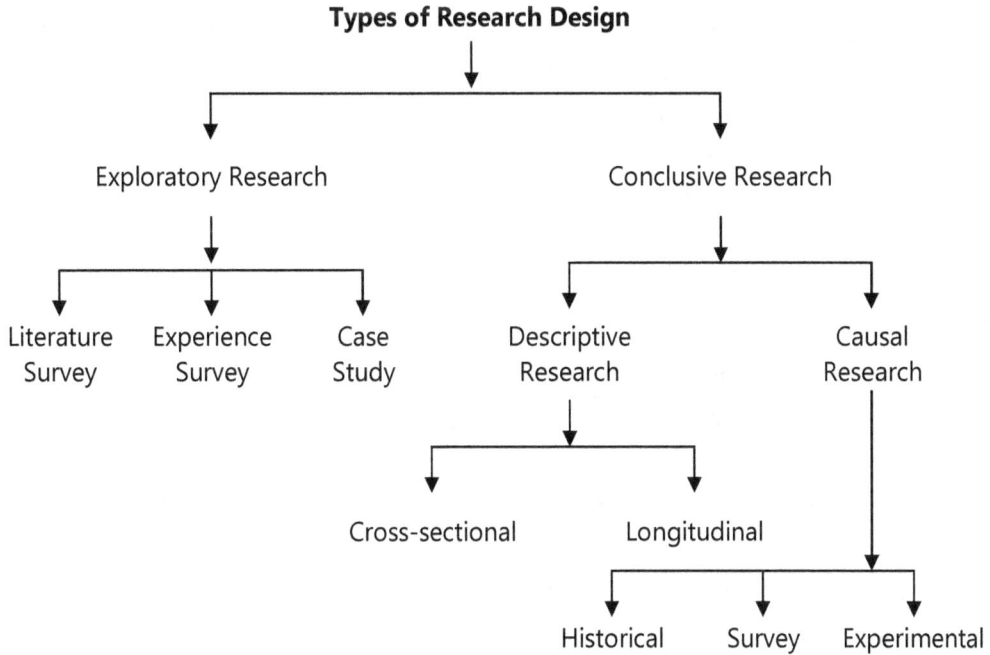

A research design is like a roadmap – you can see where you currently are, where you want to be at the completion of your journey, and can determine the best (most efficient and effective) route to take to get to your destination. Our research purpose and objectives suggest which route (design) might be best to get us where we want to go, but there is more than one way to "get there from here."

Successfully completing a research project consists of making those choices that will fulfil the research purpose and obtain answers to the research questions in an efficient and effective manner.

Choice of research design is influenced by a number of variables such as the decision maker's attitude toward risk, the types of decisions being faced, the size of the research budget, the decision-making time frame, the nature of the research objectives, and other subtle and not-so-subtle factors.

Much of the choice, however, will depend upon the fundamental objective implied by the research question:

- To conduct a general exploration of the issue, gain some broad insights into the phenomenon, and achieve a better "feel" for the subject under investigation (e.g., what do customers mean by "good value"?).
- To describe a population, event, or phenomenon in a precise manner where we can attach numbers to represent the extent to which something occurs or determine the degree two or more variables co-vary (e.g., determine the relationship between age and consumption rate).
- To attribute cause and effect relationships among two or more variables so that we can better understand and predict the outcome of one variable (e.g., sales) when varying another (e.g., advertising).

3.3 Exploratory Research Design

Exploratory Research

It is the starting point in all types of research projects and is conducted in order to find out causes/reasons behind a specific marketing problem. In the exploratory research, the possible causes will be identified, the most appropriate causes will be selected, hypothesis will be developed and research activity will be conducted accordingly. Survey of consumers, retailers, sales executives and sales-force will be useful for exploratory research. On some occasions, small scale sales survey may provide useful data for exploratory research.

The purpose of exploratory research is to know the unknown. Exploratory research is particularly useful in providing insights into the problem when the researcher lacks a clear idea of the problem. It helps the researcher develop concepts more clearly, establish priorities, develop operational definitions, and improve the final research design. Exploration may also save time and money. The information needed is only loosely defined at this stage and the research process that is adopted is flexible and unstructured. The primary data and information are qualitative in nature and are analysed accordingly.

Exploratory research requires skills like - ability to observe, get information and construct explanation. Exploratory research determines fruitful alternatives that the executive would not have perceived. This also narrows down the scope of the investigation. Exploratory research is undertaken to get the answer to the questions such as, "What alternative courses of action might solve the problem and thereby reach the final objective?" Exploratory studies are important as they may provide adequate information on a decision situation or may greatly facilitate the design of formal research studies.

In exploratory research, the stress/focus is on the discovery of ideas/causes. For example, sales may be declining for the last six months. Quick study may be conducted to find out the causes/factors responsible. Such causes will be listed. Here, an exploratory study/research may be conducted in order to find out the most likely cause so as to introduce suitable remedial measures.The secondary/published data can be used for exploratory research as such data are easily available. Exploratory study needs to be flexible in its approach.

In exploratory research one or all of the following activities may be conducted so as to understand and formulate the problem more precisely:

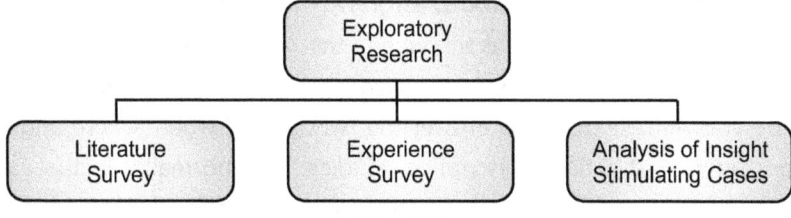

Fig. 3.1

(i) **Literature Survey:** The available literature is referred for secondary sources of data and searched for identifying the developments in the field and also to identify the research gaps.

(ii) **Experience Survey/Experts Opinion:** Experts from the relevant field are contacted to get more details about the problem at hand.

(iii) **Analysis of Insight Stimulating Cases:** For the refinement of the problem, at times it is not sufficient to have clarity of problem, and if the problem is of such a nature that specific cases may be referred to in detail so that more insights can be got into the nature and scope of the problem, then this is also carried out.

Exploratory Research is used:
- To define the problem more precisely.
- To identify relevant courses of action i.e., find the most likely alternatives, which are then turned into hypotheses.
- To isolate key variables and relationships for further examinations.
- To gain insights for developing an approach to a problem.
- To establish priorities for further research.

Exploratory research may also be involved when the perceived problem is much less general; it is used to develop the most promising hypotheses. Once a hypothesis is formulated, research is used to determine if the hypothesis was correct. The findings of exploratory research should be regarded as tentative or as an input to further research. In general, exploratory research is meaningful in any situation in which the researcher does not have enough understanding to proceed with the research project.

3.4 Descriptive Research Design

Conclusive Research Design

Conclusive Research Design is typically more formal and structured than exploratory research. It is based on large representative samples, and the data obtained are subjected to quantitative analysis. Conclusive Research is designed to assist (the decision maker in determining, evaluating and selecting the best course of action to take in a given situation. Conclusive research designs may be either descriptive or causal and descriptive designs may be either cross-sectional or longitudinal.

Descriptive Research Questions and Designs

Descriptive research is undertaken when the researcher desires to know the characteristics of certain groups such as age, gender, occupation, income or education. The objective of descriptive research is to answer the "who, what, when, where and how" of the subject under study/investigation. Descriptive studies are normally factual and simple. However, such studies can be complex, demanding scientific skill on the part of the researcher.

Descriptive research involves describing a problem, context or situation with questions that are more structured and depend on prior ideas and methods. This type of study is suitable for qualitative as well as quantitative studies.

Descriptive research is used to answer descriptive research questions such as,

What is happening? How is something happening? Why is something happening?

Example: Suppose the canteen manager is interested in finding out whether the facilities and services provided by the canteen are adequate. A descriptive study may be undertaken to determine the type of menu each student desires, whether the timings of the canteen are suitable, or if there are any problems with the physical facilities. A proper description of the canteen may provide important information and in many situations it is this descriptive information that is needed to solve business problem, although the answer to WHY is not given.

Descriptive studies are well structured. They tend to be rigid and their approach cannot be changed often and again. In descriptive studies, the researcher has to give adequate thought to framing research questions and deciding the data to be collected and the procedure to be used for this purpose. Data collected may prove to be inadequate if the researcher is not careful in the initial stages of data collection. Descriptive research designs are used for some definite purpose. Descriptive research cannot identify cause and effect relationship. Descriptive research is designed to describe the present situation or the features of a group or users of a product. In marketing, such research is undertaken to know the characteristics of certain groups or users of a product such as age, sex education, income etc. Such research studies are based on secondary data or survey research.

A major difference between exploratory and descriptive research is that descriptive research is characterised by the prior formulation of the hypotheses. Thus, the information needed is clearly defined. As a result, descriptive research is pre-planned and structured. It is typically based on large representative samples. A formal research design specifies the methods for selecting these sources of information and for collecting data from those sources.

Uses of Descriptive Research

Descriptive research may be conducted for the following reasons:

1. To describe the characteristics of relevant groups, such as consumers, sales people, or organisations, or market areas. For example, we could develop a profile of the "heavy users" (frequent shoppers) of Big Bazaar.
2. To estimate the percentage of units in a specified population exhibiting a certain behaviour,
3. To determine the perceptions of product characteristics. For example, how do households perceive the various department stores in terms of salient factors of the choice criteria?
4. To determine the degree to which marketing variables are associated. For example, to what extent is shopping at department stores related to eating out?
5. To make specific predictions. For example, what will be retail sales of shoppers stop (specific store) for fashion clothing (specific product category) in the Mumbai area (specific region)?
6. To collect demographic information of consumers/users of a product under study.
7. To find out views and attitudes of customers. For example, how many customers prefer branded goods or ISI marked goods?

8. Make predictions about future marketing trends, consumer needs or expectations or possible sales after 'n' years.
9. To discover the relationship between certain variables. For example, sale of toothpaste among rural population and urban population or rate of savings among low, middle and higher income groups.

Descriptive research designs include the following:

1. Simple descriptive
- Data are collected to describe.
- Researcher administers a survey to a random sample of autistic children in order to describe the characteristics of the population of autistic children.
  Ex1: What percent of children are autistic?
  Ex2: Given the spectrum of disorders within autism, what is the range of functioning?

2. Comparative descriptive
- Describes two or more groups for comparison.
- Researcher administers a depression inventory to popular, rejected, and neglected students.
  Ex1: What are the depression levels of popular vs. rejected vs. neglected students?
  Ex2: What is the percentage of male vs. female students who are popular?
  Ex3: What is the percentage of males vs. females who are depressed?
  Hint: It may help to think about different levels/categories of your topic and/or different subject variables.

3. Co-relational
- Describe the statistical association between two or more variables.
- Researcher measures the student-teacher ratio in each classroom in a school district and measures the average student achievement on the state assessment in each of these same classrooms. Next the researcher uses statistical techniques to measure whether the student-teacher ratio and student achievement in the school district are connected numerically; for example, when the student-teacher ratio changes in value, so does student achievement.

Descriptive Research: Cross-sectional and Longitudinal Research

Descriptive research can be further divided into the following two categories:

(i) Cross-sectional Studies

Cross-sectional study is a study involving a sample of elements from the population of interest at a single point of time. It is a study concerned with a sample of elements from a given population. Such samples may deal with households, dealers, retail stores and other entities. Information/data on a number of characteristics are collected from the sample elements. Such data are analysed for drawing conclusions. Cross-sectional studies include field studies and surveys.

Field studies are conducted the life situations such as schools, factories, institutions, etc. Here, the inter-relations among variables are studied under real setting. The cross-sectional analysis involves counting the simultaneous occurrence of the variables of interest. Field studies have certain merits and limitations.

Cross-sectional study is possible through survey. Survey research is wide in scope. Detailed information can be collected from a sample of large population. This method is also economical as more information can be collected per unit of cost. The time required for sample survey is also less than a census-inquiry. However, in survey research, more importance is given to information collection and not to in-depth analysis. Secondly, survey research needs more time and money when conducted on a large scale.

(ii) Longitudinal Studies

Longitudinal studies are based on panel methods and panel data. A panel is a sample of respondents who are interviewed not only once but thereafter from time to time. Here data to be collected relate to same variables but the measurements are taken repeatedly. For example, purchase of grocery products by families/ households at regular intervals. Such data will reflect/indicate change in the buying behaviour of families/households.

There are many advantages and limitations of panel data. Panel data are suitable when the researcher undertakes detailed analysis. Similarly, panel data are more comprehensive as compared to data collected from individual families. Finally, panel data collected is more accurate as compared to data collected through survey. These advantages of panel data improve the quality of research findings and conclusions.

There are certain limitations of panel data. For example, panels used for data collection may not be representative samples. Panel members may not be co-operative or may leave the panel membership. As a result, the representative character of the original sample may be adversely affected. Secondly, panel members may report wrong data. Their interest may reduce gradually and they may supply information in a causal manner. Their sense of participation/responsibility may reduce. This will affect the quality of data and also of findings.

3.5 Causal Research – Experimental Design

Causal Research Design

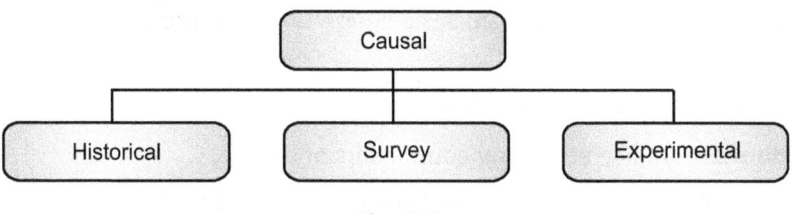

Fig. 3.2

Causal research design is the third type of research design. As the name indicates, causal design investigates the cause and effect relationship between two or more variables. This design measures the extent of relationship between the variables. Causal research designs attempt to specify the nature of functional relationship between two or more variables. For example "low pay causes people to leave", or "poor HR practices cause people to leave"

Causal research is useful to show the impact of one variable on the other. For example, price and market demand relationship or relationship between market competition and sales performance. Even the positive/negative effect of advertising on sales can be studied through causal research. The relationship between the causal factors can be studied through causal research. In addition, the variables which create effect on other variables can be studied in depth through causal research. For example, predicting the influence of price, packaging, advertising on sales.

Data for causal research can be collected through field survey with the help of a questionnaire or by conducting laboratory experiments / controlled experiments. Laboratory experiments are possible in the case of testing of new products or package design.

The causal research design is based on reasoning. The designs for causal research can be divided into three categories:

(i) Historical or case study
(ii) Survey
(iii) Experimental.

Experimental Research Designs

Experimental research is used to answer causal research questions:

Does something cause an effect? For example, does a low student-teacher ratio cause higher student achievement?

The easiest way to devise an experimental question may be to think about a question in which you can *control, manipulate,* or *assign* the independent variable. This is often done by assigning groups to treatment conditions, intervention groups, giving some information and not others.

Principles of Experimental Design: Basic design of logical proof to test hypothesis with three basic principles:

- **Replication:** Repeated several times.
- **Randomisation:** Protects extraneous factors of chance.
- **Local control:** Deliberate wide variability to measure and eliminate error.

- Helps finding causal relationship between variables, Employs a set of control and experimental groups Administers treatment / stimuli, Controlled observation of change / deviation in variables (adequate control is the essence – reduces bias increases reliability), Types: Lab experiments, Field experiments, A real life situation.

Experimental research designs include the following:

1. **True experimental (randomised trials)**
    - Researcher manipulates or varies an independent variable and measures its effects on one or more dependent variables.
    - Participants divided into groups. The treatment group receives a special reading program. Participants in the control group do not receive the treatment. Reading ability is assessed.
    - The effects of emotional counselling on the psychological well-being of children from divorced families.

2. **Quasi-experimental**
    - Random assignment not possible
    - Examining the academic achievement of two groups, one that goes to tutoring and one that doesn't. Here the groups already existed, either attended tutoring or not and were placed in groups based on this pre-existing condition.
    - The effects of academic counselling on the academic achievement of children from divorced vs. non-divorced families. Here an independent variable that cannot be randomly assigned (family status = divorced or not) is added.

Concept of Independent and Dependent Variable, Concomitant Variable, Extraneous Variable, Treatment, Control Group

- **Independent and Dependent Variables:** Every research except for descriptive research must have at least two variables. Variables may be independent or dependent. Independent variables allow for examining the cause-effect relationship and also allow more control and better inference about their impact.
- **Independent Variable:** A variable that is controlled or manipulated by the researcher and exerts effect on any other variable. It is also known as a causal variable.
- **Dependent Variable:** A variable that is influenced to some extent by one or more other variables. It is also known as an effect variable.
- **Concomitant Variable:** A variable that is observed in a statistical experiment, but it is not specifically measured or used in analysis of data. They are also known as secondary, incidental or subordinate variables. It is important to identify the concomitant variables in order to prevent distortion of results of experiment or research.

- **Extraneous Variables:** Variables that are not manipulated as part of an experiment, but may exert some influence on the dependent variable under study.
- **Treatment:** It refers to the process or intervention of interest.
- **Control Group:** A standard against which change is measured. A control group does not receive the experimental treatment. Thereafter comparisons are made between the groups.

3.6 Qualitative Research and Quantitative Research Approaches

Suppose a company is developing a hot new product for which it is preparing to commission a market research study to ensure the product meets the customers' needs. The main question which arises is to decide which method to use for the variety of choices. All market research methods can be divided into two primary types: quantitative and qualitative. The appropriate type of market research to be used can be arrived at by establishing how each method is used along with their relative merits and limitation.
- **Quantitative research** tells you WHAT your problem is.
- **Qualitative research** tells you WHY you have that problem.

3.6.1 Qualitative Research

Qualitative research is research used to gain insight into a problem, issue or theory. It aims to build an account about the issue and tries to find the reasons why something is the way it is. It is exploratory in nature and used when very few details of the problem at hand are known. i.e. when one doesn't know what to expect, to define the problem or develop an approach to the problem. Qualitative research is a highly subjective research discipline, designed to look beyond the percentages to gain an understanding of the customer's feelings, impressions and viewpoints. It looks at the "why" and "how" and involves making people to talk about their opinions so as to understand their motivations and feelings by producing observations, notes, and descriptions of behaviour and motivation.

Qualitative research was earlier used in the social sciences and now it is extensively used by market researchers, worker productivity experts, computer systems designers, and product developers to understand how people interact with things in their environment. It is especially valuable while developing new products or coming up with new marketing initiatives.

Qualitative research is concerned with the opinions, experiences and feelings of individuals and produces subjective data. Face-to-face interviews and group discussions are some ways to get in-depth feedback from customers. Other common data collection methods used in qualitative research are focus groups, triads, in-depth interviews, uninterrupted observation, bulletin boards, and ethnographic participation/observation Qualitative research has strengths like being flexible, highly-focused, and designed to be completed quickly. Because the results are seen or heard first-hand, management relates to the findings easily.

Example: Suppose a company is looking to launch a new colour version of its cell phone device. Company's objective is to evaluate end user preference for colours, customer willingness to pay a premium for their preferred colour, customer reaction to transparent flip cover overlays etc. A detailed study needs to be carried out wherein each respondent is examined, given a sample of the product for testing the device, and then asked for their personal opinions, preferences and attitudes about price, aesthetics and functionality. After careful analysis of the viewpoints expressed by the customers, company will be able to optimise the look, feel and price point of the device. This type of insightful, highly subjective personal input can be obtained through qualitative research.

Benefits

Qualitative research is characterised by the following benefits:
- Reduced respondent burden.
- Improved reliability of responses.
- Improved validity of responses.
- Reduced non-response (both unit and item).
- Reduced processing error and need for imputation.
- Improved cost efficiency.

Limitations
- Time consuming.
- Analysis is subjective and deals with a small sample size, prediction is not possible.
- Limited applicability.
- Trained moderators are essential to the success of qualitative research.

Applications

Qualitative research helps in getting insight into customer's attitudes and behaviour to know what is driving their decisions. Qualitative research methods are effective in identifying intangible factors, such as social norms, socioeconomic status, gender roles, ethnicity, and religion, whose significance in the research may not be easily evident.

Qualitative Research may be applicable to know:
- What customers or prospects think and feel about your product or service
- How customers choose between different products or suppliers; what motivates them
- How branding, design and packaging influence customers and in what way
- What sort of marketing messages have the most impact and what turns customers off completely
- How price affects their decision-making
- Whether there is demand for a new product or service

Examples of Qualitative Research
Qualitative Approach is especially useful in the following situations:
- **Talking to people who have stopped using a particular product.** Helps to find out what they thought they'd be getting when they started using it and why they stopped.
- **Watch users with particular product on a regular basis.** See where they struggle, where they seem disappointed, or where they complain that they can't do what they want. Those will all give you ideas for iterating on current features or adding new ones.
- **Watch new users** with your product and ask them what they expected from the first 15 minutes using the product. If this doesn't match what your product actually delivers, either fix the product or fix the first time user experience so that you're fulfilling users' expectations.

Hence, qualitative research is all about exploring issues, understanding phenomena, and answering questions. While there's a whole industry engaged in its pursuit, qualitative research also happens in nearly every workplace and study environment, nearly every day.

3.6.2 Quantitative Research

Quantitative research is conclusive in its purpose as it tries to quantify the problem and understand how prevalent it is by looking for projectable results to a larger population. Quantitative research can tell you when, where, how many and how often things happen. It includes research methods that produce hard numbers which can be turned into statistics. Here we collect data through surveys (online, phone, paper), audits, points of purchase (purchase transactions), and click-streams.

Quantitative research attempts precise measurement of an unknown. Quantitative research methods, including surveys and controlled experiments, originated in the natural sciences (biology, chemistry, and physics), and now they're found in nearly every professional field. In business research, quantitative methodologies usually measure consumer behaviour, knowledge, opinions, or attitudes. Such methodologies answer questions related to how much, how often, how many, when, and who.

Quantitative research statistically measures customer attitudes, behaviour, and performance. Being deeply based on numbers and statistics, quantitative research has the ability to effectively translate data into easily quantifiable charts and graphs. Real-world examples have shown the effectiveness of quantitative research in measuring product awareness, establishing customer profiles, and determining market size.

The U.S. Census is an example of large-scale quantitative research in action: census-takers survey households and then use the data to help determine the number of Congressional districts in a state, or where to allocate Federal funds.

Applications

The information gathered through quantitative research can be used in mathematical models to identify trends, or predict future performance.

- Market researchers conduct surveys to find out demographic information about their customers.
- Finance managers gather information about the performance of investments.
- Criminal justice programs compare different types of criminal offenders in terms of recidivism.

Limitations

- Large samples are required, and the logistical difficulties inherent in gathering a sufficiently large sample can sabotage the study before it even gets off the ground.
- Larger samples also tend to be more expensive.
- Prone to statistical error when handled inappropriately.
- The misuse of sampling and weighting can completely undermine the accuracy, validity, and projectability of a quantitative research study.

Types of Qualitative Techniques

(a) Projective Techniques
(b) In-Depth Interviews
(c) Experience Survey
(d) Focus Groups
(e) Observation

Methods for collecting information in qualitative research involves, focus groups, in-depth interviews, content analysis, ethnography, evaluation and semiotics etc. but qualitative research further involves the analysis of unstructured data, including, open-ended survey responses, literature reviews, audio recordings, pictures, web pages etc.

- **Projective Techniques:** A personality test designed to yield information about someone's personality on the basis of their unrestricted response to ambiguous objects or situations.
- **In-depth Interviews:** A series of structured questions or response of subject experience.
- **Focus groups:** Soliciting observations from groups of people who share a similar attribute to give opinions on a topic.
- **Observation:** Researchers watch people on their daily routine and make notes or recordings documenting their behaviour.
- **Experience Survey**: Survey of individuals who are knowledgeable about a particular research problem.

Some of the types of Qualitative Research are described below.

Projective Techniques

Projective techniques are designed to encourage the participant to reveal in detail deeply suppressed attitudes, opinions, feelings, and experiences. These may be through word or picture association, sentence completion, cartoons, the Thematic Apperception Test (TAT), imagination exercises, and sorting exercises etc. The researcher can also develop scenarios, in the form of descriptions of situations or actual pictures that are acted out for participants to observe. The participant then gives her or his interpretation of what is going on in the scenario. The participant's responses provide her or his perceptions, interpretations, and awareness of the total situation and of the interplay of the actors in the scenario.

Observation

Observation in qualitative research generally involves spending a prolonged amount of time in the setting. This method is used when the researcher wants to examine a subject in its natural environment or study behaviours without introducing personal bias into his observations.

Observation is used extensively in studies by psychologists, anthropologists, sociologists, and program evaluators. Direct observation reduces distortion between the observer and what is observed that can be produced by an instrument (e.g., questionnaire). The context or background of behaviour is included in observations of both people and their environment. Field notes are taken during the observations and at times cameras are used to record what is occurring at the research site. The task of a qualitative researcher is to make sure that the participants become comfortable to having the researcher (and, if appropriate, a recording device) around. One major drawback to observation methods is obtrusiveness. A stranger (researcher) with a pad and pencil or a camera is trying to record people's natural behaviour.

Observation may also be conducted on stationary objects, such as artifacts. When an anthropologist or archaeologist looks at an artifact and draws conclusions about the way people lived, he is performing a type of qualitative research. Similarly, when a researcher reads historical documents, histories and diaries to draw conclusions about an era, he is also performing qualitative research. However, personal bias can be an issue.

In-Depth Interviews

Interviews are the most common source of data in qualitative studies. The person-to-person format is most prevalent, but occasionally group interviews and focus groups are also conducted. Interviews may involve listening to someone recount something that happened in the past, such as a wartime experience or other event. When qualitative research takes the form of an interview, the interviewer asks open-ended questions and simply records what the participant says. Personal bias can be an issue, but other issues arise as well. For instance, the researcher may react to the subject's responses, encouraging or discouraging the dialogue in a certain direction. Moreover, the researcher has to be careful that he does not ask leading questions.

Mostly the interviewer asks the same questions of all the participants, but the order of the questions, the exact wording, and the type of follow-up questions may vary considerably. Taking notes during the interview is common. The use of a digital recorder is undoubtedly the most common method of recording interview data because it has the obvious advantage of preserving the entire verbal part of the interview for later analysis. Video recording seems to be the best method because it preserves not only what the person said but also his or her nonverbal behaviour.

Focus Groups

In a focus group, several people are interviewed at once to gain their opinions on a subject or item. This technique can be efficient because the researcher can gather information about several people in one session. The group is usually homogeneous, such as a group of students, an athletic team, etc. This method could be used to find out what people think about a product or an advertisement. Focus group interviews are usually enjoyable for the participants, and they may be less fearful of being evaluated by the interviewer because of the group setting. The group members get to hear what others in the group have to say, which may stimulate the individuals to rethink their own views. Taking notes can be difficult, but an audio or video recorder may solve that problem.

Others

Other recording devices include notebooks, narrative field logs, and diaries in which researchers record their reactions, concerns, and speculations. Printed materials such as course syllabi, team rosters, evaluation reports, participant notes and photographs of the setting and situations are examples of document data used in qualitative research.

Comparison - Pros and Cons of Qualitative and Quantitative Research Approaches

Quantitative and qualitative research methods differ primarily in:
- The objectives
- The sample
- The types of data collection instruments they use
- The forms of data they produce
- The degree of flexibility built into study design

Differences between qualitative and quantitative methods are:

Choice of appropriate method of research depends upon the problem under study and the type of information. Quantitative research is designed to reduce the complexity of studying a problem, whereas qualitative research attempts to understand, describe, and sometime explain the complexity. Quantitative research shows patterns across situations (sometimes on a large scale) whereas qualitative research has much smaller focus. Qualitative research shows details, processes at work, and the important role of individuals.

Several researchers (Merriam, 1998; Firestone, 1987 & Potter, 1996) have attempted to distinguish the key aspects of qualitative and quantitative research.

	Qualitative Research	**Quantitative Research**
Objective	<ul><li>To gain an understanding of the underlying reasons and motivations</li><li>To provide insights into the setting of a problem, generating ideas and/or hypotheses for later quantitative research</li><li>To uncover prevalent trends in thought and opinion</li></ul>	<ul><li>To quantify the data and generalise results from a sample to the population of interest</li><li>To measure the incidence of various views and opinions in a chosen sample</li><li>Sometimes followed by qualitative research which is used to explore some findings further</li></ul>
Focus	Focuses on Quality (features)	Focuses on Quantity (numbers, how much)
Purpose	Qualitative researchers are more concerned with understanding what is happening as viewed by the participants.	Quantitative researchers seek to explain the causes of change primarily through objective measurement and quantitative analysis (statistics).
Sample	Small number (purposeful) of respondents selected to fulfil a given quota.	Large number of randomly selected respondents representing the population of interest.
Data Collection	Unstructured or semi-structured techniques e.g. individual depth interviews, observation, or group discussions.	Structured techniques such as questionnaires, inventories.
Research Design	Flexible	Structured
Data Analysis	Non-statistical. Inductive (by researcher)	Statistical data is usually in the form of tabulations. Deductive.

Outcome	Exploratory and/or investigative. Findings are not conclusive and cannot be used to make generalisations about the population of interest. Develop an initial understanding and sound base for further decision making.	Findings are conclusive and usually descriptive in nature. Used to recommend a final course of action.
Researcher's Role	Immersed in the situation they are studying	Detached

A mix of research methods may be used to help gather comprehensive evidence or give a more complete picture of the problem under study. For example, in a market research scenario, after gathering quantitative information about the number of people who've bought a product in the last six months, you can then conduct qualitative interviews to find out why they bought, or didn't buy, the product, as well as how they'd heard about it.

May be Used when	**Qualitative Research**	**Quantitative Research**
	To develop initial understanding about a issue or problem.	To suggest final course of action.
	To look for a range of ideas and feeling on a subject.	To know whether there is consensus on a particular issue.
	Understand different perspectives between groups and categories of people.	Identify evidence regarding cause and effect relationship.
	Provide information needed to design a qualitative study.	Test specific hypotheses and examine specific relationships.

3.6.3 Concept of Measurement, Causality, Generalisation and Replication

Measurement assumes greater importance in the light of quantitative studies and issues of reliability and validity become more pertinent here. The extent to which the researcher is confident about the causal findings refers to the causality. Generalisation refers to the intention of the researcher to generalise the findings of quantitative studies. Generalisations can be made regarding the population characteristics and for this purpose, the sample needs to be a representative one. Replication refers to the process of reproducing the same results when a study is repeated under similar condition. It is necessary for a researcher to describe the procedures clearly so that the study can be replicated with ease and perfection.

3.6.4 Merging Quantitative and Qualitative Approaches

Though quantitative and qualitative studies have their own applications, many studies require that a combination of the two be applied so as to answer the research questions. Some ways in which the two can be combined are:
- Checking a result of qualitative research against a quantitative study.
- When qualitative research helps in identifying background information on the context and subjects, and help in formulation of hypothesis and scale construction.
- Quantitative and qualitative research is combined in order to provide a general picture about the problem.
- Quantitative research is oriented by the researcher's concerns, whereas qualitative research is based on the respondents' perspectives.
- Quantitative evidence helps in generalisation of results whereas qualitative research facilitates the interpretation of relationships between variables.
- Merging the two approaches helps to bridge the macro-micro gap.

3.7 Research Proposal

The research proposal is an activity that incorporates decisions made during the early research-project planning phases of the study including the management research question hierarchy and exploration.

A written proposal is often required when a study is being suggested. It ensures that the parties concur on the project's purpose and on the proposed methods of investigation. Time and budgets are often spelled out, as are other responsibilities and obligations. Depending on the needs and desires of the manager, substantial background detail and elaboration of proposed techniques may be included.

The length and complexity of the research proposal range widely from one to ten pages. Also, applicants for foundation or government research grants typically file a proposal in the specified format.

Every research proposal should include two basic sections: a statement of the research question and a brief description of the research methodology.

Often research proposals are much more detailed and describe specific measurement devices that will be used, time and cost budgets, sampling plans and many other details.

Purpose of Research Proposal
- To present the management question to be researched and its importance.

- To discuss the research efforts of others who have worked on related management questions.
- To suggest the data necessary for solving the management question and how the data will be gathered, treated, and interpreted.

The research proposal must present its plan, services, and credentials in the best possible way to encourage its selection over the competitors. The proposal tells us what, why, how, where, and to whom it will be done. It must also show the benefit of doing it.

Thus, the research proposal is necessary a road map, showing clearly the location where a journey begins, the destination to be reached and the method of getting there. Well prepared research proposals include potential problems that may be encountered along the way and methods for avoiding or working around them.

3.7.1 Elements of a Research Proposal

Given below are the nine elements of a research proposal. The specific format and content of the elements may vary, depending on requirements. Also remember that the elements may not always appear as separate sections or in the order listed below.

(i) Statement of the Problem

This section should include a clear and concise statement of the purpose or goal of the project. In a grant proposal, it consists of,

- The specific question(s) to be answered,
- A brief explanation of the need for or significance of the study, and
- An explanation of how the results will contribute to the existing body of knowledge.

(ii) Literature Review

A proposal should reflect the researcher's understanding of relevant bodies of literature and where his/her study fits in that context. It should be comprehensive and trace the central themes in the literature, highlight major areas of disagreement, and reflect a critical stance toward the materials reviewed.

(iii) Conceptual Framework

Here the researcher presents his/her own perspective. What theories or concepts will guide the study? How or why do they suggest the specific hypotheses or research questions? What are the strengths and weaknesses of the proposed framework?

(iv) Hypotheses or Research Questions

A clear, crisp statement of the research hypotheses, or, in the case of some qualitative studies, a concise description of the phenomena to be examined is to be included here.

Depending on the requirements of the solicitation, the hypotheses may be stated informally or formally. Finally, an explanation of why testing the hypotheses or answering the questions is appropriate for elucidating the research problems and is consistent with the conceptual framework should be included.

(v) Design - Methodology

Here the description of plans for collecting and analysing the data should be included.
- What instruments will be used?
- Why are they appropriate for this study?
- Is there evidence of the instruments' reliability and validity?
- How and to whom will they be administered?
- What procedures will be followed in the data analysis?

For qualitative studies, there should be an explanation of the purpose of observations and interviews, and, if possible, some indication of their content and format. The description of the proposed methodology should contain enough detail to indicate that the researcher knows what he/she is doing.

(vi) Task Structure (Scope of Work)

This section indicates exactly what will be done, the sequence of the various activities, and the products of deliverables that will be prepared. It is important that the proposed task structure includes all of the activities necessary for completing the project. Planning a viable schedule for carrying out the tasks is often as important as developing a comprehensive list of tasks.

(vii) Management Plan

The plan should indicate who will be responsible for each part of the work, and who will be responsible for overall coordination. The management plan should also be carefully tailored to the unique nature of the individual project.

(viii) Staff and Institutional Qualifications

This section includes a full discussion of the qualifications and experience of the proposed staff. Sometimes it is useful to include brief summaries of the staff experience in the management plan and to attach complete resumes for each member of the team as appendices to the proposal. This information is essential and should be presented in a way that demonstrates the staff has the necessary qualifications and experience to conduct the research. This section should also include complete information about the relevant qualifications of the institution where the project will be located. Research projects often require a variety of hardware or software and there should be clear evidence that adequate facilities are available to support the project.

(ix) Budget

The project budget should include clear and reasonable estimates of the costs of each element of the project, and there should be enough supporting information to indicate how the estimates were developed. Base salaries for all staff, standard charges for computer use, and allowable travel costs are a few examples of useful background information. Even if a budget is not required, it is a good idea to have a budget for internal purposes.

Key Elements of a Research Proposal

COVER PAGE / TITLE PAGE

The Executive Summary: It allows the busy manager, or sponsor to quickly understand the thrust of the proposal. It is an informative abstract - should include brief statements of the management dilemma and management question, and benefit of the researchers approach.

Introduction and Theoretical Base

Problem Statement

Purpose of Investigation

Review of Literature

Research Questions / Hypotheses

Design – Methods and Procedures (sampling, instruments, data collections and analysis)

Limitations / Delimitations

Significance of the Study

Qualifications of researchers

Budget

Schedule: Phases of Project

Facilities and special resources

References

Appendix

3.7.2 Drafting a Research Proposal

It is very important to exercise caution while drafting a research proposal. Quality writing is a must. It should be clear, concise, and free of jargon. There should be no spelling or grammatical errors, and the proposal should be easy to read.

Pilot Survey

The data collecting phase of the research process typically begins with pilot testing.

A pilot survey or preliminary survey is conducted to detect weaknesses in design and instrumentation and also provide proxy data for selection of a probability sample. It involves selecting samples from the target population and simulates the procedures designed for data collection. Data may be collected by whichever method is specified in the design. Respondents for the pilot survey do not have to be statistically selected. Pre-testing through pilot survey serves the purpose of refining a measuring instrument. Suggestions from the respondents can be used to identify and change confusing, awkward, or offensive questions and techniques. Once the researcher is satisfied that the plan is sound then data collection is started.

3.7.3 Evaluating a Research Proposal

Any research proposal can be evaluated on the following lines:

The research proposal should be thoroughly checked for the details and feasibility of the project.

Problem: It is very important that the research is focusing on some pertinent issue, and is sufficiently supported by facts for novelty of the problem. The literature review should confirm the research gaps that are indicate or the management questions that would be addressed in case of managerial dilemma. One needs to ensure that the problem is clearly stated in terms of title, objectives, hypothesis and scope.

Research Design: The research design should be well formed and clear regarding the researcher's intentions.

Time Availability: Sufficient time should be available as per the requirement of the topic being investigated.

Information: It needs to be ascertained that information required for the research is available for collection and analysis.

Strategic/Tactical Decisions: The research is addressing a pressing issue leading to strategic decisions of importance or not.

Value of Research: It is very important to ascertain that the value of research information exceeds the cost of conducting the research.

All the above will help in evaluation of the research proposal.

Points to Remember

- The research design is a plan of action indicating the specific steps that are necessary to provide answers to those questions, test the hypotheses, and thereby achieve the research purpose that helps choose among the decision alternatives to solve the management problem or capitalise on the market opportunity.
- Research design is an overall plan or scheme prepared by the researcher for executing the research study. It is an important stage in the process of conducting research as it facilitates systematic and smooth conduct of the research project. It acts as a guide for the researcher to work step by step on his research study.
- A research design refers to the preparation of sampling design, observational design, statistical design and the operational design.
- Research design is necessary because it facilitates the smooth execution of the various research activities thereby bringing efficiency and effectiveness to the study.
- A research design proves to be effective in yielding the required information within the constraints of time, money and energy. Research design helps the researcher to organise his ideas and improve upon any flaws or deviations from the right path.
- A good research design is expected to be flexible, appropriate, efficient, and economical. It should minimise the bias and maximise the reliability of the data collected and analysed, at the same time giving rise to minimum of experimental errors, if any.
- Exploratory research is particularly useful in providing insights into the problem when researcher lacks a clear idea of the problem. The purpose of exploratory research is to know the unknown.
- Descriptive research is undertaken when the researcher desires to know the characteristics of certain groups such as age, gender, occupation, income or education. The objective of descriptive research is to answer the "who, what, when, where and how" of the subject under study/investigation. Descriptive studies are normally factual and simple.
- Causal design investigates the cause and effect relationship between two or more variables. This design measures the extent of relationship between the variables. Causal research designs attempt to specify the nature of functional relationship between two or more variables.
- Experimental research is used to answer causal research questions. The easiest way to devise an experimental question may be to think about a question in which you can control, manipulate, or assign the independent variable.

- Qualitative research is a highly subjective research discipline, designed to look beyond the percentages to gain an understanding of the customer's feelings, impressions and viewpoints.
- Qualitative research is concerned with the opinions, experiences and feelings of individuals and produces subjective data. Face-to-face interviews and group discussions are some ways to get in-depth feedback from customers.
- Quantitative research is conclusive in its purpose as it tries to quantify the problem and understand how prevalent it is by looking for projectable results to a larger population.
- Quantitative research statistically measures customer attitudes, behaviour, and performance. Being deeply based on numbers and statistics, quantitative research has the ability to effectively translate data into easily quantifiable charts and graphs.
- Types of Qualitative techniques are Projective Techniques, Depth Interview, Experience Survey, Focus Groups, Observation.
- Quantitative research is designed to reduce the complexity of studying a problem, whereas qualitative research attempts to understand, describe, and sometime explain the complexity. Quantitative research shows patterns across situations (sometimes on a large scale) whereas qualitative research has a much smaller focus. Qualitative research shows details, processes at work, and the important role of individuals.
- The research proposal is an activity that incorporates decisions made during the early research-project planning phases of the study including the management research question hierarchy and exploration.
- A written proposal is often required when a study is being suggested. It ensures that the parties concur on the project's purpose and on the proposed methods of investigation.
- Every research proposal should include two basic sections: a statement of the research question and a brief description of the research methodology.
- The research proposal must present its plan, services, and credentials in the best possible way to encourage its selection over the competitors. The proposal tells us what, why, how, where, and to whom it will be done. It must also show the benefit of doing it.
- The research proposal is necessary a road map, showing clearly the location where a journey begins, the destination to be reached and the method of getting there. Well prepared research proposals include potential problems that may be encountered along the way and methods for avoiding or working around them.
- It is very important to exercise caution while drafting a research proposal. Quality writing is a must. It should be clear, concise, and free of jargon. There should be no spelling or grammatical errors, and the proposal should be easy to read.

Questions for Discussion

1. Explain what you understand by a research design.
2. Discuss the need for research design. What are the features of a good research design?
3. What do you understand by a sampling design? What points should be taken into consideration by a researcher in developing a sampling design for his research problem?
4. Highlight the basic principles of experimental designs.
5. State the components of the research design and draw a brief design for a proposed research problem of your choice.
6. Discuss giving suitable illustrations, the qualitative and quantitative research designs.
7. Explain what you understand by "Exploratory Research".
8. Discuss experimental research designs with suitable illustrations.
9. What are the various methods of conducting qualitative research? Discuss advantages and limitations of each of these methods?
10. What is a research proposal? Give the key components of a good research proposal.

Chapter 4...

Measurement and Attitude Scaling Techniques

Contents ...

Introduction

4.1 Concept of Measurement

    4.1.1 What is Measured?

    4.1.2 Problems in Measurement in Management Research - Validity and Reliability

    4.1.3 Levels of Measurement

4.2 Attitude Scaling Techniques

    4.2.1 Concept of Scale

    4.2.2 Scaling Techniques for Measuring Data gathered from Respondents

Points to Remember

Questions for Discussion

Learning Objectives

- To understand the concept of measurement in research
- To understand the need for attitude measurement
- To know the different scaling techniques

Introduction

This chapter deals with the very important component of research i.e. measurement and data collection. In every research, data is the lifeline of the study as it shapes the entire project outcome. If everything else is in place but the data are not collected keeping in mind the measurement aspects, then the entire efforts of the researcher go waste. Hence, it is very important to understand the way different scales are to be constructed to measure the qualitative data and also the techniques of collection of data.

4.1 Concept of Measurement

Measurement of variables is very crucial in research. Business research is focused around measurement and recording of observations. Measurement means the assignment of symbols to represent properties of objects, events or states. It is a system for assigning symbols, letters, or numbers to the observed properties of variables according to predefined rules. In research context, measurement involves assignment of numbers to objects in such a way that physical relationships and operations among the objects correspond to arithmetic relationships and operations among the numbers.

Definition

Measurement is defined as:

The determination of size in relation to some observed standard, for e.g., metre, kilogram, second, ampere, degree Kelvin, candela, mole, or some unit derived from these seven basic units.

"When you measure what you are speaking about and express it in numbers, you know something about it, but when you cannot (or do not) measure it, when you cannot (or do not) express it in numbers, then your knowledge is of a meager and unsatisfactory kind."

- Lord Kelvin

"Measurement is the assignment of numerals to objects or events according to rules".

- S.S. Stevens

"Measurement is the assignment of numbers to represent properties." **- Campbell**

Measurement is the process of observing and recording the observations. Measurement is the estimation or determination of extent, dimension or capacity, usually in relation to some standard or unit of measurement. The measurement is expressed as a number of units of the standard, such as distance being indicated by a number of kilometers.

4.1.1 What is Measured?

Many a times, business research involves measuring of attitudes of individuals, measurement of perceptions, cognitions, opinions, and other latent constructs that can't be measured directly. For example, it is rather difficult to measure concepts directly, e.g., efficiency, anger, etc.

In every organisation, a manager needs to take many decisions which may be related to manufacturing, marketing, hiring and so on. These decisions may be based on quantitative data or behavioural data. Whereas, quantitative data like height, weight etc. can be readily obtained through well defined measuring instruments, it is the behavioural or abstract aspects like motivation, intelligence, social conformity etc. which prove to be difficult to measure. For these, carefully designed measuring instruments need to be designed on the basis of well defined constructs.

For instance, measuring things like social conformity, intelligence, or marital adjustment is very difficult and requires much closer attention than measuring physical weight, biological age or a person's financial assets.

Measurement may be regarded as the assignment of numerals to characteristics of objects, persons, states, or events, according to rules. What is measured is not the object, person, state, or event itself but some characteristic of it. When objects are counted, for example, we do not measure the object itself but only it's characteristic of being present. We never measure people, only their age, height, weight, or some other characteristic is measured. The fundamental ideas involved in measuring are nominal, ordinal, interval and ratio which considered as four broad categories of measurements.

Tests of Sound Measurement

Any measuring instrument which is tested is required to be verified for its accuracy and appropriateness. Also, one always needs to be assured that the measure developed is a good one. For any measure to be a sound and good measure, it is desirable that it satisfies the following tests:

Test of Validity: Refers to the fact that the instrument is able to measure what it is designed for.

Test of Reliability: Means that every time the instrument is used it should give the same results.

Practicality: Means that the instrument is very easy and practical to use.

4.1.2 Problems in Measurement in Management Research - Validity and Reliability

Once the concept to be measured has been identified, the researcher is faced with the problem, "How shall the concept be measured?". Each type of measure requires specific issues that need to be addressed so as to make the measurement meaningful, accurate and efficient. Also, the 'population' for which the measure is being obtained needs to be confirmed in the context of the immediate research question at hand. And lastly, the researcher needs to confirm the purpose for which the measure is going to be used further in the context of analysis.

Once the measure has been developed the relevant questions expected are,

(a) "How do we know that we are indeed measuring what we intend to measure?" i.e., to ensure that we are measuring what we desire to measure, and

(b) "Can we be sure that if the measurement is repeated, then we will get the same results?" i.e., whether our measure is reliable.

The first question relates to validity and the second to reliability. It is the responsibility of the researcher to ensure themselves and assure to others the validity and reliability of their instruments.

Validity

Validity relates to the accuracy of the measurement. It means we are measuring what we intend to measure. Validity is the degree to which an instrument measures what it is supposed to measure and performs as it is designed to perform. It is rare, if nearly impossible, that an instrument be 100% valid, so validity is generally measured in degrees.

- **External Validity:** External validity is the extent to which the results of a study can be generalised from a sample to a population. Externally valid instrument helps to generalise results of sample to a population.
- **Content Validity**: Content validity refers to the appropriateness of the content of an instrument. It ensures whether the measures (questions, observation logs, etc.) accurately assess. For example, suppose an examiner wishes to maximise the validity of a unit test for 7th standard mathematics. Hence, this would involve taking representative questions from each of the sections of the units and evaluating them against the desired outcomes.

Reliability

Reliability of measurement means stability or consistency. Reliability is the degree to which a test consistently measures whatever it measures. It means if we measure the same object twice with our measurement device, we get the same results. Reliability is the consistency of your measurement, or the degree to which an instrument measures the same way each time it is used under the same condition with the same subjects.

The concepts of validity and reliability are closely but not symmetrically related. If a measure is valid, it should also be reliable. The reverse is not true, because a measure that's reliable is not necessarily valid. In repeating any study, you can get the same results and still not be measuring what you intend. An instrument must be reliable in order to be valid. Validity is more important than reliability but for the instrument to be most useful it should be both valid and reliable.

4.1.3 Levels of Measurement

There are four levels of measurement: nominal, ordinal, interval and ratio. Described below are the characteristics of each of these levels.

1. Nominal Measurement

Nominal measurement is the most elementary method of measurement which classifies persons, objects or events into a number of mutually exclusive and exhaustive categories on the basis of the simple presence or absence, applicability or inapplicability, possession or non-possession of certain property. Exhaustive means that there must be enough categories that all the observations will fall into some category. Mutually exclusive means that the categories must be distinct enough that no observations will fall into more than one category. It can only determine whether two observations are alike or different, for example, sorting a deck of cards into two piles: red cards and black cards.

These scales are just numerical and are the least restrictive of all the scales. Instances of Nominal Scale are - credit card numbers, bank account numbers, employee id numbers etc. Thus, the population of a town may be classified according to gender into 'males' and 'females' or according to religion into Hindus, Jains, Parsis, Muslims, Sikhs and Christians and each category of persons given certain labels either in the form of numerals (0,1,2,3) or in the form of letters (A,B,C,D).

These labels only tell us that the categories are qualitatively different from each other. They have no quantitative significance, i.e., they cannot be added, subtracted, multiplied or divided. One can, if one desires, interchange the labels of various categories for they do not signify any ranking or ordering of categories. The numeral 1 given to a certain category does not imply its superior position to other category which is given numeral 0.

Example: In a survey if variable of interest is place of residence, measured by a question on a questionnaire asking for the Pin code of the respondent's principal place of residence, observations divided into pin code categories are mutually exclusive and exhaustive. All respondents live in one pin code category (exhaustive) but no respondent lives in more than one pin code category (mutually exclusive).

There is no ordering of categories (no category is better or worse, or more or less than another).

This scale is simple and widely used when relationship between two variables is to be studied. In a Nominal Scale numbers are no more than labels and are used specifically to identify different categories of responses.

The only arithmetic operation possible in case of a nominal measurement is counting. Thus, mode is the only legitimate measure of central tendency. One can also calculate the percentage of objects failing within each category. It will not make sense to calculate the arithmetic mean of gender in a sample consisting of 45 men and 55 women. All we can say is that there are more females than males in the sample or that 45% of the sample is male.

Some examples:

Q. What is your gender?

[ ] Male   [ ] Female

Q. Suppose a survey of retail stores is done on two aspects - way of maintaining stocks and daily turnover.

How do you stock items at present?

[ ] By product category

[ ] At a centralised store

[ ] Department wise

[ ] Single warehouse

Daily turnover is?

[ ] Between 100 – 200

[ ] Between 200 – 300

[ ] Above 300

A two way classification can be made as follows:

Stock Method→ Daily Turnover	Product Category	Department wise	Centralised Store	Single Warehouse
100 – 200				
200 – 300				
Above 300				

2. Ordinal Measurement

In ordinal measurement numerals, letters or other symbols are used to rank objects. An ordinal level of measurement uses symbols to classify observations into categories that are not only mutually exclusive and exhaustive; in addition, the categories have some explicit relationship among them. For example, observations may be classified into categories such as taller and shorter, greater and lesser, faster and slower, harder and easier, and so forth. However, each observation must still fall into one of the categories (the categories are exhaustive) but no more than one (the categories are mutually exclusive). For example, asking whether one is very satisfied, satisfied, neutral, dissatisfied, or very dissatisfied with one's job is using an ordinal scale of measurement.

Ordinal measurements do not provide information on how much more or less of the characteristic various objects possess. For example, if in respect of a certain characteristic two objects have the ranks 5 and 8 and two other objects have the ranks 3 and 6; we cannot say that the differences between the two pairs are equal. There is also no way to know that any object has none of the characteristic being measured.

The most common use is of nominal data is in obtaining preferences measurements. For example, a consumer or a group of experts may be asked to rank preference for several brands, flavours, or package designs. Attitude measures are also often ordinal in nature.

Example: Rank the following attributes (1 - 5), on their importance in a refrigerator.
1. Company Name
2. Functions
3. Price
4. Comfort
5. Design

The most important attribute is ranked 1 by the respondents and the least important is ranked 5. Here, instead of numbers, letters or symbols too can be used to rate in a ordinal scale.

Example: If there are 4 different types of cement and if they are ordered on the basis of quality as Grade A, Grade B, Grade C, Grade D – then it is again an Ordinal Scale.

Example: If there are 5 different brands of Deodorant Spray and if a respondent ranks them based on say, "Freshness" into Rank 1 having maximum Freshness; Rank 2 the second maximum Freshness, and so on, an Ordinal Scale results.

The kind of descriptive statistics that can be calculated from these data are mode, median and percentages. It is meaningless to calculate a mean because the differences between ordinal scales values are not necessarily, the same.

3. **Interval Measurement**

An interval level of measurement classifies observations into categories that are not only mutually exclusive and exhaustive, and have some explicit relationship among them, but the relationship between the categories is known and exact. This is the first quantitative application of numbers.

Interval measurements represent numerals to rank objects such that numerically equal distances on the scale represent equal distances in the property being measured. The distances between numerals are meaningful because, by comparing these distances we can know how far apart the objects are with respect to the property in question. The intervals between categories are equal, but they originate from some arbitrary origin.

For example, if we are measuring the achievements of 4 students W, X, Y, and Z on an interval scale and obtain the values 1, 4, 5 and 8 respectively then by comparing the intervals, we can justifiably say that the difference between W and Y in their achievements is the same as the difference between X and Z and that the difference between X and Z is four times the difference between W and Y.

One very important drawback of this measurement, however, is that one cannot compare objects on the basis of ratios of their absolute scores. Thus, in our example, we cannot say that the achievements of X are twice as great as that of Z. The reason is that in our measurement the zero point is arbitrary so that any change in this point will change the absolute scores and the ratios between scores.

The most common examples of interval scales are the Centigrade and Fahrenheit temperature scales which start with different points of origin. The point of origin (for the same natural phenomenon, the freezing point of water) is zero on the Centigrade scale and 32 on Fahrenheit. Because of this difference the ratio between any two readings on the Centigrade scale (e.g., between 10 to 30) is not the same as that on the Fahrenheit scale as shown below. One can only talk of a 20°C rise in temperature but not of 30°C as being three times as hot as 10°C.

Centigrade: 0   10   30   100
Fahrenheit: 32   53   86   212

Unlike in Nominal or Ordinal, here the distance between the various categories, are equal in case of Interval Scales. The Interval Scales are also termed as Rating Scales.

Illustration 1: How do you rate your present refrigerator for the following qualities?

Company Name	Less Known	1	2	3	4	5	Well Known
Functions	Few	1	2	3	4	5	Many
Price	Low	1	2	3	4	5	High
Design	Poor	1	2	3	4	5	Good
Overall Satisfaction	Very Dissatisfied	1	2	3	4	5	Very Satisfied

The data obtained from the Interval Scale can be used to calculate the mean scores of each attributes over all respondents. The Standard Deviation (a measure of dispersion) can also be calculated. The most frequent of interval measurement in social sciences is index numbers which are calculated on the basis of an arbitrary zero point. Another common form of interval measurement is a Likert scale which is used in the measurement of attitudes and personality.

Virtually a wide range of statistical analysis can be applied to data measured on interval scales. One can use descriptive measures as the mean, median, mode, range and standard deviation. Bivariate correlation analysis, t-test, analysis of variance test, and most multivariate techniques applied for purposes of drawing inferences can also be used.

4. Ratio Measurement

This measurement, besides possessing the property of the interval measurement, possesses one additional property, viz., it has a true, natural or absolute zero point, from which the equal intervals between categories originate and for which there is universal agreement as to its location. A true zero means that the object measuring zero possesses none of the property in question. There is a meaningful and non-arbitrary zero point. Ratio scale possesses all the characteristics of an interval scale, and the ratios of the numbers on these scales have meaningful interpretations. Data on certain demographic or descriptive attributes, if they are obtained through open-ended questions, will have ratio-scale properties. For example, weight, area, speed, and velocity are measured on a ratio level scale. Other common examples of this type of measurement are sales, costs, number of purchasers, length, time, etc.

With a ratio measurement, the comparison between ratios of the absolute magnitude of the numbers becomes possible. Thus, a person weighing 100kg is said to be twice as heavy as one weighing 50kg and a person weighing 150kg is three times as heavy.

Further, with a ratio scale we can compare intervals, rank objects according to magnitude, or use the numbers to identify the objects. All descriptive measures and inferential techniques are applicable to ratio-measured data. For instance,

Q.1. What is your annual income before taxes? _____ rupees.

Q.2. How far is the Theatre from your home ? _____ kilometers.

Why is Level of Measurement Important?

Many variables can be easily measured by asking a single question or making one observation. Such single-item measures are most useful when a single opportunity to assess a variable's value is likely to be sufficient, including age, gender, marital status, number of children, or income. Single-item measures can be used for factual data or even for preferences such as, "Which political party do you favor for election?". It may be noted that variables measured at a higher level can always be converted to a lower level, but not vice versa. For example, observations of actual age (ratio scale) can be converted to categories of older and younger (ordinal scale), but age measured as simply older or younger cannot be converted to measures of actual age.

Knowledge about the level of measurement helps you decide how to interpret the data from that variable and also what statistical analysis is appropriate on the values that were assigned. If a measure is nominal, then you know that you would never average the data values or do a t-test on the data.

Also, there is an order implied in the level of measurement idea. At lower levels of measurement, assumptions tend to be less restrictive and data analyses tend to be less sensitive. At each level up the hierarchy, the current level includes all of the qualities of the one below it and adds something new. It is always desirable to have a higher level of measurement (e.g., interval or ratio) rather than a lower one (nominal or ordinal).

4.2 Attitude Scaling Techniques

4.2.1 Concept of Scale

A scale is a continuum that helps in making judgement about change / quality of an individual by placing him on a scale directly or by constructing a questionnaire in such a way that the score of responses assigns him a place on the scale. Scaling refers to a classification system that is used to describe the measurement of concepts or variables used in research. This classification system categorises the variables as being measured on either nominal, ordinal, interval, or ratio scale.

All measurements must take one of four forms nominal, ordinal, interval, or ratio scale. There are various forms of comparative and non-comparative namely, numeric, semantic and graphical form etc.

Types of Scales

The most frequently used scales are:
(a) Nominal Scale
(b) Ordinal Scale
(c) Interval Scale
(d) Ratio Scale

Attitude Scaling Techniques

In social and behavioural research, and in many other areas of science, sometimes the assignment of numbers to concepts under study is rather crude. An attitude scale is a measure of the relative quantity of an attitude possessed by an individual as contrasted with a reference group. They provide a quantitative measurement of attitudes, opinions or values by summarising numerical scores given by researchers to people's responses to sets of statements exploring dimensions of an underlying idea. Scaling is applied to the attempts to measure the attitude objectively. Attitude is a resultant of number of external and internal factors. Depending upon the attitude to be measured, appropriate scales are designed.

Scaling attempts one of the most difficult of research tasks – measure abstract concepts. Scaling is the type of measurement that involves the construction of an instrument that associates qualitative constructs with quantitative metric units. Scaling techniques are used for measuring qualitative responses of respondents such as those related to their feelings, perception, likes, dislikes, interests and preferences.

Concept and Applications of Attitude Scaling Techniques

Scale: During the research concerning measuring the abstract concepts, the researcher often encounters problems of valid measurements for measuring concepts like attitudes and opinions. Therefore, there is a need of techniques which may enable to measure abstract concepts more precisely. A scale is a continuum consisting of the highest point and lowest point along with several intermediate points between the extreme points indicating the degrees of a given characteristics. Scaling techniques explain the procedures of assigning numbers to various degrees of opinion, attitudes and other concepts. Hence, scaling may be defined as a procedure for the assignment of numbers to a property of objects in order to impart some of the characteristics of numbers to the properties in questions.

Applications: In business research, often the researcher needs to measure the judgement (belief) of the consumer regarding the characteristics (attributes) of product or service under consideration. The researcher is primarily interested in measuring the mental state (attitude) of the respondent. It may include the factors like awareness, attitudes and decisions processes, age, education, profession etc. of the respondents. Questionnaire Methods and Observation Methods are the commonly used techniques in attitude measurement related studies.

Applications: Useful in problems related to marketing research, behavioural studies in terms of measure of honesty, integrity, brand loyalty, brand preference, brand image etc.

Scaling can be done in the following two ways:
(i) Making a judgment about some characteristic of an individual and then placing him directly on a scale that has been defined in terms of that characteristic.
(ii) Constructing questionnaires in such a way that the score of individual's responses assigns him a place on a scale.

4.2.2 Scaling Techniques for Measuring Data gathered from Respondents

The various types of scaling techniques used in research can be classified into two categories: (a) Comparative (Ranking) scales, and (b) Non-comparative (Rating) scales.

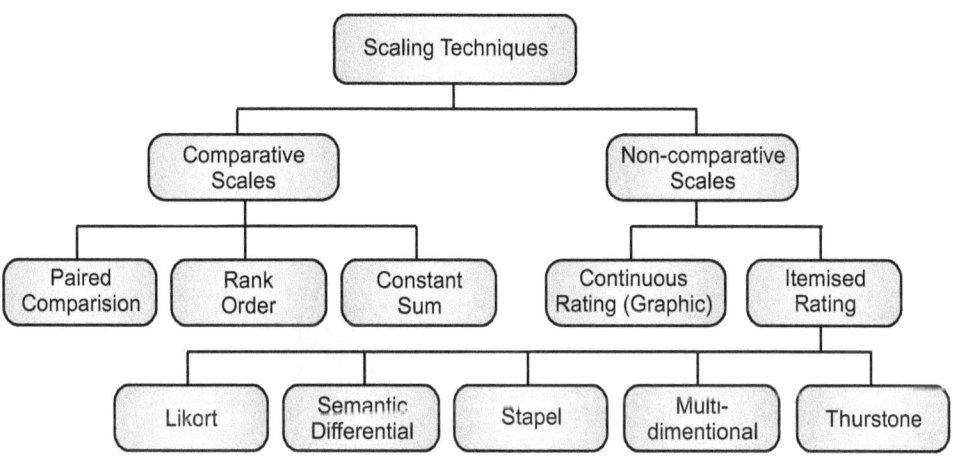

Fig. 4.1

Comparative Scales

In comparative scaling, the respondent is asked to compare one object with another. For example, the researcher can ask the respondents whether they prefer brand A or brand B of a detergent.

- Involve the respondent directly comparing stimulus objects.
- Example: How does Pepsi compare with Coke on sweetness?

Non-comparative Scales

Non-comparative scaling requires respondents to evaluate only a single object. Their evaluation is independent of the other object which the researcher is studying. Respondents using a non-comparative scale employ whatever rating standard seems appropriate to them. **Respondent scales each stimulus object independently of other objects.** Example: How would you rate the sweetness of Pepsi on a scale of 1 to 10.

Non-comparative techniques consist of continuous and itemised rating scales.

Self-Rating Scales
1. Graphic Scale
2. Itemised Scale
    (a) Likert Scale.
    (b) Semantic Differential Scale.
    (c) Stapel Scale.
    (d) Multi-dimensional Scale.
    (e) Thurstone Scale.
    (f) Guttman Scales/Scalogram Analysis.
    (g) Q Sort Technique.

Paired Comparison

Paired comparison is a widely used scaling technique wherein a respondent is presented a pair of objects to which he is supposed to provide his/her preference for the object from a pair. The data is obtained using ordinal scale. For example, a respondent may be asked to indicate his/her preference for TVs in a paired manner.

For example: Paired Comparison

Example: Please indicate which of the following televisions you prefer by circling your more preferred television in each pair:

Sony	Videocon
LG	Sony
Toshiba	Videocon
Videocon	LG
Sony	Toshiba
Toshiba	Sony

Easier format of presenting the above would be:

	Sony	LG	Toshiba	Videocon
Sony	+			
LG		−		
Toshiba			+	
Videocon				−

'+' → column brand is preferred over row brand
'−' → row brand is preferred over column brand

Research Methodology
Measurement & Attitude Scaling Techniques

Example: Paired comparison scaling

Please indicate which of following television TV sets do you prefer from the pair of brands given below?

TV	Samsung	LG	Videocon	Sony
Samsung	*	+	+	+
LG	-	*	-	-
Videocon	-	+	*	+
Sony	-	+	-	*
No. of times a brand is preferred in a pair	0	3	1	2

'+' → column brand is preferred over row brand
'-' → row brand is preferred over column brand

Paired comparison data can be analysed in several ways. In the above example, the researcher can calculate the percentage of respondents who prefer one particular brand of TV over the other. This method is useful when the number of brands is limited, as it requires direct comparison and clear choice. Also, it is a common method of taste testing, for example, the consumer is asked to taste two different brands of soft drinks and select the one with the most appealing taste.

Rank Order / Forced Ranking

This is a popular type of scaling technique used in business research wherein the respondents are offered different objects simultaneously for ranking from a list of objects presented. Forced ranking avoids the problem of every feature being scored highly. Forced ranking helps people decide which is more important by choosing one over the other, providing clearer preferences to the research team. Forced ranking scales have been used to rank a variety of dimensions such as identifying social problems considered critical by the population, providing rankings of the prestige of occupations, and ranking individuals in terms of power. In such instances, the researcher's primary goal may be simply to obtain rankings on a particular dimension. The disadvantage of forced ranking is that it does not measure how important each of the items is to the respondent. Some examples of forced ranking are discussed below.

Example: Forced Ranking.

Following is the list of colour television brands available in the market. Please rank the brands in order of your preference by assigning 1 to most preferred brand, 2 to the next preferred brand, and so forth uniquely.

Brands	Ranking
LG	…………
Samsung	…………
Sansui	…………
Videocon	…………
Sony	…………
Philips	…………

Example: Rank the following soft-drinks from 1 (best) to 5 (worst) according to your taste preference:

Coca-Cola	____
7-Up	____
Limca	____
Pepsi-Cola	____
Mountain Dew	____

Example: Indicate your preferred type of music with a 1, your second favorite with a 2, and so on for each type of music:

____	Alternative
____	Urban Contemporary
____	Classical
____	Country

Constant Sum Scales

In this method, the respondent has to allocate a constant sum of units, such as points, rupees or among a set of stimulus objects with respect to some criterion. The technique involves asking the respondents to assign 10 points to attributes of a sports utility vehicle. If the attribute is unimportant, then the respondents would want to enter zero. The attributes are scaled by counting the points assigned to each one by al the respondents and dividing the number of respondents. This predominantly uses ordinal because of its comparative nature. Constant sum scaling is advantageous, as it allows for discrimination among stimulus objects without requiring too much time.

Example: Allocate a total of 100 points among the following soft-drinks depending on how favourable you feel toward each; the more highly you think of each soft-drink, the more points you should allocate to it. (Please check that the allocated points add to 100.)

Coca-Cola	____	points
7-Up	____	points
Limca	____	points
Mountain Dew	____	points
Pepsi-Cola	____	points
	100	**points**

Example: Constant Sum Scale

Please divide 100 points among the following characteristics so the division reflects the relative importance of each characteristic to you in the selection of a bank.

	Points
Hours of service	_____
Friendliness	_____
Distance from home	_____
Investment vehicles	_____
Parking facilities	_____

Example: Constant sum scale

Following are the six attributes of a newly launched model of a car. Please indicate out of 100 points you will assign to indicate your relative preference for the particular attribute.

Attributes	Points
Price	37
Space	10
Interiors	5
Mileage	33
Colours	10
Power steering	5
Total	100

Non-comparative Scaling Techniques

These are often referred as nomadic scales as only one subject is evaluated at a time. The respondents do not compare the object being rated either to another object or to some specified standard set by the researcher. Non-comparative techniques use continuous and itemised rating scales. In such scales, each object is scaled independently of the other objects in the stimulus set, the resulting data is generally assumed to be interval or ratio scale.

1. Graphic Rating Scale

It is also called as continuous rating scale and it is used to indicate ratings of a particular attribute. It consists of points on a continuum (such as a line) and the respondents rate the objects by placing a mark at the appropriate position on a line that runs from one extreme of the criterion variable to another. Researchers develop continuous rating scale allowing the respondents to indicate their rating by placing a mark at the appropriate point on a line that runs from one end of the criterion variable to the other or a set of predetermined response categories. Here the respondents need not select marks already set the researcher.

Several variations are possible. The line may be vertical or horizontal; it may be unmarked or marked; if marked, the divisions may be few or as many as in the thermometer scale; the scale points may be in the form of numbers or brief descriptions.

Example: Please evaluate the service quality of a restaurant by placing an X at the position on the horizontal line that most reflects your feelings.

The worst--The best

Advantages
- Less time consuming to develop.
- Allow for quantitative comparison.
- They are easy to use and cost little to develop.

Disadvantages
- Less uniformity as different persons will use the same graphic scales in different ways.
- There is possibility of differences in interpretations of scale item meanings and scale ranges.
- Scoring can be cumbersome.

Errors or problems in rating
(a) Halo effects
(b) Leniency
(c) Strictness
(d) Central tendency
(e) Personal bias
(f) Recency

Example: Indicate your overall opinion about ice-ream brand by placing a tick mark at appropriate position on the line.

← -- →
Poor   **Good**

This line can be vertical or horizontal and scale points may be provided. No other indication is there on the continuous scale. A range is provided. To quantify the responses to question that "indicate your overall opinion about ice-cream Brand by placing a tick mark at appropriate position on the line", we measure the physical distance between the left extreme position and the response position on the line; the greater the distance, the more favourable is the response or attitude towards the brand. Limitation of this scale is that coding and analysis requires substantial amount of time, as first we need to measure the physical distances on the scale for each respondent.

2. Itemised Rating Scales

These scales are widely used in business research. The respondents are provided with a scale that has a number or brief description associated with each category. They essentially take the form of the multiple category questions usually five to seven categories (rarely ten). The categories are ordered in terms of scale position; and the respondents are required to select the specified category that best describes the object being rated. The categories are given verbal description, although this is not absolutely necessary. These scales are widely used in research and nowadays, more complex types such as multi-item rating scales are used. Variations among the itemised rating scales are - Likert, Semantic, Staple, Multi-dimensional, etc.

(a) Likert Scale

Likert Scale was developed by **Rensis Likert**. It is the most widely used scale in business research particularly in testing models. In contrast to a simple "yes / no" question, a Likert scale allows to reveal degrees of opinion. A Likert scale measures attitudes and behaviours using answer choices that range from one extreme to another (for example, not at all likely to extremely likely). This can be particularly helpful for sensitive or challenging topics or subject matter. The respondents are asked to indicate a degree of agreement and disagreement with each of a series of statement. Each scale item has 5 response categories ranging from strongly agree to strongly disagree. Analysis can be done by either using profile analysis or summated analysis. Profile analysis is item by item analysis where respondent's scores are obtained for each item of the scale and analysis is done on individual items. Alternatively, the scores are obtained from respondents and sum is obtained across the scale items. On summing, average is obtained for all the respondents. Likert scale is also referred to as summated scale.

Having a range of responses helps to identify areas of improvement easily; for example, sending out a questionnaire to understand the levels of effectiveness of the course being taught or gathering clients' opinions on the quality of service at a fast food joint.

Example: Listed below are the tangibility of service rendered by a bank. Please indicate how strongly you agree or disagree with each by using the following scale:

1 = Strongly disagree
2 = Disagree
3 = Neither agree nor disagree
4 = Agree
5 = Strongly agree

Attributes	5 Strongly agree	4 Agree	3 Indifferent	2 Disagree	1 Strongly disagree
1.					
2.					
3.					
4.					
5.					

To analyse the data generated using this scale, each statement is assigned a numerical score ranging either from -2 to +2 through a zero or 1 to 5. The analysis can be conducted item wise or a total score (summated) or a mean can be calculated for each respondent by summing or averaging across items. It is important in Likert scale that a consistent scoring procedure is adopted so that a high score reflects favourable response and a low score reflects unfavourable response.

Example: Following are the statements related to a microwave oven produced by a company. Indicate your answer in terms or agreement or disagreement on the statement by ticking the concerned number as described below:

	5 Strongly agree	4 Agree	3 Indifferent	2 Disagree	1 Strongly disagree
Price range of microwave is appropriate					
After sales service is good					
Ad campaign is effective					
Sales executives are very co-operative					
Showroom demonstration is appropriate					

The practical range of response choices for Likert scale items is from three to seven. Fewer than three responses limit the researcher to a dichotomy, and the scale becomes a simple summated ratings scale. With more than seven choices, and perhaps with fewer, it becomes difficult to make adequate distinctions along the response continuum.

(b) Semantic Differential Scale

Semantic differential is a popular scaling technique that usually takes a 5 or 7 point bipolar labels (adjective scales) that have semantic meaning. It refers to a questionnaire format in which the respondent is asked to rate something in terms of two opposite adjectives. The respondents rate objects on a number of itemised, seven point rating scales bounded at each end by one of two bipolar adjectives such as "Excellent" and "Very bad". The respondents indicate their response choosing the one that best describes their choice. The points are marked either from - 3 to +3 through a zero or from 1 to 7. The middle value maybe treated as a neutral position. The value zero in the first type is the neutral point and 4 in the second type is the neutral point. The resulting data are commonly analysed through profile analysis wherein the means or median values on each rating scale are calculated and compared by plotting or statistical analysis. This helps the researcher to determine the overall differences and similarities among the objects. The purpose of this technique is to discover underlying meanings of concepts or objects for individuals and groups.

	Very Much	Somewhat	Neither	Somewhat	Very Much	
Enjoyable	☐	☐	☐	☐	☐	Unenjoyable
Simple	☐	☐	☐	☐	☐	Complex
Harsh	☐	☐	☐	☐	☐	Gentle
Traditional	☐	☐	☐	☐	☐	Modern

Example: Suppose we want to know personality of a particular person. We have options, like

(i) Unpleasant/Submissive
(ii) Pleasant/Dominant

This is a seven point scale and the end points of the scale are associated with bipolar labels.

1 Unpleasant Submissive	2	3	4	5	6	7 Pleasant Dominant

Research Methodology — Measurement & Attitude Scaling Techniques

Advantages and Limitations of Semantic Differential

This scale is simple to construct and it provides a good basis for comparing images of two or more items while developing image profile. It is easy and fast to administer, but it is also sensitive to small differences in attitude, highly versatile, reliable and generally valid.

The semantic differential requires respondents that are intelligent and co-operative. Also, it requires respondents with a good knowledge of language, who are willing and able to make fine distinctions. It is not appropriate for children, unless presented in a simplified form.

(c) Stapel Scale

This scale was developed by **Jan Stapel**. It is a variation of semantic differential scale with unipolar rating scale having generally 10 categories from -5 to 5 without a zero point. The scale is usually presented vertically and respondents choose their response based on how accurately or inaccurately each item describes the object by selecting an appropriate numerical response category. It is easy to administer. The higher number indicates more accurate description of the object and lower number indicates lower description of the object.

Distinct Features of Stapel Scale are,

- Each item has only one word/phrase indicating the dimension it represents.
- Each item has ten response categories.
- Each item has an even number of categories.
- The response categories have numerical labels but no verbal labels.

    +5
    +4
    +3
    +2
    +1

- High Quality

    -1
    -2
    -3
    -4
    -5

- This is a unipolar rating scale.

(d) Multi-dimensional Scaling

It consists of a group of analytical techniques which are used to study consumer attitudes related to perceptions and preferences. It is a computer based technique. The respondents are asked to place the various brands into different groups like similar, very similar, not similar, and so on. A goodness of fit is traded off on a large number of attributes. Then a lack of fit index is calculated by computer program. The purpose is to find a reasonably small number of dimensions which will eliminate most of the stress. These techniques attempt to identify the product attributes that are important to consumers and to measure their relative importance. There are many possible uses of such scaling like in market segmentation, product life cycle, vendor evaluations and advertising media selection.

The limitation of this scale is that it is difficult to clearly define the concept of similarities and preferences. Further the distances between the items are seen as different.

It is useful in studies like;

(i) To study which brand competes most directly with each other.
(ii) To find out whether the consumers would like a new brand with a combination of characteristics not found in the market.
(iii) What would be the consumer's ideal combination of product attributes.
(iv) What sales and advertising messages are compatible with consumers brand perceptions.

This scaling involves a unrealistic assumption that a consumer who compares different brands would perceive the differences on the basis of only one attribute.

For example, what are the attributes for joining MBA course?

The responses may be;

- To do PG,
- To get knowledge,
- To aim for doctoral studies, etc.

(e) Thurstone Scales

These are also known as equal appearing interval scales. They are used to measure the attitude towards a given concept or construct. A large number of statements are collected that relate to the concept or construct being measured. A panel of judges rate these statements along an 11 category scale in which each category expresses a different degree of favourableness towards the concept. The items are then ranked according to the mean or median ratings assigned by the panel of judges and are used to construct questionnaire of twenty to thirty items that are chosen more or less evenly across the range of ratings. The statements are worded in such a way so that a person can agree or disagree with them. The scale is then administered to assemble of respondents whose scores are determined by computing the mean or median value of the items agreed with. A person who disagrees with all the items has a score of zero. So, the advantage of this scale is that it is an interval measurement scale. It is the time consuming method and commonly used in psychology and education research.

(f) Guttman Scales/Scalogram Analysis

It is based on the idea that items can be arranged along a continuum in such a way that a person who agrees with an item or finds an item acceptable will also agree with or find acceptable all other items expressing a less extreme position. For example - children should not be allowed to watch violent programmes or government should ban these programmes or they are not allowed to air on the television. They all are related to one aspect. In this scale each score represents a unique set of responses and therefore the total score of every individual is obtained. This scale takes a lot of time and effort in development. They are very commonly used in political science, anthropology, public opinion, research and psychology.

Points to Remember

- Measurement of variables is very crucial in research. Business research is focused around measurement and recording of observations. Measurement means the assignment of symbols to represent properties of objects, events or states.
- It is a system for assigning symbols, letters, or numbers to observed properties of variables according to predefined rules.
- Measurement may be regarded as the assignment of numerals to characteristics of objects, persons, states, or events, according to rules. What is measured is not the object, person, state, or event itself but some characteristic of it.
- Validity relates to the accuracy of the measurement. It means we are measuring what we intend to measure. Validity is the degree to which an instrument measures what it is supposed to measure and performs as it is designed to perform.
- Reliability of measurement means stability or consistency. Reliability is the degree to which a test consistently measures whatever it measures.
- There are four levels of measurement: nominal, ordinal, interval and ratio.

- Nominal measurement is the most elementary method of measurement which classifies persons, objects or events into a number of mutually exclusive and exhaustive categories on the basis of the simple presence or absence, applicability or inapplicability, possession or non-possession of certain property.
- In ordinal measurement numerals, letters or other symbols are used to rank objects.
- An interval level of measurement classifies observations into categories that are not only mutually exclusive and exhaustive, and have some explicit relationship among them, but the relationship between the categories is known and exact.
- Ratio measurement, besides possessing the property of the interval measurement, possesses one additional property, viz., it has a true, natural or absolute zero point, from which the equal intervals between categories originate and for which there is universal agreement as to its location.
- A scale is a continuum that helps in making judgement about change / quality of an individual by placing him on a scale directly or by constructing a questionnaire in such a way that the score of responses assigns him a place on the scale. Scaling refers to a classification system that is used to describe the measurement of concepts or variables used in research.
- An attitude scale is a measure of the relative quantity of an attitude possessed by an individual as contrasted with a reference group. They provide a quantitative measurement of attitudes, opinions or values by summarising numerical scores given by researchers to people's responses to sets of statements exploring dimensions of an underlying idea.
- In comparative scaling, the respondent is asked to compare one object with another. Non-comparative scaling requires respondents to evaluate only a single object. Their evaluation is independent of the other object which the researcher is studying. Respondents using a non-comparative scale employ whatever rating standard seems appropriate to them.
- Forced ranking is a popular type of scaling technique used in business research wherein the respondents are presented different objects simultaneously for ranking from a list of objects presented. Forced ranking avoids the problem of every feature being scored highly.
- In constant sum scales the respondent has to allocate a constant sum of units, such as points, rupees or among a set of stimulus objects with respect to some criterion.

- Graphic Rating Scale is also called as continuous rating scale and it is used to indicate ratings of a particular attribute. It consists of points on a continuum (such as a line) and the respondents rate the objects by placing a mark at the appropriate position on a line that runs from one extreme of the criterion variable to another.
- Itemised Rating Scales are widely used in business research. The respondents are provided with a scale that has a number or brief description associated with each category. They essentially take the form of the multiple category questions usually five to seven categories (rarely ten). The categories are ordered in terms of scale position; and the respondents are required to select the specified category that best describes the object being rated.
- Variations among the itemised rating scales are - Likert, Semantic, Staple, Multi-dimensional, etc.
- Likert scale was developed by Rensis Likert. It is the most widely used scale in business research particularly in testing models. In contrast to a simple "yes / no" question, a Likert scale allows to reveal degrees of opinion.
- Semantic differential is a popular scaling technique that usually takes a 5 or 7 point bipolar labels (adjective scales) that have semantic meaning. It refers to a questionnaire format in which the respondent is asked to rate something in terms of two opposite adjectives.
- Stapel scale was developed by Jan Stapel. It is a variation of semantic differential scale with unipolar rating scale having generally 10 categories from -5 to 5 without a zero point.
- Multi-dimensional scaling consists of a group of analytical techniques which are used to study consumer attitudes related to perceptions and preferences. It is a computer based technique. The respondents are asked to place the various brands into different groups like similar, very similar, not similar, and so on.
- Thurstone scales are also known as equal appearing interval scales. They are used to measure the attitude towards a given concept or construct.
- Guttman scales/Scalogram analysis is based on the idea that items can be arranged along a continuum in such a way that a person who agrees with an item or finds an item acceptable will also agree with or find acceptable all other items expressing a less extreme position.

Questions for Discussion

1. Define 'measurement' in research. What are the different levels of measurement?
2. Explain the different sources of error in measurement.
3. Discuss any two scaling techniques.
4. What are the four different levels of measurement? Discuss the mathematical operations which may or may not be used under each level of measurement?
5. Explain the concept of validity and reliability in research.
6. What is scaling? How is it useful in research?
7. Discuss the rating and ranking scaling techniques.
8. Explain any two scaling techniques giving suitable illustrations.

Chapter 5...

Types of Data, Sampling and Analysis of Data

Contents ...

Introduction

5.1 Types of Data
    5.1.1 Secondary Data
    5.1.2 Definition of Secondary Data
    5.1.3 Sources of Secondary Data
    5.1.4 Characteristics of Secondary Data
    5.1.5 Searching World Wide Web for Data
    5.1.6 Sufficiency, Adequacy, Reliability and Consistency of Secondary Data

5.2 Primary Data

5.3 Observation Method

5.4 Questionnaire Method
    5.4.1 Collection of Data through Questionnaires
    5.4.2 Questionnaire Construction

5.5 Personal Interviews

5.6 Telephonic Survey / Interviewing

5.7 Schedules through Enumerators

5.8 Email/Internet Surveys, Online Survey Sites

5.9 Sampling Techniques

5.10 Basic Concepts of Sampling
    5.10.1 Defining the Universe, Survey, Census and Sampling
    5.10.2 Concepts of Statistical Population and Sample
    5.10.3 Characteristics of a Good Sample
    5.10.4 Sampling Frame
    5.10.5 Sampling Errors
    5.10.6 Non-sampling Errors
    5.10.7 Methods to Reduce Errors
    5.10.8 Sample Size Constraints
    5.10.9 Non-response

5.11 Probability Sample
5.12 Non-probability Sample
5.13 Data Analysis
    5.13.1 Processing of Data - Editing, Coding, Classifications and Tabulation
    5.13.2 Univariate, Bivariate and Multivariate Analysis of Data
    5.13.3 Construction of Frequency Distributions
5.14 Graphical Representation of Data
    5.14.1 Univariate Analysis - Measures of Central Tendency – Mean, Median and Mode
5.15 Bivariate Analysis
    5.15.1 Bivariate Analysis: Cross Tabulations
    5.15.2 Karl Pearson's Coefficient of Correlation and Spearman's Rank Correlation and Scatter Plots
    5.15.3 Chi square Test
5.16 Linear Regression Analysis
5.17 Test of Significance
5.18 Interpretation of Results
5.19 Research Reports
    5.19.1 Structure of Research Report
    5.19.2 Report Writing and Presentation
5.20 Use of Computers in Research
5.21 Importance of MS Excel and SPSS for Research Data Analysis
    Points to Remember
    Questions for Discussion

Learning Objectives

- To learn the different methods of collecting data
- To understand the basic concepts and importance of sampling techniques in research
- To get acquainted with the steps involved in processing of data
- To understand the tools for analysis of data
- To become aware of the proper way of reporting the research

Introduction

In every research, data is the lifeline of the study as it shapes the entire project outcome. The entire efforts of the researcher will go waste if everything else is in place but the data are not collected appropriately.

Once the collection of data is over, the next step is to organise the data so that meaningful conclusions may be drawn. The data collected from the field has to be processed and analysed as per the research plan. This is possible only through systematic processing of data. Data processing involves editing, coding, classification and tabulation of the data collected so that they are amenable to further analysis. In this chapter, the different stages of processing of data, the tools available for analysis of data and the intricacies involved in writing of the research report are discussed in detail.

5.1 Types of Data

Data collection is a very important activity in the task of any research and the quality of data collected affects the results. Each research project uses a data collection technique appropriate to the particular research design.

Quantitative and Qualitative Data Collection Methods

Quantitative data collection methods rely on random sampling and structured data collection instruments that fit diverse experiences into predetermined response categories. They produce results that are easy to summarise, compare, and generalise.

Quantitative research is concerned with testing hypotheses derived from theory and/or being able to estimate the size of a phenomenon of interest. If the intent is to generalise from the research participants to a larger population, the researcher will employ probability sampling to select participants.

Typical quantitative data gathering strategies include:
- Experiments/clinical trials.
- Observing and recording well-defined events (e.g., counting the number of patients waiting in emergency at specified times of the day).
- Obtaining relevant data from management information systems.
- Administering surveys with closed-ended questions (e.g., face-to face and telephone interviews, questionnaires etc).

Qualitative data collection methods play an important role in impact evaluation by providing information useful to understand the processes behind observed results and assess changes in people's perceptions of their well-being. Furthermore qualitative methods can be used to improve the quality of survey-based quantitative evaluations by helping generate evaluation hypothesis; strengthening the design of survey questionnaires and expanding or clarifying quantitative evaluation findings. They rely heavily on interactive interviews; respondents may be interviewed several times to follow up on a particular issue, clarify concepts or check the reliability of data. Generally the findings cannot be generalised to any specific population, rather each case study produces a single piece of evidence that can be used to seek general patterns among different studies of the same issue. Data collection in a qualitative study takes a great deal of time. The researcher needs to record any potentially useful data thoroughly, accurately, and systematically, using field notes, sketches, audiotapes, photographs and other suitable means. The data collection methods must observe the ethical principles of research.

Primary and Secondary Data

Data, or facts, may be derived from several sources. Data can be classified as primary data and secondary data. Primary data is data gathered for the first time by the researcher; secondary data is data taken by the researcher from secondary sources, internal or external.

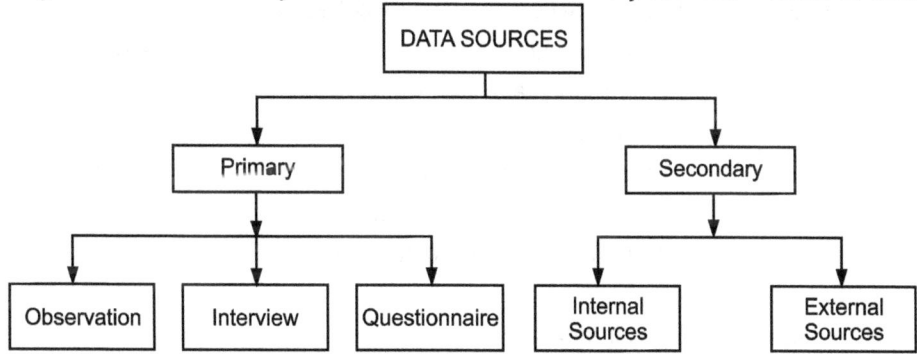

Fig. 5.1 : Sources of Data Collection

5.1.1 Secondary Data

There is a large amount of data that has already been collected by others, although it may not necessarily have been analysed or published. Locating these sources and retrieving the information is a good starting point in any data collection effort. The most widely used method for collecting data is through secondary data collection, commonly called secondary research.

Secondary data refer to the fact when the investigator does not collect the data himself for the research enquiry but uses data already collected and available in published or unpublished forms. This means finding information from third-party sources such as marketing research reports, company websites, magazine articles, and other sources. The advantage of using secondary data is that collection is inexpensive in terms of time, money and energy. However, it is sometimes difficult to gain access to the records or reports required, and the data may not always be complete and precise enough, or too disorganised.

The researcher must thoroughly search secondary data sources before commissioning any efforts for collecting primary data. There are many advantages in searching for and analysing data before attempting the collection of primary data. In some cases, the secondary data itself may be sufficient to solve the problem. Usually the cost of gathering secondary data is much lower than the cost of organising primary data. Moreover, secondary data has several supplementary uses. It also helps to plan the collection of primary data, in case, it becomes necessary. We shall therefore discuss secondary data first and then take up primary data in the next chapter. Use of secondary data in a research enquiry saves time, finance and labour. However, some people doubt the accuracy of secondary data. If reliable and suitable secondary data is available, there is no harm in using secondary data for any research enquiry.

5.1.2 Definition of Secondary Data

Secondary data is the data that have been already collected by and readily available from other sources. Such data are cheaper and more quickly obtainable than the primary data and also may be available when primary data cannot be obtained at all. For example, data collected by a hotel on its customers through its guest history system, data supplied by marketing organisations, annual company reports, government statistics etc. Sources of secondary data include the internet, libraries, museums, company reports, newspaper etc. The data collected is useful as it allows the researcher to see the prevailing thoughts about his/her area of study.

Secondary data can be used in different ways:
- When the researcher merely wants to report the data in its original format, then it is most likely that the place for this data will be in the main introduction or literature review as support or evidence for the researcher's argument.
- If the researcher uses it (analyses it or re-interprets it) for a different purpose to the original then the most likely place would be in the 'Analysis of findings' section of the dissertation.

It is always a good idea to use data collected by someone else if it exists – it may be on a much larger scale and could contribute to the findings considerably.

Advantages of Secondary Data

Secondary data collection methods have various advantages. These are discussed below:
- It is highly convenient to use secondary data.
- Use of secondary data saves time.
- Very convenient and necessary when primary data cannot be collected.

- **Ease of Access:** In years past accessing good secondary data required researchers to visit libraries or wait until a report was shipped by mail. However, the Internet has changed the way of accessing secondary research by offering convenience (e.g., online access from many locations) and generally standardised usage methods for all data sources.
- **Low Cost to Acquire:** Obtaining this data is much less expensive than primary data.
- **Help Clarify Research Question:** Secondary research is often used prior to larger scale primary research to help clarify what is to be learned. For instance, a researcher doing competitor analysis, but who is not familiar with competitors in a market, could access secondary sources to locate a list of potential competitors.
- **Answer Research Question:** It is often used to help set the stage for primary research. Researchers may find that the exact information they were looking for is available via secondary sources thus eliminating the need and expense to carrying out their own primary research.
- **Indicate Difficulties (if any) in conducting Primary Research:** The originators of secondary research often provide details on how the information was collected and difficulties encountered while collecting data. This may help the researcher to weigh the appropriate worth of going further.

Disadvantages of Secondary Data

Researcher needs to be careful while using secondary data due to the following reasons:
- Degree of accuracy of secondary data is not as high as in primary data.
- It is very difficult to find secondary data which exactly fit the needs of the present investigation.
- Secondary data are not available for all types of enquiries.
- **Quality:** The quality of secondary research should be scrutinised closely since the origins of the information may be questionable with regards to the validity and reliability of the information.
- **Not Specific to Researcher's Needs:** Secondary data is often not presented in a form that exactly meets the researcher's needs.
- **Incomplete Information:** Many a times it may happen that the data referred to as secondary data may only be a part of the entire data collected and presented in the report. Such data would be incomplete information for the researcher and it would be necessary to access the full report to gain the full value of the study.
- **Time:** Out-of-date information may offer little value especially for companies competing in fast changing markets.

Relative Advantages and Disadvantages of Secondary Data

Advantages	Disadvantages
1. Easy availability	1. May be obsolete i.e. old and outdated.
2. Take relatively less time to collect	2. May not be relevant to problem at hand
3. Promptly available	3. May not be valid or reliable, depending on how they were collected
4. Exploration possible	4. May be less accurate
	5. Possibility of Bias

5.1.3 Sources of Secondary Data

When the researcher uses secondary data, then he has to look into various sources from where he can obtain them. Secondary data may be either published or unpublished data usually published data are available in various publications of the central, state and local government, foreign government or of international bodies and their subsidiary organisation; Technical and trade journals, Books magazines and newspapers, Reports publication of various associations connected with business and industry, banks, stocks exchanges etc. reports prepared by various scholars' universities economists etc. in different fields or in the form of public records and statistics, historical documents etc. The sources of unpublished data may be found in diaries, letters, unpublished biographies and autobiographies and also may be available with scholar's research workers, trade organisation, labour bureaus and other public/private organisations.

The secondary sources of information may be divided into two categories: internal sources and external sources.

- **Internal Sources:** Data from within the organisation.
- **External Sources:** Data from outside the organisation.

Internal Sources of Data

Internal secondary data may be obtained with less time, effort and money than the external secondary data. In addition, they may also be more appropriate to the situation at hand since they are from within the organisation. These sources include sales record, sales force reports, operating statements, budgets, previous research reports and the likes. The most useful type of internal information is generally sales data. Internal data must be collected in a usable format and must be analysed to be of value. Many firms have useful but unutilised data. By changing the format of collection forms (sales invoices, salesman call reports, etc) other useful data can be often collected.

The Internal Sources include:

1. **Accounting resources:** Gives information which can be used to know about the internal factors.
2. **Sales Force report:** It gives information about the sale of a product outside the organisation. Organisations frequently overlook this valuable resource by not beginning their search of secondary sources with an internal audit of sales invoices, orders, inquiries about products not stocked, returns from customers and sales force customer calling sheets. Much information can be obtained from sales orders and invoices:
   - Sales by territory
   - Sales by customer type
   - Prices and discounts
   - Average size of order by customer, customer type, geographical area
   - Average sales by sales person and
   - Sales by pack size and pack type, etc.

   This type of data is useful for identifying an organisation's most profitable product and customers. It can also serve to track trends within the enterprise's existing customer group.
3. **Financial data:** Data within its files on the cost of producing, storing, transporting and marketing each of its products and product lines.
4. **Transport data:** Companies that keep good records relating to their transport operations are well placed to establish which are the most profitable routes, and loads, as well as the most cost effective routing patterns.
5. **Storage data:** The rate of inventory, stock turn, stock handling costs, assessing the efficiency of certain marketing operations and the efficiency of the marketing system as a whole.
6. **Internal experts:** These are people who are heading the various departments and can give a fair idea of how a particular thing is working.
7. **Miscellaneous reports:** Information obtained from operational reports. Miscellaneous reports include previous marketing research studies, special audits, and reports purchased from outside for prior problems may have relevance for current problems.

External Sources of Data

External Sources are sources which are outside the company in a larger environment. Collection of external data is more difficult due to varied nature and sources.

1. Demographic Information
2. Company Information

3. Government Publications
4. Non-Government Publications
5. Syndicated Services
6. International Organisations
7. Trade Associations
8. Commercial Services

External sources of data are discussed below:

1. Demographic Information: Demographics or demographic data are the characteristics of a human population as used in government, marketing or opinion research, or the demographic profiles used in such research. Demographics are frequently used in economic and marketing research. Commonly used demographics include sex, race, age, income, disabilities, mobility (in terms of travel time to work or number of vehicles available), educational attainment, home ownership, employment status, and even location. The main sources of social and demographic data are population and housing censuses, administrative records and household sample surveys. These three sources, if well planned and executed, can be complementary in an integrated programme of data collection and compilation.

2. Company Information: A company provides on its own information through:

(i) Company Websites: Company websites are mostly packed with information.

(ii) Annual Reports: These reports mention the company's market position within a particular product category and also suggest spending levels for marketing efforts as well as problems the company experienced while selling within a market. Most publicly traded companies place their annual reports on their website but there are also one-stop clearing houses that collect these reports.

(iii) Press Release: A press release is a document intended to gain news media attention or to provide information to other company stakeholders (e.g., customers, investors). For those seeking metrics for an overall market or industry the most useful releases are those provided by market research firms who are using the release to sell their research reports. Most companies that issue press releases post them on their website often within a media section where publicly issued documents are located.

(iv) White Papers: White papers are detailed, sometimes highly researched, documents intended to offer a much fuller picture of the capabilities of a product or company. They often contain good information, especially in terms of results of customer surveys, sales trends, and industry forecasts. Unlike an advertisement or press release, white papers are normally not promotional (though certainly some are) but rather, through strong writing and hopefully good research, these documents attempt to establish a level of credibility for a company and its products or services.

(v) Presentations: In addition to white papers, more companies are including presentations on their websites. Most of these are in the form of slide presentations (e.g., PowerPoint) with many also including audio voice-over. A growing trend is to exhibit presentations in an online video format by either converting a basic slide presentation to video or actually filming a live presentation. To locate video presentations researchers can search key video upload sites and video search engines.

3. Government Publications: Government sources provide an extremely rich pool of data for the researchers. In addition, many of these data are available free of cost on internet websites. Government at all levels; i.e. municipal; district, state and union publish thousands of documents in a year. However, from the viewpoint of users, Indian government documents can be divided into following major groups:

- **Administrative Reports:** These are generally published annually containing summary records of the activities and achievements of government agencies.
- **Statistical Publications:** Results of statistical operations such as sample surveys, censuses and statistical series derived out of administrative records of regulatory agencies of government come under this category.
- **Commission and Committee Reports:** Ministries, departments and their subordinate bodies frequently appoint committees and commissions consisting of one or more members. The theme and content of such publications are valuable sources of information.
- **Research Reports:** The results of government sponsored research projects fall under this category. Many government agencies have their own research wing and some of these assign their research projects to autonomous institutions.

In terms of utility and actual use, statistical publications can be reckoned as the most important category of government publications. In the Indian context, Central Statistical Organisation (CSO) and National Sample Survey Organisation (NSSO) two major agencies responsible for collection, processing and dissemination of data on important socio-economic variables.

(i) Central Statistical Organisation (CSO)

It co-ordinates the statistical activities of central, and state agencies, and keeps a close liaison with international agencies. Major databases developed by CSO include:

- National Accounts Statistics (NAS).
- Annual Survey of Industries (ASI).
- Index of Industrial Production (IIP).
- Economic Census (EC).
- Consumer Prices Index for Urban Non-Manual Employees (CPIUNME).

- National Sample Survey Organisation (NSSO) conducts multi-subject household inquiries in randomly selected villages and urban blocks spread all over the country. In each round of its survey, NSSO takes a sample of 12,000 to 14,000 villages and blocks in its central sample and 14,000 to 16,000 villages and blocks in its state sample.
- Registrar General of India (RGI), Directorate General of Commercial Intelligence and Statistics (DGCIS), Directorate of Economics and Statistics (DES), Timely Reporting Scheme (TRS) and General Crop Estimation Survey (GCES), The Labour Bureau etc. are some more organisations collecting and publishing relevant statistics.

Some major publications are:
(a) Statistical Abstract of India (Annual).
(b) Statistical Abstract of Maharashtra (Annual).
(c) Monthly Abstract of Statistics.
(d) Economic Survey (Annual).
(d) Agricultural Statistics of India.
(f) Indian Trade Journal.
(g) National Income Statistics.
(h) Vital Statistics of India (Annual).
(i) Population Census (after ten years).
(j) Plan Drafts.

(ii) Semi-Government Publications

Very useful information is provided by the publications of semi-government organisations, For example, Reserve Bank of India (R.B.I.), The Institute of Economic Growth (I.E.G.), The Institute of Foreign Trade (I.F.T.) and Indian Council of Research in Social Sciences (I.C.S.S.R.). The main publications are:

(a) R.B.I. Bulletin (Monthly).
(b) Annual Report of R.B.I.
(c) Currency and Finance Report (Published by R.B.I.)
(d) Foreign Trade Review. (Published by I.I.F.T.)

(iii) Publications of Universities and Research Institutions

Individual research scholars, the different departments in the universities and various research organisations and institutes like Indian Statistical Institute (I.S.I.), National Council of Educational Research and Training (N.C.E.R.T.), National Council of Applied Economic Research (N.C.A.E.R.), Indian Council of Agricultural Research (I.C.A.R.), publish findings of their research programmes in the form of research papers, journals which are very useful sources of secondary data.

The main publications are:
(a) Indian Journal of Economics.
(b) Indian Journal of Quantitative Economics.
(c) Indian Economic Journal.

(iv) Publications of Commercial and Financial Institutions

A number of private commercial and trade institutions like Federation of Indian Chamber of Commerce and Industries (F.I.C.C.I.) Institute of Chartered Accountants of India Trade Unions, Stock Exchanges, etc. Published data and reports on current economic and business issues. These are very useful sources of secondary data.

(v) Reports of Committees and Commissions

Reports of the special committees and commissions appointed by government contain valuable data. The reports of National Labour Commission, Monopolies Commission, Finance Commission. National Agricultural Commission etc. are the store-house of secondary data.

(vi) Newspapers and Periodicals

Different newspapers and periodicals collect and publish data related to different fields. For example, Economic Times, Financial Express, Commerce, Southern Economist, India Today, Probe, Economic and Political Weekly, Facts for You etc.

(vii) Publications of International Bodies

Official publications of different international bodies like U.N.O., I.L.O., I.M.F., I.B.R.D., U.N.C.T.A.D. etc. contain valuable international statistics. The main publications are:
(a) Annual Reports
(b) International Financial Statistics
(c) World Development Report
(d) Finance and Development
(e) I.M.F. Survey
(f) Handbook of International Trade and Development Statistics
(g) I.M.F. Staff Papers etc.

(viii) Unpublished Sources

All statistical material is not always published. There are various sources of unpublished data, such as records maintained by various government and post offices, studies made by research institutions, scholars etc. Such sources can be used where necessary.

4. Non-Government Publications

These includes publications of various industrial and trade associations, such as
- The Indian Cotton Mill Association
- Various chambers of commerce

- The Bombay Stock Exchange (it publishes a directory containing financial accounts, key profitability and other relevant matter)
- Various Associations of Press Media
- Export Promotion Council
- Confederation of Indian Industries (CII)
- Small Industries Development Board of India

The only disadvantage of the above sources is that the data may be biased.

5. Syndicated Services

A wide array of data on both consumer and industrial markets is collected and sold by commercial organisations which collect and tabulate the marketing information on a regular basis for a number of clients who are the subscribers to these services. So the services are designed in such a way that the information suits the subscriber. These services are useful in television viewing, movement of consumer goods etc. These syndicate services provide information data from both household as well as institution. A number of firms regularly collect data of relevance to marketers that they sell on a subscription basis. Two types of syndicated services are widely used by marketing researchers – channel information and omnibus surveys. Channel information is available to the firm at four levels – manufacturers, intermediaries, retailers and consumers.

At the intermediary or wholesale level, several syndicated firms provide information on the flow of products and brands to retail outlets. Store audits provide data on the movement of brands through retail outlets. At the consumer level, consumer panels provide data on both purchasing pattern and media habits.

Advantages of Syndicate Services

Syndicate services are becoming popular since the constraints of decision making are changing and we need more of specific decision-making in the light of changing environment. Also Syndicate services are able to provide information to the industries at a low unit cost.

Disadvantages of Syndicate Services

The information provided is not exclusive. A number of research agencies provide customised services which suits the requirement of each individual organisation.

6. International Organisations

Bank economic reviews, university research reports, journals and articles are all useful sources to contact. International agencies such as World Bank, IMF, IFAD, UNDP, ITC, FAO and ILO produce a plethora of secondary data which can prove extremely useful. Some of these are:

- **The International Labour Organisation (ILO):** It publishes data on the total and active population, employment, unemployment, wages and consumer prices.
- **The Organisation for Economic Co-operation and Development (OECD):** It publishes data on foreign trade, industry, food, transport, and science and technology.
- **The International Monetary Fund (IMFA):** It publishes reports on national and international foreign exchange regulations.

7. Trade Associations

Trade associations are generally membership-supported organisations whose mission is to offer assistance and represent the interests of those operating in a specific industry. One of the many tasks performed by trade associations is to provide research information and industry metrics through such as conducting member surveys. Trade associations differ widely in the extent of their data collection and information dissemination activities. However, it is worth checking with them to determine what they publish. Also they would publish a trade directory and a yearbook.

8. Commercial Services

Published market research reports and other publications are available from a wide range of organisations which charge for their information. Typically, marketing people are interested in media statistics and consumer information which has been obtained from large scale consumer or farmer panels.

9. Other External Media

(i) **News and Media Outlets:** Possibly the most widely used method for acquiring secondary research is through articles and other reports found through commercial news sources. Options include magazines, newspapers, television news, and other video/audio programming. Nearly all of these sources are available online.

(ii) **Magazines and Newspapers:** Journalists who write about industries and markets often have access to expensive market research reports parts of which may be mentioned in an article.

(iii) **Television News Sites:** Many of the leading television news networks have built elaborate websites and populated these with original materials produced by their own reporters. Just as journalists for magazines and newspapers include research information in their print pieces, reporters for television news do the same. In many cases television news sites present news reports in video format and also in text transcript.

(iv) Video and Audio News Programming: Search engines are quickly evolving to allow for the search of content within video and audio programming. Several search tools make it easy to search video clips, such as news reports, university lectures, presentations on corporate websites, and much more.

(v) Other Low Cost Research Sources: While the options listed above are the most widely used methods for obtaining low cost market research, there are a few additional options to consider.

- **Cause-Related Groups:** Many non-profit groups have an organisational mission directed at supporting causes they feel are not well-supported in society. Examples include groups focusing on the environment, education, and health care. As would be expected a considerable portion of their focus looks at how business impacts these issues.
- **Expert Sites:** Several websites allow information seekers to post questions to supposed experts in a field. On an effectiveness scale these sites probably do not rate very high for providing hard numbers and whether someone responding is truly an expert is open for debate. But those responding to a user's question may still provide value in offering direction to someone seeking information.
- **Old reports:** In some cases, where a market is not prone to rapid change, older market reports could hold enough information to answer a research question. While new reports are often very expensive, the research company may sell previous reports for a heavy discount.

5.1.4 Characteristics of Secondary Data

Secondary data are collected with specific objectives by the researcher.
- Useful to gain initial insight into the research problem.
- Easy to access and convenient to use secondary data.
- Very convenient and necessary when primary data cannot be collected.
- Help clarify research question: Secondary research is often used prior to larger scale primary research to help clarify what is to be learned. For instance, a researcher doing competitor analysis, but who is not familiar with competitors in a market, could access secondary sources to locate a list of potential competitors.
- Answer research question: It is often used to help set the stage for primary research. Researchers may find that the exact information they were looking for is available via secondary sources thus eliminating the need and expense to carry out their own primary research.

Such data help the researcher to clearly understand the issues faced in collecting the data and also prepare him for further difficulties if similar data need to be collected.

5.1.5 Searching World Wide Web for Data

Gathering and referring secondary data is essential in almost any research project and it was seen as a tedious and boring job in earlier days. Until a few years back, accessing good secondary data required researchers to visit libraries or wait until reports were shipped by mail. The researcher often had to write to government agencies, trade associations, or other secondary data providers and then wait days or weeks for a reply that might never come. Often, the researcher made one or more trips to the library, only to find out that the needed reports were checked out or missing. However, beginning in the late 1990s, with the rapid development of the Internet and the World Wide Web, the access and use of secondary data has evolved! It has eliminated the drudgery by offering convenience of time and place (e.g., online access from many locations). This secondary data source continues to expand, with publicly available documents on the Web doubling every 18 months.

Finding Secondary Data on the Internet

Internet refers to a computer network consisting of smaller, interconnected networks world over. This network consists of two or more computers connected to one another for the purpose of sharing communication and resources. It links both public and private computer systems to allow users to access information and documents from distant sources. World Wide Web (WWW) is part of the Internet servers that organises information into thousands of interconnected pages or documents called Web pages. Content providers are parties that provide information on the WWW known as Web sites, which consist of one or more Web pages with related information about a particular topic. Search engine refers to a computerised directory that allows users to search the WWW for information in a systematic way. For example Google, Yahoo!, MSN, America Online, Alta Vista, Lycos, and Ask Jeeves, etc. Companies, direct marketers, electronic retailers (e-tailers) and many other organisations have their own Websites that contain secondary data.

Information may be searched on the Internet through:
- Directed search through key terms in search engines.
- Browsing or surfing for casual search: Browsing relies heavily on hyperlinks between documents, allowing the browser to navigate through cyberspace in a non-sequential manner.
- Government data on the internet.
- Discussion Groups: Internet sites devoted to a specific topic where people/ professionals can read and post messages. These act like bulletin boards where people visit to read messages left by other people, post responses to others' questions, and send rebuttals to comments with which they disagree. For example, Usenet.
- Chat Rooms: Function as virtual focus groups operating in near-continual session, enabling companies to track consumer buzz as it develops.

5.1.6 Sufficiency, Adequacy, Reliability and Consistency of Secondary Data

Issues to be considered for Secondary Data – Sufficiency, Adequacy, Reliability, Consistency.

As secondary data has been collected for a different purpose to the researcher's, the researcher should treat it with care. Secondary data should be thoroughly checked for the following parameters:

- Applicability of research objective.
- Cost of acquisition.
- Accuracy of data.

The basic questions the researcher should ask are:

Reliability: The researcher must check for the reliability of the data by finding answers to questions like:

- Where has the data come from?
- Does it cover the correct geographical location?
- Is it current (not too out of date)?
- If the data is going to be combined with other data are the data the same (for example, units, time, etc.)?
- If the data is going to be compared with other data is the researcher comparing like with like?

Applicability of research objective: The researcher should make a detailed examination of the following:

- Title (for example, the time period that the data refers to and the geographical coverage).
- Units of the data.
- Source (some secondary data is already secondary data).
- Column and row headings, if presented in tabular form.
- Definitions and abbreviations. For example, how is 'small' defined in the phrase 'small hotel'? Is 'small' based on the number of rooms, value of sales, number of employees, profit, turnover, square metres of space, etc., and do different sources use the word 'small' in different ways? Even if the same unit of measurement is used, there still could be problems.

It is observed that it is never safe to take published statistics at their face value without knowing their meaning and limitation.

Availability: Check whether the data pertaining to the research is available or not. If not, then primary data has to be collected.

Sufficiency: Adequate data should be available.

Relevancy: Refers to the extent to which the data fits the information needs of research problem. Relevance of the data can be ensured by checking:
- that the units of measurement are the same.
- concepts used and currency of data are same and latest.

Accuracy: Accuracy of the data should be ensured by considering:
- Specification and methodology used.
- Margin of error should be examined.
- The dependability of the source must be seen.

Suitability of Data: The researcher must carefully scrutinise the definition of various units and terms of collection used at the time of collecting the data from the primary source originally. Similarly the object scope and nature of original enquiry must also be studied.

Generally, problems reduce the relevance of the secondary data thus making them unfit for use. Like for instance, there is often a difference in the units of measurement or definition of the classes which may reduce the relevancy of the data making them misfit for use. While using secondary data, the original source should be used if possible.

5.2 Primary Data

Definition

Primary data are those which are collected for the first time by the researcher himself, and thus happen to be original in character.

These are collected for a specific purpose, or to solve a specific problem and are expensive and time consuming, but more focused than secondary research. Secondary data, on the other hand, are those which have already been collected by someone else for some other purpose and which have already been processed earlier.

Primary data collection begins when a researcher is not able to find the data required for his research from secondary sources or the nature of the problem demands that primary data be used. Business researchers are interested in a variety of primary data about demographic/socioeconomic characteristics, attitudes/opinions/interests, awareness/knowledge, intentions, motivation and behaviour.

Advantages and Disadvantages of Primary data

Advantages	Disadvantages
Level of accuracy is high.	Requires more time.
Data can be collected as per the requirement and objectives.	Requires trained personnel to collect data through different methods.
Very useful when secondary data are not available as per the objectives of the study.	Proves to be costly to collect primary data.
Original and direct from the population.	Surveyor's influence on the data quality.

Based on the type of data needed by the researcher and nature of study, the researcher will decide which method of data collection to use. The various methods of collecting primary data are:
(i) Observation
(ii) Interviews – Personal and Telephonic
(iii) Questionnaires
(iv) Schedules through enumerators and
(v) Mail surveys – Email / Internet surveys
(vi) Other methods

Other methods include,
    (a) Warranty cards;
    (b) Distributor audits;
    (c) Pantry audits;
    (d) Consumer panels;
    (e) Mechanical devices;
    (f) Projective techniques;
    (g) Depth interviews,
    (h) Content analysis.

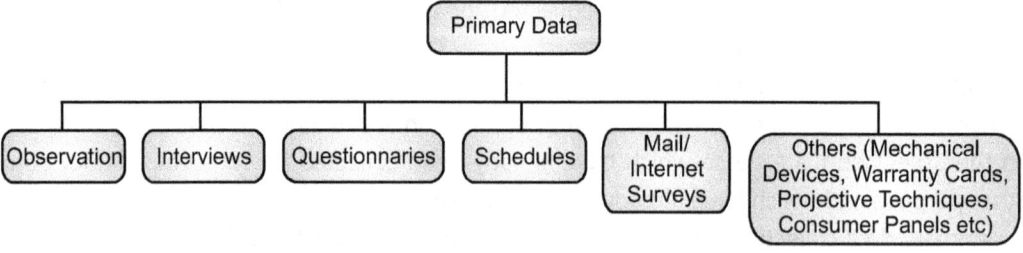

Fig. 5.2

Primary data can be obtained by:
- **Communication**: It involves questioning respondents either verbally or in writing. This method is versatile, since only one need to ask for the required information; however, the response may not be accurate. Communication usually is quicker and cheaper than observation.
- **Observation:** It involves the recording of actions and is performed by either a person or some mechanical or electronic device like: Observation is less versatile than communication, since some attributes of a person may not be readily observable, such as attitudes, awareness, knowledge, intentions, and motivation. Observation also might take longer since observers may have to wait for appropriate events to occur, though observation using scanner data might be quicker and more cost effective. Observation typically is more accurate than communication.

- **Personal Interviews**: Have an interviewer bias that mail-in questionnaires do not have. For example, in a personal interview the respondent's perception of the interviewer may affect the responses.
- **Questionnaire**: The questionnaire is an important tool for gathering primary data. Poorly constructed questions can result in large errors and invalidate the research data, so significant efforts should be put into the Questionnaire.

5.3 Observation Method

In this method the data is collected by the researcher by observing or watching the units/respondents under study. Researcher may need to observe physical actions maybe for observing pattern of working, watching TV etc. Verbal behaviour i.e. conversations between respondents may also be observed or expressive behaviour like voice tone, facial expressions may be observed.

Observation may be, (a) Direct Observation, (b) Indirect observation

(a) **Direct Observation :** Here the respondent is aware that he is being observed for the required information. For example, behavioural studies, group discussions, etc.

(b) **Indirect Observation :** Here the respondent is not aware that he is being observed and neither he is actively involved. For example – observing the buying behaviour of people in a supermarket. Observing the behaviour of school children etc.

	Advantages	Disadvantages
1.	Directness : There is a directness involved which allows the research to observe the respondent in a particular situation, instead of asking his responses which may not be unbiased.	Time consuming and difficult to pursue when time and resources are very limited.
2.	Flexibility of keeping the observation to be structured or informal.	Success of this method depends upon the skill of the observer.
3.	Can be used in combination of other methods for better data capturing.	Susceptible to reliability and validity issues as there are chances of observer bias.

Observation method is also very useful when children are involved as respondents and behavioural patterns need to be studied. The researcher needs to be very skilled if this is being applied.

5.4 Questionnaire Method

5.4.1 Collection of Data through Questionnaires

Questionnaire is a data collection tool in which written questions are presented that are to be answered by the respondents in written form. This method of data collection is quite popular, particularly in case of big enquiries. This method is particularly useful to reach out to a large number of respondents in a short time. It is mostly adopted by private individuals, research workers, private and public organisations and even by governments. In this method a questionnaire is sent (usually by post) to the persons concerned with a request to answer the questions and return the questionnaire.

A questionnaire consists of a number of questions printed or typed in a definite order on a form or set of forms. The questionnaire is mailed to respondents who are expected to read and understand the questions and write down the relevant answers in the questionnaire itself. The respondents have to answer the questions on their own. The questions can be either open-ended or closed ended. Questionnaires may be administered by mail, over the telephone, by computer, or in person.

The design of a questionnaire depends on whether the researcher wishes to collect exploratory information (i.e. qualitative information for the purposes of better understanding or the generation of hypotheses on a subject) or quantitative information (to test specific hypotheses that have previously been generated).

Questionnaires can be classified into four types:
1. Structured Non-disguised,
2. Structured Disguised,
3. Non-structured Non-disguised,
4. Non-structured Disguised.

Non-disguised are the direct questions and the object of enquiry is revealed to the respondent. Disguised are the indirect questions where the object of enquiry is not revealed to the respondent. In a structured questionnaire the questions are asked in a pre-determined order.

Formal Standardised Questionnaires

If the data is required to be analysed statistically, a formal standardised questionnaire is designed. The points to be remembered while designing such questionnaires are:
- The questionnaire has to be framed in such a manner that each respondent receives the same stimuli.
- The questionnaire has to be well-defined so that the interviewer is able to answer the respondent's clarifications, if necessary.

- The response format must be easy to complete during the interviewing process.
- A well-designed questionnaire should primarily meet the research objectives.
- A questionnaire should obtain the most complete and accurate information possible.
- The questionnaire should be brief and to the point and be so arranged that the respondent remains interested throughout the interview.

5.4.2 Questionnaire Construction

The following steps are involved in the development of a questionnaire:

1. Choose and decide on the information required: The objective behind the survey should be kept in mind while designing a questionnaire. Through the secondary data, the researcher should be aware of what work has been done on the same or similar problems in the past, what factors have not yet been examined, and how the present survey questionnaire can build on what has already been discovered.

2. Define the target respondents: The researcher must define the population that he wishes to collect the data from. While designing the questionnaire we must take into account factors such as the age, education, etc. of the target respondents.

3. Selection of methodology to reach the target segment: This will influence not only the questions the researcher is able to ask but the phrasing of those questions.

4. Decide on question content: Researcher must look at whether the question is really required and if it can be used in testing one or more of the hypotheses established during the research design.

5. Decide type of questions: The questions can be classified into two forms, i.e. closed and open-ended. In a closed type of question, the respondent chooses between an alternative already stated. He does not get a chance to answer in a descriptive manner.

For example. : Do you use Brand X ? Yes _____ No_____.

The **closed** type of questioning has a number of important advantages:
- It is easy for the respondent to answer. He does not have to think and answer.
- It 'prompts' the respondent so that the respondent has to rely less on memory while answering a question.
- Analysis is easier as responses can be easily classified.
- It permits categorisation of the response to specify the answer categories.

It also has some disadvantages:
- It does not allow the respondent the opportunity to give a different response to those suggested.
- They 'suggest' answers that respondents may not have considered before.

In an **open-ended** question, the respondent is asked to give a reply to a question in his/her own words. No answers are suggested. These responses are explanatory in nature and give some insights from the respondents end.

Example: "What do you like most about this Product ?"

Open-ended questions have advantages when used in a questionnaire:
- They allow the respondent to answer in his own words, with no influence by any specific alternatives suggested by the interviewer.
- They often reveal the issues which are most important to the respondent, and this may reveal findings which were not originally anticipated when the survey was initiated.
- Respondents can qualify their answers or emphasise their opinions.

The inherent problem of an open-ended question is that they must be treated with caution as:
- Respondents may find it difficult to 'articulate' their responses i.e., to properly and fully explain their attitudes or motivations.
- Respondents may not give a full answer simply because they may forget to mention important points. Some respondents need prompting of the types of answer they could give.
- Data collected is in the form of verbatim comments - it has to be coded and reduced to manageable categories. This can be time consuming for analysis and there are numerous opportunities for error in recording and interpreting the answers given on the part of interviewers.
- Respondents will tend to answer open questions in different dimensions. Such responses need to be probed further for clarity on response.

However, disadvantage of this form of question is that it requires the researcher to have a good prior knowledge of the subject in order to generate realistic/likely response options before printing the questionnaire. In many situations a questionnaire will need to incorporate all these forms of question, because some forms are more appropriate for seeking particular forms of response.

6. **Putting questions into a meaningful order and format:**
   - **Opening questions:** Opening questions generally should be easy to answer and not in any way threatening to the respondents.
   - **Question flow:** Questions should flow in some kind of psychological order, so that one leads easily and naturally to the next. There could be a continuity maintained on the flow of the questions where the response from one leads to the other.

- **Question variety:** Questions need to be carefully keyed in to maintain the interest throughout the interview.

7. **Closing questions:** By the time the respondent comes to the end of the questionnaire it is quite natural for a respondent to become increasingly indifferent to the questionnaire. This is mainly due to impatience or fatigue. He might give careless answers to the later questions. Hence such questions should be included in the earlier part of the questionnaire.

8. **Physical appearance of the questionnaire:** The physical appearance of a questionnaire has a significant effect upon both the quantity and quality of data obtained. In general, it is best for a questionnaire to be as short as possible. A long questionnaire leads to a long interview and this may lead to decreasing interest on the part of the respondent.

9. **Piloting the questionnaires:** Piloting is very mush essential to test whether the desired responses are being obtained for the questions. Many a time, the perception of the respondents varies from those of the researcher. Hence these issues can be corrected in the initial stage itself so that the research process is facilitated. The purpose of pre-testing the questionnaire is to determine:
    - If the wordings used help in achieving the desired results.
    - Are the questions in the right order?
    - Are the questions easy to understand?
    - Is any question needed to be added or deleted?

Administering the Questionnaire
- Sending questionnaires by mail with clear instructions on how to answer the questions and requesting for mailed responses;
- Gathering all or part of the respondents in one place at one time, giving oral or written instructions, and letting the respondents fill out the questionnaires;
- Hand-delivering questionnaires to respondents and collecting them later;
- E-mailing the questionnaire to respondents and asking for return of the same through e-mail.

Essentials of a Good Questionnaire

Questionnaires are a popular means of collecting data, but are difficult to design and often require many rewrites before an acceptable questionnaire is produced. To be successful, the following points may be borne in mind while designing the questionnaire:
- The size of the questionnaire should be kept to the minimum i.e., questionnaire should be comparatively short and simple.
- The language used in the questionnaire should be simple and clear.
- Questions should proceed in a logical sequence moving from easy to more difficult questions.

- Personal and intimate questions should be asked only if necessary and included at the end.
- Technical terms and vague expressions capable of different interpretations should be avoided in a questionnaire.
- Questions may be dichotomous (yes or no answers), multiple choice (alternative answer listed) or open-ended. The latter types of questions are often difficult to analyse and hence should be avoided in a questionnaire to the extent possible.
- There should be some control questions in the questionnaire which indicate the reliability of the respondent. For instance, a question designed to determine the consumption of particular material may be asked first in terms of financial expenditure and later in terms of weight.
- There should be a way to control questions, maybe by introducing a cross-check to see whether the information collected is correct or not.
- Questions affecting the sentiments of respondents should be avoided.
- Adequate space for answers should be provided in the questionnaire to help editing and tabulation.
- There should always be provision for indications of uncertainty, e.g., "do not know", "no preference" and so on.
- Brief directions with regard to filling up the questionnaire should invariably be given in the questionnaire itself.

Hence, qualities of a good questionnaire are:
(1) Explain purpose
(2) Define terms
(3) Assure confidentiality
(4) Minimise questions
(5) Simple questions
(6) Logically arranged questions
(7) Suitable type of questions
(8) Avoid personal questions
(9) Avoid sentimental questions
(10) Avoid calculative questions
(11) Apply crosschecks
(12) Attractive look

Advantages of Questionnaires
- Can be used as a method in its own right or as a basis for interviewing or a telephone survey.
- Can be posted, e-mailed or faxed.

- Can cover a large number of people or organisations, thus, covering wide geographic coverage.
- Relatively cheap.
- Anonymity of respondents, avoids embarrassment on the part of the respondent.
- Respondent can consider responses.
- No interviewer bias.

Disadvantages of Questionnaires
- Design problems.
- Questions have to be relatively simple.
- Historically low response rate hence inducements may help.
- Time delay while waiting for responses to be returned.
- Require a return deadline, several reminders may be required.
- Assumes no literacy problems.
- No control over who completes it.
- Not possible to give assistance if required.
- Problems with incomplete questionnaires.
- Replies not spontaneous and independent of each other.
- Respondent can read all questions beforehand and then decide whether to complete or not. For example, perhaps because it is too long, too complex, uninteresting, or too personal.
- Problem of non-response, difficulty of verification, inflexible in accuracy.
- Suitable when respondents are spread over large geographic area, resources are limited; matter of interest for respondents, legal compulsion to respond, high accuracy is not expected.

5.5 Personal Interviews

An interview is a data-collection technique that involves orally questioning respondents, either individually or as a group. It is primarily used to gain an understanding of the underlying reasons and motivations for people's attitudes, preferences or behaviour.

Interviewing is one of the most common methods for collecting data in qualitative research. Interviews allow participants to provide rich, contextual descriptions of events. The process of interviewing is time-consuming, and the quality of data often is dependent on the aptitude of the interviewer. Interviews can be undertaken on a personal one-to-one basis or in a group. They can be conducted at work, at home, in the street or in a shopping centre, or some other agreed location.

In this method the interviewer asks questions generally in a face-to-face contact to the other person or persons. Answers to the questions posed during an interview can be recorded by writing them down (either during the interview itself or immediately after the interview) or by tape-recording the responses, or by a combination of both.

Advantages
- (a) Information obtained is accurate due to direct contact with the respondent.
- (b) Response rate for personal interviews is good.
- (c) In-depth questions can be asked to get better insight into the respondent's characteristics under study.
- (d) The interviewer is in control and can effectively lead the data collection.
- (e) Motives and feelings can be investigated.
- (f) Recording equipment can be used to record responses efficiently.
- (g) Characteristics of respondent like tone of voice, facial expression, hesitation, etc. can be assessed.
- (h) Uniformity of results can be achieved if single interviewer is used.

Disadvantages
- (a) Interviews need to be formally set up.
- (b) They are time consuming.
- (c) Geographic limitations.
- (d) Expensive affair.
- (e) Chances of respondent bias due to tendency to please or impress, create false personal image, or end interview quickly.
- (f) Personal questions may prove to be embarrassing.
- (g) Trained interviewers are a must for success of this method.

Guidelines for Conducting the Interviews Successfully
1. Interviewer must plan in advance and should fully know the problems under consideration.
2. Interviewer's approach must be friendly and informal.
3. All possible efforts should be made to establish proper rapport with the interviewee; people are motivated to communicate when the atmosphere is favourable.
4. Interviewer must have the ability to listen with understanding, respect and curiosity, since it is the gateway to communication, and hence must act accordingly during the interview.
5. There should be a free-flowing interview to the maximum extent possible, and the questions must be well phrased in order to have full co-operation of the interviewee.

6. In case of big enquiries, where the task of collecting information is to be accomplished by several interviewers, there should be an interview guide to be observed by all so as to ensure reasonable uniformity in respect of all important points in the study.
7. Before selecting interviewing as a data collection method, the researcher must determine whether the research question can be answered appropriately by interviewing people who have experienced the phenomenon of interest. The first step in all research is to conduct a pilot study. The researcher should practice how he or she will gain access to a sample, conduct interviews, transcribe and analyse the data. Different approaches may exist depending on the methodology used. A consistent approach should be used with both the pilot and actual study.

Scheduling the Interview

Pre-interview: Before the scheduled interview, pre-interview contact or introduction should be made may be through telephone. The potential participant should be given information regarding the study, protection of privacy, and also informed what will and will not be done with the data. If the potential participant agrees to participate in the study, a mutually agreed time and place for the interview should be decided.

Conducting the interview: The place of interview should be free of distractions. Tape recorder should be appropriately placed to capture the voices clearly. The interviewer should be in a position suitable to note nonverbal cues, such as eye contact, crying, laughing, or hand gestures.

Interviews can be conducted with varying degrees of flexibility. Interview may be in direct personal interview or an indirect oral investigation (Telephonic).

Direct Personal Interviews: In the case of direct personal investigation the interviewer has to collect the information personally from the sources concerned. He has to be on the spot and has to meet people from whom data have to be collected. This method is particularly suitable for intensive investigations.

Structured and Unstructured Interviews

Interview is a widely used tool to access people's experiences and their inner perceptions, attitudes, and feelings of reality. The type of interview will be determined by the research question, methodology, and literature insight. Based on the degree of structuring, interview can be: Structured Interview and Unstructured Interview.

Structured Interviews: Structured interview is similar to survey and questionnaire except that it is administrated orally rather than in writing. In a structured interview, the researcher asks explicit questions consistently to all participants. Structured interviews are popular for several reasons. First, interviewers who aren't comfortable interviewing people can hide behind them. Second, there are so many legal constraints on what you can ask in an interview that some otherwise articulate interviewers are tongue-tied.

Unstructured Interviews: An unstructured interview is an interview that has no format and the interviewer chooses the questions depending on the interviewee and the situation i.e., questions can be changed and adapted based on the candidate's answers to determine intelligence, understanding and suitability. Questions at an unstructured interview therefore tend to be more open ended requiring open answers that mean the candidate can reveal more about themselves. The researcher's probes then are related directly to the participant's answers. Alternately unstructured interviews are referred to as informal conversational interview, in-depth interview, non-standardised interview, and ethnographic interview in an interchangeable manner.

Advantages of Unstructured Interviews
- Rapport is build up because the respondent has trust in the interviewer, so the validity of the findings is high and a good technique for sensitive areas of sociology e.g., domestic violence and eating disorders.
- There is huge potential for flexibility as the respondent leads the interview.

Disadvantages of Unstructured Interviews
- Difficult to generalise as it is suitable only for small sample size due to detailed and time consuming nature of this technique.
- It is not a systematic method so it is difficult to verify and reliability is inevitable lowered.
- It may lack objectivity, because the way in which the interviewer asks the questions may affect the results.
- The interviewer may offer their opinion without realising consequences which may bias the results.

A lot of interviewers today mix both structured and unstructured interviews. e.g., competency based interviews where the areas the employers want to ask questions are categorised and set however, they then adapt questions under these headings to each candidate based on their responses. This also gives the candidate the opportunity to sell themselves much better than with structured interviews.

5.6 Telephonic Survey / Interviewing

When information required is very short and structured, with large number of respondents then telephonic interview may be used. Telephonic interview is an alternative form of interview to the personal, face-to-face interview and most useful in case of structured and minimal information required from respondents.

Advantages of Telephonic Interviews
- It is relatively cheaper than personal interview.
- Quick responses can be had.

- Large numbers of people or organisations spread over wide geographic area can be covered.
- Spontaneous response can be had.
- Responses can be taped.
- Sometimes respondents are more comfortable and frank during telephonic interviews than with personal interviews if nature of questions is personal.

Disadvantages of Telephonic Interviews
- Often connected with selling.
- Structured and straightforward set of questions required.
- Respondent needs to be connected through telephone.
- Repeat calls are necessary due to non-availability to get response.
- Sometimes it proves to be wastage of time due to non-response.
- Respondent gets less time to think.
- Visual aids cannot be used.
- Can cause irritation.
- Good telephone etiquettes are required.
- Question of authority.

Tips for Successful Telephonic Interviews

Locate the respondent: If the researcher is trying to contact people in organisations where one has to go through secretaries, then repeat calls may be necessary. An advance letter explaining the purpose of the research and informing the respondent about the telephone contact may be sent in advance. There is the possibility of interviewing the wrong person as the interviewer may not know the person.

Invoke to Participate: The purpose of the call should be clear enough to prompt the respondent to agree for the interview. Respondents will normally listen to this introduction before they decide to co-operate or refuse.

Ensuring quality: Design the questionnaire in such a way that it must be easy to move through so as to avoid long silences on the telephone. Also the ability of interviewer is necessary to ensure the success of the interview.

Implementation: Interview record: Each interview schedule should have a cover page with number, name and address having provisions to record the call details, the interviewer details, the outcome of the call and space to note down specific times at which a call-back has been arranged. Space should be provided to record the final outcome of the call – was an interview refused, contact never made, number disconnected, etc.

Procedure for call-backs: A system for call-back needs to be implemented. Interview schedules should be sorted according to their status: weekday call-back, evening call-back, weekend call-back, specific time call-back.

Technique	Advantages	Possible constraints
Using available information	Is inexpensive, because data is already there. Permits examination of trends over the past.	Data is not always easily accessible. Ethical issues concerning confidentiality may arise. Information may be imprecise or incomplete.
Observing	Gives more detailed and context-related information. Permits collection of information on facts not mentioned in an interview. Permits tests of reliability of responses to questionnaire	Ethical issues concerning confidentiality or privacy may arise. Observer bias may occur. (Observer may only notice what interests him or her). The presence of the data collector can influence the situation observed. Through training of research assistants is required.
Interviewing	Is suitable for use with both literates and illiterates. Permits collection of questions. Has higher response rate than written questionnaires.	The presence of the interviewer can influence responses. Reports of events may be less complete than information gained through observations.
Small scale flexible interview	Permits collection of in-depth information and exploration of spontaneous remarks by respondents.	The interviewer may inadvertently influence the respondents. Analysis of open-ended data is more difficult and time-consuming.
Administering written questionnaires	Is less expensive. Permits anonymity and may result in more honest response. Does not require research assistants. Eliminates bias due to phrasing questions differently with different respondents.	Cannot be used with illiterate respondents. There is often a low rate of response. Questions may be misunderstood.
Participatory and projective methods	Provide rich data and may have positive sign offs for knowledge and skills by researchers and informants.	Require some extra training of researchers.

5.7 Schedules through Enumerators

In this method, a schedule i.e. a questionnaire containing questions is prepared and filled in by the investigator/researcher himself or by enumerators (persons appointed by the researcher) to contact each and every respondent and fill up the schedule. This method is used when the information being collected is of very critical nature and cannot be compromised with. It has the advantages of both personal interview and questionnaire. Example of schedule filling is when the Census of India is collected every ten years through enumerators appointed by the Government of India.

Advantages of Schedules	Disadvantages of Schedules
Accuracy of information is assured as first hand information is collected by the researcher.	It is time consuming and expensive as each respondent needs to be contacted personally.
Doubts can be cleared or facial expressions can be observed.	Problem of no response can occur when respondent may not be willing to cooperate.
Detailed information can be collected and data on different dimensions can be obtained.	Enumerator needs to be skilled and trained.

5.8 Email/Internet Surveys, Online Survey Sites

Online surveys are a great option for companies to conduct their own research as online survey tools make it possible for these business owners to perform market research at a fraction of the usual cost. Surveys conducted over the email or internet are becoming more and more popular these days. They can easily be conducted online or over e-mail. More and more companies are using the online surveys for their market research purposes as they are cost effective and time saving. Companies offer the respondents / consumers an incentive to fill out online surveys. Online surveys with rewards are a potential win-win situation for companies and consumers as the company gets valuable market research and the consumer is paid for his time through discounts and freebies on products he likes.

Online surveys make it faster and cheaper to contact the respondents than to make phone calls or send postal mail surveys. Also, e-mail has a higher incidence (response) rate than other survey methods. People are more likely to respond to online or e-mail surveys because they can finish them on their own time, unlike phone surveys, and also e-mails are relatively painless to fill out and send back.

Advantages of Online Surveys

1. **Time Saving:** Less time is required generally to complete an online survey that traditional surveys. The researcher does not have to wait for the questionnaires to be returned as these are automatically returned. The response rate is almost instant. Time required for data analysis is also very less.
2. **Cost Effective:** Using online questionnaires can save money on postage. The responses are processed automatically, and the results are easily accessible.
3. **More Accurate:** Less margin of error as participants can enter their responses directly into the system.
4. **Faster Analysis:** Results of the online survey are ready to be analysed quickly and data can be presented in graphs or tables.
5. **Easy to Use for Participants:** With an online survey participants can pick a time that suits them best, and the time needed to complete the survey is much shorter.
6. **Customised Formats:** An online survey can be styled to match business' website with choice of colours, layout, images, audio, or video to the questions.
8. **Honest:** Participants in online surveys usually provide truthful and better answers as they feel safe in the anonymous environment of the Internet and open up easily.
9. **Selective:** Participants can be screened as per needs thus allowing to target specific issues and questions to only those who can give you the correct answers.
10. **Flexible:** Online surveys are flexible in their design and administering.

To sum up, online surveys are less time consuming, cheaper, and give faster results that can be stored and transferred.

Some examples of online survey sites are: surveymonkey.com, esurveyspro.com, freeonlinesurveys.com etc.

Constraints

Though online surveys are very appropriate for collecting information in a faster and cheaper manner they are bound with constraints too. It is necessary that the target respondents are connected through internet. Also, there is no way to confirm the identity of the respondent where it is important.

Other Methods

Other methods for collecting primary data include, but are not restricted to:

Mechanical Devices: Mechanical device refers to a CCTV camera. Mechanical devices are used at exhibitions and other places to capture the details of respondents Also, content analysis, projective techniques etc. are used as per the requirement of the study.

5.9 Sampling Techniques

Sampling assumes much importance in research studies. This following sections will enable one to comprehend the basic concepts of sampling and the different techniques available for sampling. Also, it will be possible to identify and understand the considerations for sample size and sampling frame. Knowledge about the different errors possible due to sampling will also be dealt with.

5.10 Basic Concepts of Sampling

Introduction

While conducting a research study, data about the population characteristics is required to be collected. Often it is impossible or too expensive to study the entire population for the decision-maker to understand the market. Here the researcher may use data collected by somebody else (secondary data) or collect the data himself (primary data) through surveys. Again while collecting primary data through surveys, researcher has the option whether to collect data from all the units of the population (census survey) or from a target population (sample survey), i.e., before deciding the method of collection of data through experimentation, observation, questionnaire, or interview schedule, the researcher has to decide whether he wants to collect data from every unit of the universe or whether he will use only a portion of the universe.

An important step before the data collection process is sampling. Sampling is the process of selecting a representative part of a population, studying it and thereby drawing conclusions about the population itself. Sampling is a very important aspect of research and due care has to be taken to arrive at the right sample to be studied. It is an important concept that we practice even in our routine life. Sampling involves selecting a relatively small number of elements from a larger defined group of elements and expecting that the information gathered from the small group will allow judgements to be made about the larger group.

If all the respondents in a population are asked to provide information, such survey is called a census. Information obtained from a subset of the population is known as the statistic (from sample). Researchers then attempt to make an inference about the population parameter with the knowledge of the relevant sample statistic. Sampling is often used when conducting a census is impossible or unreasonable. When using a census, the researcher is interested in collecting primary data about or from every member of the defined target population.

5.10.1 Defining the Universe, Survey, Census and Sampling

Survey

Survey is a very important part of research. Survey research covers any measurement procedures that involve asking questions of respondents. A survey can be anything from a short paper-and-pencil feedback form to an intensive one-on-one in-depth interview. The term survey is applied to a wide variety of investigations, such as the poverty surveys, market research, census and sample surveys. Surveys are concerned with examining the nature of and relationships among demographic characteristics, social conditions and activities, opinions and attitudes of a group of people etc. Surveys are always carried out in a field situation and could be either descriptive or analytical.

A census is a collection of data from the entire population. A survey is a collection of data from a sample of the population.

Census

Census refers to the complete enumeration of all the units in the population. Since each and every unit of the population is considered here, more accuracy is presumed in such survey data collected. But this may not be true always, as even a slight element of bias will go on increasing with each element covered. Also, such a survey involves more amount of time, money and energy. This type of survey is suitable when the population size is very small. For example, the complete list of registered voters or person with active driving licenses. But there would be no records of a complete list of homeless people! So if a study requires input from homeless persons, one may need to go and find the respondents personally and not through mail surveys or telephone interviews. Census is carried out for population census and conducted once in every ten years. It is usually very expensive and time consuming to collect information from every member of the population, exceptions being the General Election and the Census.

Sample: A subset or set of units of the population which is drawn by some sampling technique to study about the population.

Sampling

Sampling techniques are especially useful in business research as many times large amount of data are generated and researcher thinks of using a more manageable subset of data that they believe accurately represents the trends in the larger collection.

Sampling may be defined as the process of selecting units (people, organisations etc.) from a population of interest so that by examining the sample units, results may be generalised about the population. It helps to identify the target population to be considered for collection of data. It involves the selection of some part of an aggregate or totality on the basis of which a judgement or inference about the aggregate or totality is made. In most of the research work and surveys, the usual approach happens to make generalisations or inferences based on samples about the parameters of population from which the samples are taken.

Sampling is an essential part of all scientific procedures. It is well developed in the field of biology, physics, chemistry and social science research. Some general examples of sampling are:

- To confirm whether the rice is cooked or not, the housewife checks only a few grains of the rice from the pot and concludes about the entire contents whether the rice is properly cooked or not.
- A doctor, whether doubtful about something infections / diseases affecting a person, suggests for blood tests to be undergone which employs samples of blood to be studied.
- While preparing tea, coffee or cold drinks, we can check the taste by just tasting a spoonful of the same and infer whether it is of suitable taste, flavour, temperature etc.
- While buying a novel or book, a reader can judge about it by reading a couple of pages or briefly going through the language, print, contents etc.

Advantages of Sampling

Sampling from a population is advantageous due to the following:

- We can get information from large populations
- It is cost effective
- Saves time
- Proves to be more accurate
- Many tools available.

Sampling is an attractive alternative to the census method because:

1. **Resource Constraints:** Due to limited amount of resources (time and money) available to a researcher/decision-maker, it is not feasible to conduct a census study. Here sampling provides the required information though with some uncertainty, within the given resource constraints.
2. **Accuracy:** Choosing the right sample and sampling method, the researcher can provide information within the given tolerable of error so as to arrive at an acceptably accurate answer.
3. **Impossibility:** Sampling is a must when at times it is impossible to take a census, particularly in natural sciences.

4. **Destructive measurement:** A measurement can often involve destruction of the element and sampling proves to be a better option.
5. **Quality:** Since samples are smaller than the population, it is possible to be more thorough in a sample study than in a study of the population. This results in higher quality of the information obtained.

5.10.2 Concepts of Statistical Population and Sample

Key terms in Sampling
- **Population:** All the units in the field of inquiry constitute a 'Universe' or 'Population'. The population is defined in keeping with the objectives of the study. Population refers to the collection of all the items about which researcher wants to study some characteristics and need not be human. For example, hospital patients, pet owners, unoccupied property etc.
- **Sample:** 'Sample' refers to a part of the population which is selected to be studied. As the name implies, 'sample' is a smaller representation of a larger whole. It is composed of some fractions or part of the total number of elements or units in a defined population. Sampling therefore is a method of selecting some fraction of a population.
- **Need for Sampling:** Normally, the population is too large for the researcher to survey each and every unit in the population. When studying a part of the population is sufficient to conclude about the whole, then sampling may be resorted to obtain a sample. A small, but carefully chosen sample can be used to represent the population. The sample reflects the characteristics of the population from which it is drawn. In case of field studies carried out, considerations of time and cost lead to selection of a sample to study the population characteristic. The skill in sampling lies in choosing a sample that will be as representative as possible. As a general rule the larger the sample, the better it is for estimating characteristics of the population.
- **Sampling Frame:** Sampling frame or sample frame, survey frame is the actual set of units from which a sample has been drawn. It is necessary that the sampling frame should be comprehensive, correct, reliable and appropriate.
- **Sampling Design:** A sample design refers to the technique or the procedure the researcher would adopt in selecting items for the sample. It is determined before the data are collected.

Key Considerations for Developing a Sampling Design
The following points must be kept in mind while developing a sampling design:
   (a) **Type of Universe:** Finite /infinite. The universe or population to be studied should be clearly defined – it may be finite or infinite. For example – number of employees in an organisation is finite whereas listeners of a specific radio programme etc. are infinite.

(b) **Sampling Unit:** Family, school, state, district. Sampling unit may be geographical, whether district, state etc. or a social unit such as family, institution etc.

Sampling units may be of the following types:

Geographical units - Such as state, districts, town etc.

Construction units - Such as house, flat etc.

Social units - Such as family, club, schools etc.

(c) **Source List or Sampling Frame:** It is a list which contains the names of all the units of the finite population / universe from which the sample is to be drawn. Sampling frame should be comprehensive, correct, reliable and appropriate.

(d) **Sample size:** Sample size refers to the number of items to be selected from the universe and is very important for the researcher. The sample size should not be very small, neither too large. An optimum sample size is the number which satisfies the requirements of efficiency, representativeness, reliability and flexibility. The size of the population, the parameter under study, time and cost estimates, budgetary constraints etc. play an important role in determining the size of the sample.

Factors Determining Size of a Sample

(i) **Parameters of Interest:** The nature of the parameter of interest is also to be considered while deciding the sample size whether it is required to study some average, or proportion etc.

(ii) **Budgetary Constraints:** Cost considerations also affect the sample size and also the type of sampling method to be used.

(iii) **Sampling Procedure:** The researcher needs to identify which sampling technique should be used so that it results in minimum of sampling error.

(iv) **Representative Sample:** A sample is expected to represent the population to the maximum extent as possible, means, the information derived from the sample is expected to be the same had a complete census of the target population been carried out.

5.10.3 Characteristics of a Good Sample

Characteristics/Features/Attributes of a Good Sample

A good sample should be truly representative of the population. It has the following characteristics:

1. **Accurate and Representative of the Universe:** The selected sample should be an accurate representative of the population from which it is taken. It will be truly representative only when it represents all types of units or groups in the total population in fair proportions. In short, sample should be selected carefully as improper sampling is

a source of error in the survey. A good sample should be able to specify the accuracy and precision associated with it, i.e., it should enable researchers to specify the degree of confidence that can be placed in its parameter estimate.

2. **Goal-oriented:** A sample design should be goal oriented / focused. It is essential that the sample selected should be oriented to the research objectives and focused to the survey conditions. For example, if a research is being conducted to study job satisfaction in police force; then the sample members must be the police personnel belonging to different levels in the police force.

3. **Economical:** A sample selected should be economical. The objectives of the survey should be achieved with minimum cost and effort.

4. **Precision:** A good sample should be precise, i.e. it should have a low standard error of its estimate. A good sample should be large enough to ensure precision. For instance, if a research is undertaken to find out the impact of inflation on the poor, then the sample size would be larger, as there are more poor households in India.

5. **Random Selection:** A sample should be selected at random so as to ensure representativeness.

6. **Proportional:** A sample should be proportional to the universe so as to provide reliability. The sample size should give accuracy required for the purpose of particular study. Flexibility in determining the sample size should be adopted so as to achieve a representative sample.

7. **Proper Selection of Sample Units**: The sample units should be properly selected based on the objectives and the desired information. For example, if study related to bank employees, further male/female, junior, senior etc. should be clearly selected as per the objectives.

8. **Low Sampling Error, High Confidence Level and Least Degree of Variability:** It is desirable that a sample selected should result in low sampling error, high confidence level and least degree of variability. It should represent all types of units or groups in the total population in fair proportions. In brief, sample should be selected carefully as improper sampling is a source of error in the survey.

9. **Practical:** A sample design should be practical. The sample design should be simple i.e. it should be capable of being understood and followed in the fieldwork.

10. **Actual Information Provider:** A sample should be designed so as to provide actual information required for the study and also provide an adequate basis for the measurement of its own reliability.

5.10.4 Sampling Frame

The sampling frame is an important component of sampling design. Sampling frame or sample frame, survey frame is the actual set of units from which a sample would be drawn. It helps the researcher in identifying and locating the population elements and other related information necessary for clustering and stratifying. Hence, a sampling frame is a complete list of all the members of the population that we wish to study. The sampling frame should uniquely list each and every unit of the population. It is necessary that the sampling frame is comprehensive, correct, reliable and appropriate.

Sampling and Non-sampling errors

The two components of total survey error, random sampling error and non-sampling error are present in all the surveys. Random sampling error is encountered in survey research because the sample selected is not a perfect representation of the test population. Non-sampling error is caused by phenomenon such as subject non response and misreporting of answers that are not associated with the actual sampling procedure.

5.10.5 Sampling Errors

Sampling error arises from the fact that samples differ from their populations as they are small sub-sets of the total population. Sampling error refers to differences between the sample and the population that exist only because of the observations that happened to be selected for the sample. Sampling errors occur because inferences about the entire population are based on information obtained from only a sample of that population.

For example, if one measures the weight of a hundred individuals from a population of five thousand, the average weight of the hundred (i.e. sample) is not typically the same that of all five thousand (i.e. Population). Since sampling is typically done to determine the characteristics of a whole population, the difference between the sample and population values is known as sampling error. Sampling error cannot be measured exactly, as the population parameter is unknown, but it can be estimated.

5.10.6 Non-sampling Errors

Non-sampling errors are much serious and occur due to mistakes made while collecting the data or sample observations incorrectly. Non-sampling errors refer to the deviations from the true values which are not a function of the sample chosen. Non-sampling errors are the remaining errors after accounting for sampling errors and include all the biases that can affect surveys. They are even possible in complete censuses. These types of errors are difficult to quantify than sampling errors and can error at every/any stage of a survey process. The persons responsible for committing these types of errors may be survey designers, trainers, enumerators, respondents, printers, analysts, managers, manual writers, data entry operators etc. Non-sampling errors may include data entry errors, biased questions in a questionnaire, poorly worded questions, biased processing/decision making, improperly trained personnel, false information provided by respondents or even badly defined concepts etc. Increasing the sample size will not reduce this type of error and it is very difficult to eliminate the non-sampling errors entirely.

Some examples of non-sampling errors are:

(1) Non-response errors in the form of refusals, not-at-homes, unreturned or lost questionnaires.
(2) Long or repeated interviews which result in inaccurate responses.
(3) The wording of the question causes the respondent to misunderstand the concept.
(4) Incorrect decimal placement during key entry, etc.

Non-sampling errors may occur due to the following reasons:
- Errors in data acquisition,
- Non-response, and
- Selection bias.

Response and Non-response Errors

(i) Non-response error occurs when some sample members do not respond causing responses to be an unreliable representation of the selected sample.
(ii) Response error occurs when sample members respond inaccurately; because members purposely misreport their answers, have faulty recall, are fatigued, are affected by interviewers or are influenced by host of other environmental factors.

Non-sampling errors can be divided into coverage errors, measurement errors (respondent, interviewer, questionnaire and collection method), non-response errors and processing errors.

Types of Non-sampling Errors

Non-sampling errors may be of various types depending upon the causes:

(a) Coverage (or Frame) Errors / Selection Bias
(b) Non-Response
(c) Errors in Data Acquisition / Measurement
(d) Data Handling / Processing

(a) Coverage (or Frame) Errors / Selection Bias: These may be due to under-coverage (missing elements) or over-coverage (duplicates) of units.

(b) Non-Response: Non-response errors may be due to,
- **Unit non-response:** Inability to obtain response from the pre-chosen sampling unit or population
- **Item non-response:** Failure to get response to a specific question or item in the data recording form

(c) **Measurement Errors - Errors in Data Acquisition/Measurement:** These occur when recorded response differs from the actual response and may arise due to reasons like
- **Respondent** – false information provided by respondent due to,
    o Prestige issues, sensitivity or social undesirability of question.
    o Misunderstanding the requirements.
    o Lack of motivation to give an accurate answer or "lazy" respondent gives an "average" answer.
    o Question requires memory/recall.
    o Proxy respondents - taking answers from someone other than the respondent.
- **Instrument** – question error
    o Unclear, ambiguous or difficult to answer questions.
    o Incomplete list of possible answers suggested in the recording instrument.
    o Requested information assumes a framework unfamiliar to the respondent.
    o The definitions used are different from those commonly understood by the respondent.
- **Interviewer error**
    o Inadequate training of interviewers.
    o Different interviewers administer a survey in different ways.
    o Stressed interviewer.

(d) **Data Handling/Processing Errors:** These errors can occur at any stage of the process and may be due to,
- Errors in transmission of data from the field to the office.
- Errors in coding, data entry or during data analysis.

5.10.7 Methods to Reduce Errors

In order to reduce the non-sampling errors it is important to understand them completely in the context of the survey being undertaken. For this, the researcher must take the following steps:
- Investigate the entire survey process and identifying the sources of the error.
- Understand the cause of the error.
- Identify the impact of the error so as to decide the extent.

Measures suggested to control non-sampling errors

The researcher needs to take the different measures to tackle the sources, causes and extent of the non-sampling errors. The following actions would be useful:
- Clarify the purpose and objectives of the survey.
- Pay utmost care and attention to confidentiality concerns.
- Verification of coding procedures and use of tested and verified software and instruments.
- Impart training to the concerned personnel.
- At planning stage, list all potential non-sampling errors.
- Question procedures adopted for data collection, and data verification at each step of the data chain.
- Critically view the data collected and attempt to resolve queries immediately they arise.
- Document sources of non-sampling errors so that results presented can be interpreted meaningfully.

5.10.8 Sample Size Constraints

Sample size represents the number of observations taken to conduct a statistical analysis. Sample sizes can be composed of people, animals, food batches, machines, batteries or whatever population is being evaluated. Sample size plays an important role in research. A very small sample is likely to skew the results of an experiment. The basic rule for sample size is the larger the better because as sample size increases, the estimates become more accurate. But as the size of the sample increases, it means more expensive in terms of time and money. Hence the appropriate size depends upon the purpose and objective of the research along with the variability of the population characteristics.

5.10.9 Non-response

For a researcher, it is very important to manage and minimize the non-response. Response rates in a survey can be improved through good survey design, clarity of purpose, questions etc. Assurances of privacy and confidentiality are very important along with follow-ups and rapport with the respondents can improve the response rates considerably.

Following are some suggested measures for minimising the non-response during personal or phone contact:
- Try to identify the reasons for refusal and attempt to address the same.
- Stress upon the importance of the survey and explain role of the respondents in the survey.
- Explain the importance of their response as representation of the sample.

- Use positive language.
- Highlight the benefits from the survey results.
- Assure confidentiality of the responses.

Some other measures that may improve respondent co-operation and maximise response are:

- Use of Media: News releases, media interview and articles may be released so as to create public awareness and informing community about the survey, identifying issues of concern so as to address them.
- Advance notice to selected units explaining the purposes of the survey and how the survey is going to be conducted may be given to increase the response.

5.11 Probability Sample

Different Types of Sampling Techniques/Methods

The purpose of any sampling method is to obtain a sample that is representative of the target population. Sampling methods are classified as either probability or non-probability. Probability sampling is based on the concept of random selection, whereas non-probability sampling is 'non-random' sampling.

(i) Probability Sampling

Probability sampling also known as random sampling or chance sampling is one in which every unit in the population has a non-zero chance of being selected in the sample, and this probability can be accurately determined. In probability sampling design, the population must be clearly defined and list of target population must be available. Probability sampling allows for estimation of sampling errors.

In Probability Sampling:
1. Every element has a known non-zero probability of being selected, and
2. It involves random selection at some point.

Probability sampling includes:
- Simple Random Sampling,
- Systematic Sampling,
- Stratified Sampling and
- Cluster or Multistage Sampling.

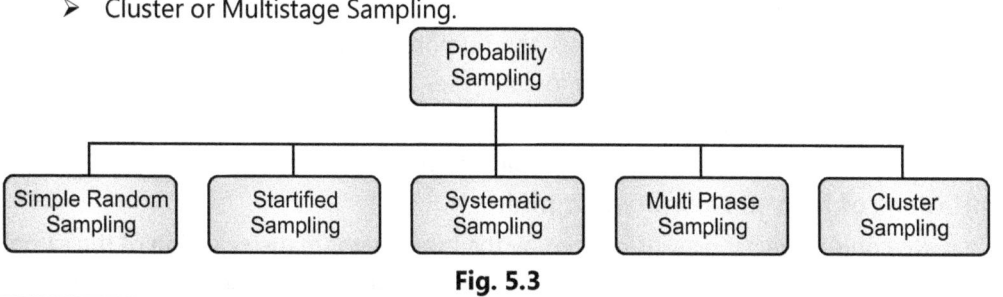

Fig. 5.3

(ii) Non-probability Sampling

Non-probability sampling simply means sampling without using random selection methods. In this type of sampling, items for the sample are selected deliberately by the researcher and his choice concerning the items remains absolute. With non-probability sampling methods, the probability of being included in the sample is unknown. In non-probability sampling, members are selected from the population in some non-random manner usually on the basis of their accessibility or by the purposive personal judgement of the researcher. The non-random selection of elements does not allow the estimation of sampling errors. These conditions give rise to exclusion bias, placing limits on how much information a sample can provide about the population. Information about the relationship between sample and population is limited.

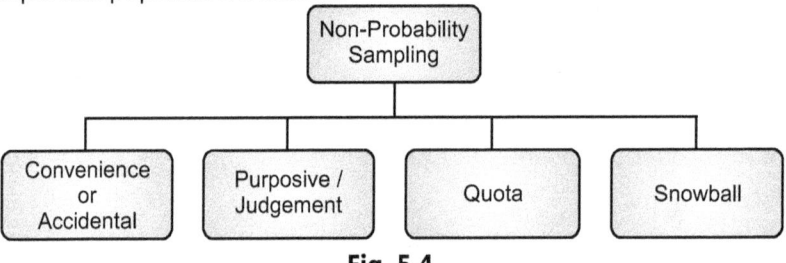

Fig. 5.4

Non-probability sampling includes: Deliberate (purposive sampling), Accidental Sampling, Quota Sampling, Judgement Sampling, Convenience Sampling and Snowball Sampling.

Non-probability Sampling convenience samples and volunteers. For example, people who volunteer are frequently different in many respects from those who do not.

If we visit every household in a given street, and interview the first person to answer the door, this is a non-probability sample, because some people are more likely to answer the door (e.g. an unemployed person who spends most of their time at home is more likely to answer than an employed housemate who might be at work when the interviewer calls) and it's not practical to calculate these probabilities.

Sometimes non-probability methods may be used if the purpose of the research is to explore some topic maybe, to identify key concepts or to test respondents' understanding of items to be used in a scale. In such cases, the purpose is not to generalise, which requires a random sample, but to learn something for later use.

Also, when a sampling frame does not exist and cluster sampling is impractical, non-probability methods are the only way to obtain a sample.

Limitations of Non-probability Sampling

- No control against bias introduced by the investigator in the selection of the sample
- Results cannot be safely generalised beyond the specific sample that was used.

Methods of Probability Sampling

Probability sampling methods:
1. Simple Random Sampling,
2. Systematic Sampling,
3. Stratified Sampling and
4. Area and Cluster or Multistage Sampling.

1. Random Sampling

Random sampling is the simplest and purest form of probability sampling. It is a technique in which every unit in population has equal and known chance of being included in sample. A simple random sample is free from sampling bias. The selections that make up the sample are made independently; that is, the choice of one unit will not affect the chance of another unit being selected.

When the population is very large, it is often difficult or impossible to identify every member of the population. If the sample is to be collected by a person untrained in statistics, then instructions may be misinterpreted and selections may be made improperly.

Features of Random Sampling
1. Every element has a known non-zero probability of being selected.
2. It involves random selection at some point.
3. It is not haphazard but follows a sound procedure to ensure chance selection.
4. Items are selected independent of each other.
5. There is no bias in selection of units.

Merits
1. It is a scientific method.
2. No scope for personal bias.
3. Economical in nature.
4. Uses theory of probability – random and reliable.
5. Ensures accuracy.

Demerits
1. Complete listing is required i.e. sampling frame necessary.
2. Unsuitable for heterogeneous population.
3. Problem of non-response may occur.

Steps in Selecting a Simple Random Sample are:
1. Define the target population and sampling element;
2. Select a sampling frame; and
3. Select the sample.

Methods of Simple Random Sampling

In simple random sampling, units are selected through the Lottery Method or by referring to Random Numbers Table.

(i) Lottery Method: It is the simplest way of selection a random sample. The number of items in a universe (i.e., population) are written on sheets of paper or cards and these are then shuffled in a box. Then, at random, the cards/chits of papers are drawn from the box. As many cards as the required sample sizes are drawn and the corresponding unit of the population forms the sample.

Instead of pieces of paper, plastic discs or coins can also be used. This method is suitable for drawing a small number of samples from a small universe.

The following example will illustrate this method clearly.

If we want to take a sample of 10 persons out of a population of 100, the procedure is to write the names of all the 100 persons on separate slips of paper, fold these slips, mix them thoroughly, and then make a random selection of 10 slips.

(ii) Random Numbers Method: When the population / universe is very large then it is not practical to write down slips for each member of the universe. Instead, the random numbers method can be used. In this method the statistical tables of random numbers (or even available from calculators) in the range of 000 to 999 or 9999 etc. are selected randomly to form the sample. Random numbers may be between 0 – 9 or between 0 – 99 or between 0 – 999 as the universe (N – 10, 100, 1000 etc.) may be. Random numbers method is quite suitable if the size of the population is large.

For example: If a researcher wants to select 200 employees from a total of 8000 employees in an organisation. He may number the employees from 000 to 7999 and then he can refer to the random numbers between 0000 to 7999 and select the 200 random numbers in this range only. The corresponding employees would form the sample.

Advantages of Simple Random Sampling

The advantages of this method are:
1. No advance knowledge of the characteristics of the population is necessary.
2. Assessment of the accuracy of the results is possible by sample error estimation.
3. It is representative of the universe.
4. Bias due to human preferences and influences is eliminated.
5. It is a simple and easily practicable procedure if the population is not large.
6. It is less expensive as compared to other methods.

Limitations of Simple Random Sampling

The limitations of this method are:
1. Definition of the universe at many times is inadequate.
2. The ready lists of universe are not always available. Serialising the large population is also difficult.
3. Sampling is likely to be biased at the survey stage; because of non-availability of or no response from the sample units.

2. Stratified Sampling

In this method the heterogeneous population is divided into distinct, non-overlapping homogenous subgroups called "strata"; according to some important characteristics or variable like income, education, age, etc., and then a random sample is selected from within each subgroup. A stratum is a subset of the population that shares at least one common characteristic i.e. homogenous in nature. Hence, now the population is formed of different strata. A stratified sample is obtained by independently selecting a separate simple random sample from each population stratum. From each stratum, sample units are randomly selected to form the sample. Stratified sampling is commonly used probability method that is superior to random sampling because it reduces sampling error.

The investigator can use this method to ensure that each subgroup of interest is represented in the sample. This method generally produces more precise estimates of the characteristics of the target population, unless very small number of units is selected within individual strata.

Examples of stratums might be according to gender-males and females, or cadre-managers and non-managers. The researcher first identifies the relevant stratums and their actual representation in the population. Random sampling is then used to select a sufficient number of subjects from each stratum. "Sufficient" refers to a sample size large enough for us to be reasonably confident that the stratum represents the population. Stratified sampling is often used when one or more of the stratums in the population have a low incidence relative to the other stratums.

Methods of Stratified Sampling

(i) **Non-Proportionate Allocation Method:** In this method, after dividing the population into strata, equal number of sample points from each stratum are selected to form the complete sample. Hence, irrespective of the size of the strata, the equal number of units will form the sample. In this case, there are chances of error creeping in because the strata with less number of units may also be wrongly represented and lead to further bias.

(ii) Proportionate Allocation Method: In this method, after dividing the population into strata, the number of sample points from each stratum are selected in proportion to the size of the strata. This eliminates the error of non-representative sample. Hence, each strata representation in the sample is in proportion to its size.

Example: Let a population of 100 employees be divided into the following manner:

Group / Strata	Characteristic (Experience in years)	Number of employees	Non-proportional allocation	20 % sample Proportional allocation
A	Less than 5 years	10	5	2
B	5 to 10 years	30	5	6
C	10-20 years	40	5	8
D	20 and above	20	5	4
	Total	100	20	20

Suppose it is desired to draw a stratified random sample of size 20.

(i.e. sample size = 20%). This may be done as follows:

(i) Simply 5 employees from each group may be selected randomly – giving rise to non proportional allocation. (See column 4)

OR

(ii) 20% from each strata may be selected i.e. 2 from A, (See column 5) leading to stratified proportional allocation.

Merits
- Suitable for heterogeneous population.
- No personal bias.
- Accuracy.
- Uses theory of probability.
- Results in representative sample.
- Economical.
- Suitable for skewed and heterogeneous universe.

Demerits
- Complex Method.
- Choice of strata is difficult at times.
- Complete information about population is necessary.

3. Systematic Sampling

Systematic sampling is often used instead of random sampling. Systematic sampling is frequently used to select a specified number of records from a computer file. It is also called an nth name selection technique. A systematic random sample is obtained by selecting one unit on a random basis and choosing additional elementary units at evenly spaced intervals until the desired number of units is obtained.

In this method list of population units is arranged in some order and every k^{th} item is selected from the population where k is sampling interval, $k = \dfrac{\text{Size of population}}{\text{Size of sample}}$. Typically, the integer k is estimated by dividing the size of the target population by the desired sample size. First item is drawn at random. This method of sampling is easy to implement in practice, and the sampling frame can be compiled as the study progresses. As long as the list does not contain any hidden order, this sampling method is as good as the random sampling method. Its only advantage over the random sampling technique is simplicity.

For example, suppose we want to draw sample of 20 from 100 employees then we arrange the employees according some manner say alphabetically and assign numbers to each employee. Here, k = 100/20 = 5. To choose a systematic random sample, randomly select any number between 1 and 5. Suppose the number picked is 4, hence that will be the starting number. So employee number 4 has been selected. From there every 5th name be selected until we reach the last number i.e., 100. Thus, selection of 20 employees is completed.

Merits
- Economical.
- Human bias is not involved.
- Representative sample.
- Ensures Accuracy.

Demerits
- Complete listing required.
- Sampling error not available.
- Periodicity.

4. **Cluster Sampling**

In this method the population is divided into heterogeneous groups called clusters. A cluster is then randomly selected from population and further sampling or complete enumeration of clusters done. This method divides the population into clusters at each stage and draws sample of required size at each stage. Sampling is done in multistage.

Elements within a cluster are as heterogeneous as possible, but there should be homogeneity between clusters. Each cluster is a small scale representation of the total population. The clusters are mutually exclusive and collectively exhaustive.

A random sampling technique is then used on any relevant clusters to choose which clusters to include in the study. In single-stage cluster sampling, all the elements from each of the selected clusters are used. In two-stage cluster sampling, a random sampling technique is applied to the elements from each of the selected clusters.

Cluster sampling may be used if the study units form natural groups or if an adequate list of the entire population is difficult to compile. In a national survey, for example, clusters may comprise individuals in a localised geographic area. The clusters or regions are selected, preferably at random, and the persons are enumerated in each selected region and random samples are drawn from these units of the population. Because sampling is performed at multiple levels, this method is sometimes referred to as multistage sampling.

For example, a cluster may be a village or a school, a state. So you decide all the elementary schools in Maharashtra are clusters. You want 20 schools selected. You can use simple or systematic random sampling to select the schools and then every school selected becomes a cluster. If your interest is to interview teachers on their opinion of some new programme which has been introduced, then all the teachers in a cluster must be interviewed. Though every economical, cluster sampling is very susceptible to sampling bias. Like for the above case, you are likely to get similar responses from teachers in one school due to the fact that they interact with one another.

Cluster sampling is used to estimate high mortalities in cases such as wars, famines, natural disasters etc.

Multistage Sampling

Sometimes the sample unit needs to be selected in stages while ensuring randomness at every stage. The population is regarded as being composed of a number of first stage or Primary Sampling Units (PSUs) each of them being made up of a number of second stage units in each selected PSU and so the procedure continues down to the final sampling unit, with the sampling ideally being random at each stage.

For example, primary sampling units for national surveys may be administrative districts, urban districts or parliamentary constituencies. Within the selected PSU one may go direct to the final sampling units, such as individuals, households or addresses, in which case we have a two-stage sample.

Area Sampling

Area sampling is a method in which the area to be sampled is subdivided into smaller blocks that are further selected at random, and sub-sampled or surveyed. Area sampling is a form of multistage sampling in which maps rather than lists serve as sampling frame. This is very useful in developing countries where population lists are lacking. The areas are divided into sub-areas from which a sample is selected at random.

5.12 Non-probability Sample

Methods of Non-probability Sampling

Due to practical considerations, one often uses non-probability sampling even though it is technically inferior to probability sampling. It is useful when researchers do not need to generalise the results. Since cost and time-saving are high in non-probability sampling, it is a valuable tool in certain cases. This method is also useful when the entire population is not available for the study. In all the above cases, non-probability sampling is favoured.

Non-probability sampling typically is used in following situations:
(i) The exploratory stages of a research project,
(ii) Pre-testing a questionnaire,
(iii) Dealing with a homogeneous population,
(iv) When a researcher lacks statistical knowledge,
(v) When operational ease is required.

1. Convenience Sampling

Convenience sampling (or accidental sampling) is a method in which samples are drawn at the convenience of the researcher or interviewer. The assumptions are that the target population is homogeneous and the individuals interviewed are similar to the overall defined target population with regard to the characteristics being studied.

Advantages and Disadvantages

Convenience sampling allows a large number of respondents to be interviewed in a relatively short time. For this reason, it is commonly used in the early stages of research. The use of convenience samples in the development phases of constructs and scale measurements can have a seriously negative impact on the overall reliability and validity of those measures and instruments used to collect raw data. Another major disadvantage of convenience samples is that the raw data and results are not generalised to the defined target population with any measure of precision. It is not possible to measure the representativeness of the sample, because sampling error estimates cannot be accurately determined.

2. Judgement Sampling

In judgement sampling or purposive sampling, participants are selected according to an experienced individual belief that they will meet the requirements of the study. Judgemental sampling is associated with a variety of biases. For example, shopping center intercept interviewing can over-sample those who shop frequently, who appear friendly, and who have uncertainty, because the sampling frame is unknown and the sampling procedure is not well specified. There are times when probability sampling is either not feasible or expensive.

For example, a list of sidewalk vendors might be impossible to obtain, and a judgemental sample might be appropriate in that case. Secondly, if the sample size is to be very small - suppose 10, then, a judgemental sample usually will be more reliable and representative than a probability sample.

Also, sometimes it is useful to obtain a deliberately biased sample. If, for example, a product or service modification is to be evaluated, it might be possible to identify a group that, by its very nature, should be disposed towards the modification. It is also very useful when a limited number of individuals possess the trait of interest and is the most suitable sampling technique in obtaining information from a particular group of people.

Advantages and Disadvantages

If the judgement of the researcher or expert is correct, then the sample generated from judgement sampling will be much better than one generated by convenience sampling. But, it is not possible to measure the representativeness of the sample. The raw data and information collected from sampling units generated though the judgement sampling method should be interpreted as nothing more preliminary insights.

3. Purposive Sampling

Purposive Sampling is also known as judgemental, selective or subjective sampling. Selection of the sample is largely dependent on the judgement of the researcher (e.g., people, cases/organisations, events, pieces of data) that are to be studied. Usually, the sample being investigated is quite small, especially when compared with probability sampling techniques. In purposive sampling, sample is selected with a purpose in mind. Purposive sampling can be very useful for situations where you need to reach a targeted sample quickly and where sampling for proportionality is not the primary concern.

Advantages and Disadvantages

This type of sampling is very useful in qualitative studies as there are various means available to select the appropriate sample. For example, maximum variation sampling, homogenous sampling, typical case sampling, expert sampling etc.

On the other hand, this purposive sampling can be highly prone to researcher bias. Also, since it is affected by the subjectivity and is non-probability based, the representativeness of the sample is of much concern.

4. Quota Sampling

The quota sampling method involves the selection of prospective participants according to pre-specified quota regarding either demographic characteristics (e.g., age, race, gender, income), specific attitudes (e.g., satisfied/dissatisfied, liking/disliking, great/marginal/no quality), or specific behaviours (e.g., regular/occasional/rare customer, product user/non user). The underlying purpose of quota sampling is to provide an assurance that pre-specified sub-groups of the defined target population are represented on pertinent sampling factors that are determined by the researcher or client. Surveys frequently use quotas that have been determined by the specific nature of the research objectives.

In order to meet the quotas, researcher using quota sampling sometimes overlooks the problems associated with adhering to the quotas.

Advantages and Disadvantages

The greatest advantage of quota sampling is that the sample generated contains specific sub-groups in the proportions desired by researchers. In those research projects that require interviews, the use of quotas ensures that the appropriate sub-groups are identified and included in the survey. The quota sampling method may eliminate or reduce selection bias on the part of the field workers. An inherent limitation of quota sampling is that the success of the study will be dependent on subjective decisions made by the researchers. Also, it is incapable of measuring the true representativeness of the sample or accuracy of the estimate obtained. Hence, attempts to generalise data results beyond those respondents who were sampled and interviewed become very questionable and may misrepresent the defined target population.

5. Snowball Sampling

Snowball Sampling involves the practice of identifying and qualifying a set of initial prospective respondents who can, in turn, help the researcher identify additional people to be included in the study. This method of sampling is also called referral sampling, because one respondent refers other potential respondents. Snowball sampling is typically used in research situations:

(i) The defined target population is very small and unique, and

(ii) Compiling a complete list of sampling units is a nearly impossible task.

The snowball method would yield better results at a much lower cost. Here the researcher would identify and interview one qualified respondent, then solicit his or her help in identifying other people with similar characteristics. The main underlying logic of this method is that rare groups of people tend to form their own unique social circles.

Advantages and Disadvantages

Snowball sampling is a reasonable method of identifying and selecting prospective respondents who are members of small, possessing rare characteristics, hard-to-reach, and uniquely defined target population. It is most useful in qualitative research practices, like focus group interviews. Reduced sample sizes and costs are primary advantages to this sampling method.

It may be difficult or costly to locate the respondents and snowball sampling relies on referrals to generate further sample points. Snowball sampling definitely allows bias to enter the overall research study.

Determining size of the sample - Practical considerations in sampling and sample size

The procedures used to select a sample require some prior knowledge of the target population, which allows a determination of the size of the sample needed to achieve a reasonable estimate (with accepted precision and accuracy) of the characteristics of the population. Kent illustrates how the purpose of the research affects sample size through the following examples:

- To generate new product ideas or obtain feedback from customers, a sample of 30 is probably sufficient.
- For quantitative analysis a sample of at least 100 should be obtained, even to calculate only percentages.
- If subgroups are distinguished, each subgroup should have a large enough sample. If variables are to be cross tabulated, then larger samples are required, say 300 minimum.
- In most surveys samples of less than 1,000 persons are consequently of limited use for exploring variations within the total population.

So, it may be concluded that the sample size should be chosen by keeping considerations for time, energy, money, labor, equipment and access available. Most approaches assume normality of parent population and 95% confidence interval.

5.13 Data Analysis

Data preparation or Data processing is a stage between data collection and data analysis. The data collected for the research is in an unorganised form and needs to be processed so as to reveal unknown and unseen information. The results obtained from analysis are interpreted to some extent by the researcher. Once the analysis is done and the interpretation is made, the researcher needs to report the research to the decision maker. The rest of the interpretation is done by the decision-maker himself, as he understands the problem situation more clearly than the researcher. Different tools and techniques are available to the researcher for analysis. A proper understanding of each is desirable so as to efficiently analyse the data and get appropriate results.

5.13.1 Processing of Data - Editing, Coding, Classifications and Tabulation

(A) Editing

Editing is the first stage in data processing. Editing may be broadly defined to be a procedure, which uses available information and assumptions to substitute inconsistent values in a data set. In other words, editing is the process of examining the data collected through various methods to detect errors and omissions and correct them for further

analysis. While editing, care has to be taken to see that the data are accurate and complete. The following practical guidelines may be handy while editing the data:
1. The editor should have a copy of the instructions given to the interviewers.
2. The editor should not destroy or erase the original entry. Original entry should be crossed out in such a manner that they are still legible.
3. All answers, which are modified or filled in afresh by the editor, have to be indicated.
4. All completed schedules should have the signature of the editor and the date.

For checking the quality of data collected, it is advisable to take a small sample of the questionnaire and examine it thoroughly. This helps in understanding the following types of problems:
1. Whether all the questions are answered,
2. Whether the answers are properly recorded,
3. Whether there is any bias,
4. Whether there are inconsistencies.

Types of Editing
1. **Field editing:** Preliminary editing by a field supervisor, during the interview to catch technical omissions, check legibility of hand writing and clarify responses that are logically inconsistent. Field editing consists of the review of the reporting forms by the investigator, for completing (translating or rewriting) what the latter has written in abbreviated and / or in illegible form at the time of recording the respondents' responses. This type of editing is necessary in view of the fact that individual writing styles often can be difficult for others to decipher.
2. **In-house editing:** is a rigorous editing job performed by a centralised office staff. The researcher normally has centralised office staff, to perform editing and coding. All completed schedules/questionnaires should be thoroughly checked for completeness, accuracy and uniformity.

(B) Coding

Coding refers to the process by which data are categorised into groups and numerals or other symbols or both are assigned to each item depending on the class it falls in. Hence, coding involves:
- Deciding the categories to be used, and
- Assigning individual codes to them.

Coding is done by using a code book, code sheet, and a computer card. Coding is done on the basis of the instructions given in the codebook. The code book gives a numerical code for each variable. For open-ended questions, however, post-coding is necessary. In such cases, all answers to open-ended questions are placed in categories and each category is assigned a code.

Manual processing is employed when qualitative methods are used or when in quantitative studies, a small sample is used, or when the questionnaire/schedule has a large number of open-ended questions, or when accessibility to computers is difficult or inappropriate.

In general, coding reduces the huge amount of information collected into a form that is amenable to analysis.

(C) Classification

The process of dividing the data into different groups (viz. classes) which are homogeneous within but heterogeneous between them is called a classification. It helps in understanding the salient features of the data and also the comparison with similar data. For a final analysis it is the best friend of a statistician.

Classification refers to the process of arranging data in groups or classes on the basis of common characteristics. Most research studies result in a large volume of raw data which must be reduced into homogeneous groups if we are to get meaningful relationships. Data having common characteristics are placed in one class and in this way the entire data get divided into a number of groups or classes. Classification may be according to attributes, or class intervals.

When to classify: Classification can be done at any stage prior to the tabulation. Certain items like gender, age, type of house, and the like, are structured and pre classified in the data collection form itself. The responses to open-ended questions are classified at the processing stage.

Number of categories: How many categories should a scheme include? It is preferable to include many categories rather than a few, since reducing the number later is easier than splitting an already classified group of responses. However, the number of categories is limited by the number of cases and the anticipated statistical analysis. The data may be classified in the following ways:

Qualitative Classification

According to attributes or qualities this is divided into two parts:
- Simple classification
- Multiple classifications

When facts are grouped according to the qualities (attributes) like religion, literacy, business etc., the classification is called as qualitative classification.

Simple Classification

It is also known as classification according to **Dichotomy**. When data (facts) are divided into groups according to their qualities, the classification is called as 'Simple Classification'. Qualities are denoted by capital letters (A, B, C, D ......) while the absence of these qualities are denoted by lower case letters (a, b, c, d, ... etc.)

Manifold or Multiple Classification

In this method data is classified using one or more qualities. First, the data is divided into two groups (classes) using one of the qualities. Then using the remaining qualities, the data is divided into different subgroups. For example, the population of a country is classified using three attributes: gender, literacy and business.

Classification according to Class Intervals or Variables

The data which is expressed is classified according to class-intervals. While grouping the data into classes, the number of classes should not be too large or too small. As a rule one should have between 10 and 25 classes, the actual number depending on the total frequency. Further, classes should be exhaustive; they should not be overlapping, so that no observed value falls in more than one class. Apart from exceptions, all classes should have the same length.

(D) Tabulation

It is the systematic and orderly presentation of classified data in a definite form so as to elucidate the characteristics of the data. Tabulation is an orderly arrangement of data in columns and rows. Tabulation thus refers to the process of arranging the classified data in some kind of concise and logical order. In statistical tables the numerical information is presented in such a form that the information so presented turns to be readily understandable.

Usefulness of Tables

Tables are useful to the researchers and the readers in three ways:
1. They present an overall view of findings in a simpler way.
2. They identify trends.
3. They display relationships in a comparable way between parts of the findings.

By convention, the dependent variable is presented in the rows and the independent variable in the columns. Tables facilitate comprehending masses of data at a glance; they conserve space and reduce explanations and descriptions to a minimum; they give a visual picture of relationships between variables and categories; they facilitate summation of items and the detection of errors and omissions; and they provide a basis for computations. A good statistical table must contain at least the following components:

(A) Heading
1. Table number
2. Title of the table
3. Designation of units

(B) Body
1. Stub-head - heading of all rows or blocks of stub items
2. Box head - headings of all columns or main captions and their sub captions
3. Field or body - the cells in rows and columns

(C) Notations
1. Footnotes, if necessary
2. Source

These are discussed below in detail.

1. **Table number:** A table should always be numbered for easy identification and reference in future.
2. **Title of the table:** A table must have a suitable title. Title is the description of the contents of the table. So the title should be clear, brief and self-explanatory.
3. **Caption:** Caption refers to the column headings. It explains what the column represents. A caption should be brief, concise and self-explanatory. Captions are usually written in the middle of the columns in small letters to economise space.
4. **Stubs:** These refer to the headings of horizontal rows. They are at the extreme left.
5. **Body:** The body of the table contains the numerical information. This is the most vital part of the table. Data presented in the body arranged according to descriptions are classifications of the captions and stubs.
6. **Head note:** It is a brief explanatory statement applying to all or a major part of the material in the table, and is placed below the title and enclosed in brackets.
7. **Footnote:** Anything in a table that the reader may find difficult to understand from the title, captions and stubs should be explained in footnotes. If footnotes are needed, they are placed directly below the body of the table. In most cases footnotes are used to mention the source of data especially in case of secondary data.

Utility of Tabulation

After the collection of data, the next step is to present them in some suitable form, where statistical table is one of them. Tabulation enables the numerical facts to be presented in such a way that their analysis, interpretation and subsequent computation become easier. Decision makers neither have the opportunity nor have enough time to go through bulky data. They want the information in a precise form so that conclusions can be drawn from them without much wastage of time and energy. Tabulation is thought to be a useful tool in this respect.

- The condensed facts presented in the table can be easily visualised and the needed information can be easily sorted out.
- The comparability of the data increases significantly when they are placed side by side in a table. This also helps the establishment of relationship between different phenomena.
- Tabulation paves the way for further condensation of the data by presenting them in suitable forms for mathematical treatment.
- Statistical tables conserve space and reduce explanatory and descriptive statements to a minimum.

- The visualisation of relations and process of comparison are greatly facilitated by tables.
- Tabulated data can be more easily remembered than data that are not tabulated.
- A tabular arrangement facilitates the summation of items and the detection of errors and omissions and statistical tables provide a basis for computations.

Two-way tables: Distribution in terms of two or more variables and the relationship between two variables are shown in two-way tables. The categories of one variable are presented, one below another, on the left margin of the table, and those of another variable at the upper part of the table, side by side of one another. The cells represent particular combinations of both variables. To compare the distribution of cases raw numbers are converted into percentages based on the number of cases in each category.

Univariate analysis – Tabular representation of data, frequency tables

5.13.2 Univariate, Bivariate and Multivariate Analysis of Data

Univariate, bivariate and multivariate are the various types of data that are based on the number of variables under study.

Univariate Data Analysis

Univariate data is the simplest form of analysis in which data are analysed based on one variable only. Univariate data analysis is applicable when the study concerns only single variable. The basic steps involve, forming the frequency tables. Analysis may be supported by diagrammatic and graphic representation of data, using bar chart or any other graphical representation of data. Other methods include measures of central tendency, dispersion, skewness, kurtosis etc.

Bivariate Data

Bivariate data analysis is used when the data analysis are based on two variables per observation simultaneously. Tools available for bivariate analysis of data are Cross tabulation, correlations, regression, association of attributes, contingency table analysis, use of percentages etc.

Multivariate Data

Multivariate data is the data in which analysis are based on more than two variables per observation. Usually multivariate data is used for explanatory purposes. Methods used re ANOVA, MANOVA etc.

5.13.3 Construction of Frequency Distributions

While preparing the data for analysis, the frequency distribution is formed so as to condense the large amount of data. This frequency distribution is represented through the frequency distribution tables. Frequency distribution is a simple way for Univariate Analysis of data.

Frequency Distribution and Class-intervals

A frequency distribution table is a method to organise data so that it makes more sense. Variables that are classified according to magnitude or size are often arranged in the form of a frequency table. Some frequency tables present the distribution of cases on only a single dimension or variable. For example, distribution of respondents by gender, distribution of respondents by religion, socio-economic status of respondents and the like are shown in one-way tables. Frequency tables may be - discrete frequency distribution or continuous frequency distribution. In constructing a table it is necessary to determine the number of class-intervals to be used and the size of the class-intervals. Ordinarily the number of class-intervals may not be less than 5 and not more than 15, depending on the nature of the data and the number of cases being studied. After noting the highest and lowest values and the features of the data, the number of intervals can be easily determined by dividing the range with class interval decided.

Relative Frequency and Percentage Frequency Table

The frequency distribution may be constructed by using the actual frequency, relative frequency or the percentage frequency. Simple frequency relates to the number of occurrences of the variable. Relative frequency refers to the frequency of the class divided by total frequency and percentage frequency refers to percentage of the proportion of occurrences.

For example, if f is the frequency of any variable X, then,

(Variable X)	(Number of Tyres)	(Relative frequency)	(Percentage frequency)
Life of Tyres	Frequency (f)	= (f/N)	= (f/N) * 100

Where N = total frequency

Univariate data analysis is applicable when the study concerns only single variable. The basic steps involve, forming the frequency tables, using bar chart or any other graphical representation of data.

5.14 Graphical Representation of Data

Diagrammatic and Graphic Representation of Data

After the data has been processed through editing, coding, classification and tabulation, the next step is to analyse it. Graphic representation is the simplest way to show the information of the data. It helps the researcher to view the behaviour of the data at a glance and notice the overall picture. It helps to point out the various properties of the data regarding trends, variation etc. Graphing is a way of visually presenting the data. Graphic presentation involves use of graphs, charts and other pictorial representation. They help to reduce large masses of statistical data to a form that can be quickly understood at a glance whereas meaning of the figures in tabular form may be difficult for the mind to grasp or retain. The purpose of graphing is to present, summarise, describe and explore the data so as to enable comparisons easily.

Graphs are very helpful in,
- Discovering new facts and in developing hypotheses.
- Conveying information to non-technical people or general public.
- Emphasising points more effectively.
- People can grasp the information presented in a graph better than in a text format.

Types

The most commonly used graphic forms are:
- Line graphs or charts
- Bar charts
- Pie Charts (Segmental representations)
- Histograms
- Pictographs
- Leaf and Stem
- Candle Stick
- Box Plots

Line Graph or Chart

The line graph is useful for showing changes in data relationships over a period of time. In this graph the values of the independent variable are plotted on the X axis and the values of the other variable are plotted on the Y axis. The line graph is useful in studying the trend and behaviour of a variable over a period of time or relationship between two variables.

Bar Charts

Bar Charts consist of representation of data through vertical or horizontal bars, wherein the length of the bars is proportional to the values of the variable. Bar charts are very effective for comparing data. Patterns of dots, dashes, shades etc. may be used to depict the bars more attractively. Bar Charts are of different forms:
- One-dimensional,
- Two-dimensional, and
- Three-dimensional, etc.

Also, the actual numerical values pertaining to the variables may be shown on the X-axis or Y-axis, as the case may be, or at the immediate ends of the bars. Bar charts may further be classified as being simple, multiple, subdivided or percentage bar charts.

Simple bar chart is shown below:

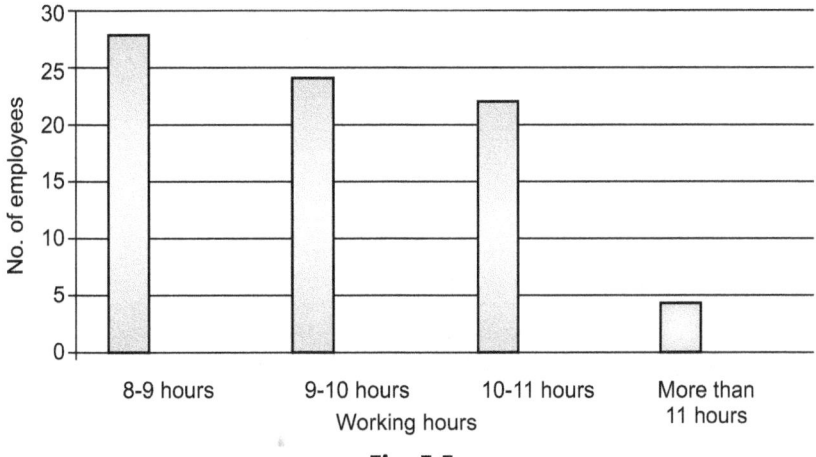

Fig. 5.5

Age groups of children of employees from various sectors

Age group	IT	Service	Education	Manufacturing	Total
0-5 years	3	4	6	4	17
5-10 years	9	10	12	6	37
10-15 years	3	6	8	3	20
15 onwards	1	2	8	0	11
Total	16	22	34	13	85

Subdivided bar chart for the given table is shown below:

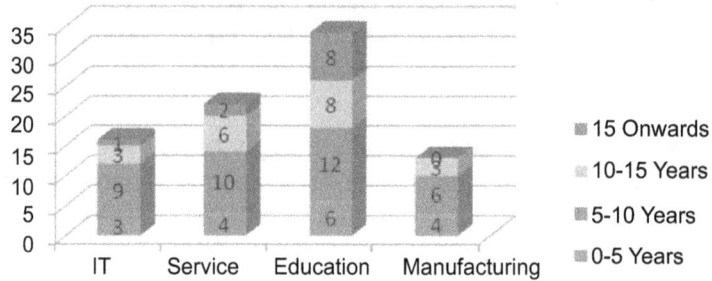

Fig. 5.6

Pie or Circle Charts

The circle or pie chart is a component parts chart. The component parts form the segments of the circle. The circle chart is usually a percentage chart. The data are converted to percentage of the total; and the proportional segments, therefore, give a clear picture of the relationship among the component parts. Pie chart is very useful to depict the composition or components of whole.

Sector	Sample Size
IT	30
Service	50
Education	50
Manufacturing	20
Total	150

Pie chart for the above data is given below:

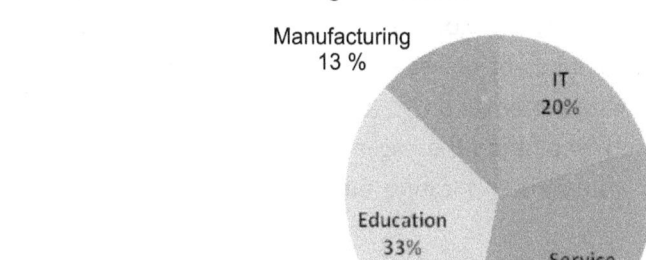

Fig. 5.7

Pictograms / Pictographs

A pictogram is a variation of the bar chart in which the variable values are represented by relevant symbol or pictures. Each symbol represents a fixed size of the variable. The symbols used may be appropriate to the type of data. For example, representing the population through a human being symbol, data related to cars through symbol of cars where each car may represent 10, 100 or more of cars.

Histogram

A Histogram refers to the graph obtained by plotting adjacent rectangles where base of the rectangle is equal to class interval and height proportionate to class frequency. Histogram enables visual impact of representation of classes. Also, it is possible to locate mode graphically on a Histogram. Histogram enables the reader to visualise the volume of the variable instead of just the magnitude.

Frequency Polygons

It is often more convenient to draw a frequency polygon instead of drawing a histogram of a distribution. In laying out a frequency polygon, the frequency of each class is located at the midpoint of the interval and the plotted points are then connected by straight lines. If two or more series are shown on the same graph, the curves can be made with different kinds of ruling. If the total number of cases in the two series is of different size, the frequencies are often reduced to percentages. The frequency polygon is particularly appropriate for portraying continuous series. It is sometimes desirable to portray the data by a smoothed curve. The chart is then called a frequency curve. Frequency polygons are very useful for comparing multiple distributions and their characteristics.

Ogive Curves

Ogive Curve is the graph obtained by plotting class limits on X axis and cumulative frequencies on Y axis. There are 2 types of ogives – 'less than' and 'more than'. Less than Ogive is obtained by plotting the upper limits on 'X' axis and cumulative frequencies on 'Y' axis. More than Ogive is obtained by plotting the lower limits on 'X' axis and De-cumulative frequencies on 'Y' axis. Ogives are useful in locating median and also reading/interpreting data between the lines.

It is useful in representing population, per capita income, per capita earnings etc. Two or more distributions may be compared by converting the data of the distributions to percentages of the total, then cumulating the percentages and plotting the ogives on the same grid. The differences in steepness and shape of the ogives facilitate comparative observations. The point of intersection of two ogives gives the median value. Also, it is possible to find the number of observations, below or above a given value.

Leaf and Stem

Stem and leaf is used to classify variables and organise data as they are collected. Stem-and-leaf refers to a table where each data value is split into a "leaf" (usually the last digit) and a "stem" (the other digits). A stem and leaf plot looks something like a bar graph. Each number in the data is broken down into a stem and a leaf, thus the name. The stem of the number includes all but the last digit. The leaf of the number will always be a single digit. It is advantageous because it overcomes the drawback of loss of data faced due to use of frequency distribution tables or histograms.

Candlestick

Candle sticks are an interesting way of representing data – especially the financial data.

First used in the 1700s by legendary Japanese rice trader named Homma, these techniques later developed into the candlestick techniques used by the technical analysts on the Japanese stock market in the 1870s. Today, these techniques are a part of technical analysis and charting used in the stock market, forex market and all other markets, and can be used in all time frames either for long term investments or for swing trading or day trading! The power of candlesticks (also called Japanese candlestick charts) is that they excel at giving market turning points and when used properly can potentially decrease market risk exposure. Candlestick charts are used by swing traders, day traders, investors and premier financial institutions.

Advantages:
- Easy to understand.
- Provides earlier indications of market turning points i.e. Traditional indicators, which helps to enter and exit the market with better timing.

- Furnish unique market insights.
- Give timing and trading benefits.
- Can be used in all markets such as the stock market, forex market, futures or commodity markets, and can be a powerful trading tool for option trading.

Box Plots

Box Plots are commonly used in the display of statistical analyses. A box plot is a graphical representation of statistical data based on the minimum, first quartile, median, third quartile, and maximum. The term "box plot" comes from the fact that the graph looks like a rectangle with lines extending from the top and bottom. Because of the extending lines, this type of graph is sometimes called a box-and-whisker plot. In a typical box plot, the top of the rectangle indicates the third quartile, a horizontal line near the middle of the rectangle indicates the median, and the bottom of the rectangle indicates the first quartile. A vertical line extends from the top of the rectangle to indicate the maximum value, and another vertical line extends from the bottom of the rectangle to indicate the minimum value. Box plots are useful for identifying outliers and for comparing distributions.

5.14.1 Univariate Analysis - Measures of Central Tendency – Mean, Median and Mode

In addition to the use of graphs for univariate analysis, measures of central tendency are commonly used for analysis. Measures of Central Tendency commonly used are **mean, median and mode.** These are useful in summarising the extent to which the data are clustered around a central value (mean, median or mode).

Arithmetic Mean: The arithmetic mean refers to a unique number that represents the set of data.

Merits of arithmetic mean	Demerits
It is rigidly defined.	Cannot be determined graphically.
Easy to calculate and simple to understand.	Cannot be computed for qualitative data. E.g. Honesty, intelligence etc.
It is unique and useful in comparing sets of data.	It is very much affected by extreme values.
It is based on all the observations.	Cannot be computed for open ended class intervals.
Capable of further algebraic treatment.	
Least affected by fluctuations of sampling.	

Median: The middlemost observation of a series of observations. It divides the series into two equal parts.

Merits of Median	Demerits
Simple to locate.	Not based on all the observations hence, it is not as popular as the mean.
Not affected by extreme values.	Not capable of further algebraic treatment
There is only one median and hence can be used to compare data.	
Can be located graphically.	
Can be estimated for open ended classes.	

Mode: The most frequently occurring observation in the data series.

Merits of Mode	Demerits
Simple and popular measure.	Not necessarily unique. There may be bimodal or multimodal data.
Not affected by extreme values.	It is difficult to interpret and/or compare.
Can be located graphically.	Not capable of further algebraic treatment.

Other Measures

The statistical measures that help to describe the tendency and extent of scattering of observations from the central value are the measures of dispersion. These measures include range, semi-interquartile range, and standard deviation. Skewness and Kurtosis are the measures that describe how data are distributed and spread across the central values.

5.15 Bivariate Analysis

5.15.1 Bivariate Analysis: Cross Tabulations

Cross tabulation is one of the most useful analytical tools. A typical frequency distribution is used to describe one variable at a time, whereas a cross tabulation describes two or more variables simultaneously. It is one of the most basic methods that show how variable X varies with respect to Y. Hence, cross tabulation refers to a two (or more) dimensional table that records the number of respondents with specific characteristics as described in the cells of the table. These tables help to unearth information about relationships between variables. Also known as contingency table analysis, it is most often used to analyse nominal data. This too is most widely used in market research. Related terms used in cross tabulation are "Banners", "stubs", "Chi Square Statistic" and "Expected Values".

Cross tabulation: Use of Percentages

Many a times in the tabular display, relationships are not clearly visible because of wide ranging frequencies or due to large number of categories. At such times, computing and observing the row or column percentages can make the task of interpretation easier.

Each frequency in the cross tabulation table can be expressed as a percentage to facilitate comparisons with other data. Three types of percentages are commonly computed:
- Column Percentages
- Row Percentages
- Total Percentages

Bivariate Correlation Analysis - Meaning and Types of Correlation

Bivariate correlation and regression evaluate the degree of relationship between two or more than two variables without distinguishing between dependent or independent variables. Correlation analysis refers to the study of relationship between two or more than two variables. It is a popular technique for indicating the relationship of one variable to another and a correlation coefficient is a statistical measure of co-variation, or association between two variables.

The correlation may be of different types:
- Positive and negative correlation
- Simple, partial and multiple correlation
- Linear and non-linear correlation.

Positive and negative correlation: When two variables vary in the same directions i.e. increase in one causes increase in the other then we say that they are positively correlated. Whereas, when two variables vary in the opposite directions i.e. increase in one causes decrease in the other, then we say that they are negatively correlated.

Simple, partial and multiple correlation: When the study of correlation involves exactly two variables then it is a study of simple correlation. On the other hand, when the study involves more than two variables, but we are studying only two at a time, then it is known as partial correlation. And when the study involves the simultaneous study of relationship between multiple variables at a time, then it is referred to as multiple correlation analysis.

Linear and non-linear correlation: When correlation relationship is of linear nature then it is called linear relationship otherwise, it is known as non-linear relationship.

5.15.2 Karl Pearson's Coefficient of Correlation and Spearman's Rank Correlation and Scatter Plots

Methods of Studying Correlation
  (a) Scatter Diagram (Scatter Plots)
  (b) Karl Pearson's Coefficient of Correlation
  (c) Spearman's Coefficient of Rank Correlation

(a) **Scatter Diagram (Scatter Plot, Dot Diagram)** : A scatter plot is a graph that enables to visualise the simultaneous changes taking place in two variables. Scatter diagram is the simplest method of studying correlation. These are used to investigate the possible relationships between two variables. In this method graph is plotted for paired values of the two variables. The points so obtained are observed for the scatter and depending on the nature of the scatter of the plotted points, one can say whether there is relationship indicated between the variables or not. A straight line of best fit (regression line) is often included. Correlations indicated may be positive (rising), negative (falling), or null (uncorrelated). If the pattern of dots slopes from lower left to upper right, it suggests a positive correlation between the variables being studied. If the pattern of dots slopes from upper left to lower right, it suggests a negative correlation. A straight line of best fit (using the least squares method) is often included.

Advantages
- Very quick method to identify relationship exists or not.
- Degree and direction of relation can be ascertained.
- Outliers can be observed.
- Suitable for large amount of data to see at a glance.

Disadvantages
- The magnitude of relationship is not indicated.
- Very crude method. Can only indicate the degree and direction, not the magnitude of correlation.

(b) **Karl Pearson's Coefficient of Correlation:** Karl Pearson's correlation coefficient is used when the data are ratio scale. This correlation coefficient is denoted by 'r' and assumes a value between −1 and +1. When r = +1 it means there is perfect positive correlation between the variables and when r = −1, it indicates perfect negative relationship between the variables.

(c) **Spearman's Coefficient of Rank Correlation:** Spearman's coefficient of rank correlation is used when data are qualitative in nature or the ranks for variable series are given.

5.15.3 Chi-square Test

The Chi-Square (χ^2–test)

The chi-square test (denoted as ((χ^2) is an important test amongst the several tests of significance developed by statisticians. Chi-square, symbolically written as χ^2 (Pronounced as Ki-square), is a statistical measure used in the context of sampling analysis for comparing a variance to a theoretical variance. Also, it is one of the most popular non-parametric tests. It is used to make comparisons between two or more nominal variables. It is used to determine if categorical data shows dependency or the two classifications are independent. It is also used to make comparisons between frequencies rather than mean scores. Thus, the Chi-Square test is used to,

(i) test the goodness of fit;
(ii) test the significance of association between two attributes, and
(iii) test the homogeneity or the significance of population variance.

Steps for Applying Chi-square Test

The various steps involved are as follows:

(i) State the null and alternate hypothesis
(ii) Decide the level of significance
(iii) Compute the degrees of freedom = $(r-1) \times (c-1)$
(iv) Where r = no. of rows and c = no. of columns
(v) Find tabulated value of Chi-Square
(vi) Calculate the expected frequencies. Usually in case of a 2×2 or any contingency table, the expected frequency for any given cell is worked out as under:

$$\text{Expected Frequency of any cell} = \left[\frac{\text{(Row total for the row of that cell)} \times \text{(Column total for the column of that cell)}}{\text{(Grand Total)}}\right]$$

(vii) Obtain the difference between observed and expected frequencies and find out the squares of such differences i.e. calculate $(O_{ij} - E_{ij})^2$.
(viii) Divide the quantity $(O_{ij} - E_{ij})^2$ obtained as stated above by the corresponding expected frequency to get $(O_{ij} - E_{ij})^2 / E_{ij}$ and this should be done for all the cell frequencies or the group frequencies.
(ix) Find the summation of $(O_{ij} - E_{ij})^2 / E_{ij}$ values or what we call calculated value of Chi-Square.

$$\frac{(O_{ij} - E_{ij})^2}{E_{ij}} \Sigma \text{ This is the required } \chi^2 \text{ value.}$$

$$\chi^2 = \frac{\Sigma(F_o - F_e)^2}{F_e}$$

where, F_o = Observed Frequency
F_e = Expected frequency

(x) Compare the tabulated and the computed values.
(xi) Reject H_0 if Calculated value > tabulated value, otherwise accept H_0.

For using χ^2 test, data should be nominal, at least 2×2 contingency table should be there, no expected frequency should be less than 5.

The table below shows the differences between Univariate and Bivariate

Univariate Analysis	Bivariate Analysis
Involves study of single variable.	Involves two variables. Analysis of two variables simultaneously.
Does not involve concern with causes or relationships.	Concerned with causes or relationships.
Major purpose is to describe.	Major purpose is to explain.
Measures used are • Central tendency – mean, median, mode • Dispersion – range, variance, maximum, minimum, quartiles, standard deviation • Graphs – Bar graph, histogram, pie chart, line graph, box plot	• Measures • Correlations • Comparison, cause and effect relation-ships • Contingency tables

Exercise

1. An experiment was conducted to test the efficacy of chloromycetin in checking typhoid. In a certain hospital, chloromycetin was given to 285 out of 392 patients suffering from typhoid. The number of typhoid cases were :

	Typhoid	No Typhoid	Total
Chloromycetin	35	250	285
No chloromycetin	50	57	107

   With the help of chi-square, test the effectiveness of chloromycetin in checking typhoid.

2. Test whether the two attributes are independent or not:

Condition of child	Condition of Home		Total
	Clean	Dirty	
Clean	70	50	**120**
Fairly clean	80	20	**100**
Dirty	35	45	**80**
	185	**115**	**300**

3.
	Passed	Failed
Day classes	10	20
Evening classes	4	66

   State whether if any association is there, between passing in an examination and studying in day classes is significant using Chi-square test.

4. An insurance company has introduced a new insurance scheme for employees. Independent random samples of 100 males and 120 females when examined to know their views about the new scheme yielded the following results.

	For	Against	Indifferent
Male	25	40	35
Female	35	55	30

Test the hypothesis at $\chi = 0.01$, that the 2 samples have come from homogenous population.

5. 200 central government employees were classified according to the level of their salaries (high and low) and their reactions (as favourable & unfavourable) to a new formula for determining the dearness pay.

Test to know if any relationship of dependency exists between the level of salaries and the employees' reactions to the new dearness pay formula.

	Low salaried	High salaried
Favourable reaction	60	30
Unfavourable	50	60

5.16 Linear Regression Analysis

Regression Analysis

Regression Analysis is a statistical tool to find relationships between independent and dependent variables. Bivariate regression studies the average relationship between the variables and uses this to further predict the values of the unknown (dependent) variable from values of the known (independent) variable. It is used to measure the degree of relationship between two or more ratio variables. The dependent variable is generally denoted by Y and independent by X.

Regression Lines

Regressions lines are the linear equations which are used to express the linear relationship between the variables. There are two regression lines:
   (i) Regression line Y on X
   (ii) Regression line Y on X

Properties of Regression Lines
   (i) There are two regression lines and hence two regression coefficients viz regression coefficients of y on x denoted by byx and regression coefficient of x on y i.e. bxy.
   (ii) Both regression coefficients have the same sign.
   (iii) Both regression lines intersect at the point (X,Y) (symbol Xbar, Ybar).

(iv) The geometric mean of two regression coefficients is the correlation coefficient with sign of the regression coefficients.

Regression Analysis is applicable to almost all the fields. Regression analysis is very useful for predictive studies. Business Forecasting is an important component of any business for predicting the future trends or performance. Regression analysis measures the strength or correlation between the dependent and independent variables. Governments and businesses use regression analysis as a predictive tool for forecasting purposes.

Relationship between Correlation and Regression co-efficient

Correlation analysis is very helpful in identifying the significant relationships among the variables. From among the various variables that affect a decision variable, correlation helps to identify the most influential ones. Regression analysis uses the underlying correlation between the variables and estimates an average relationship that is further useful for predicting the dependent variable values. Also, the geometric mean of two regression coefficients is the correlation coefficient with sign of the regression coefficients.

5.17 Test of Significance

Parametric and Non-parametric Tests

Parametric Tests: These tests depend on the parameters of the population. In this type of tests, the population from which the samples are drawn are assumed to be normally distributed and the data collected are of interval level. These tests are very powerful in nature.

Non-Parametric Tests: These tests are also known as distribution-free tests as they are not based on the characteristics of the parent population. No assumption of normality is there.

Small Sample Tests: t (Mean, proportion) and F-tests, Z-test, Non-parametric tests:

The Z-Test: This test was given by R.A. Fisher. It is based on the Normal distribution. It is widely used for testing the significance of several statistics such as mean, mode, correlation coefficient and others. The calculated test statistic (i.e. Z_{cal}) is compared with its probable value from normal distribution table at specified level of significance.

Z-TEST Rejection criterion for Z-test

H_1	1%	5%	10%
$\mu \neq \mu_0$	$|Z| \geq 2.58$	$|Z| \geq 1.96$	$|Z| \geq 1.645$
$\mu > \mu_0$	$Z > 2.33$	$Z > 1.645$	$Z > 1.28$
$\mu < \mu_0$	$Z \leq -2.33$	$Z \leq -1.645$	$Z \leq -1.28$

The t-test: This test was given by W. S. Gosset who wrote under the pen-name of *'student'*. It is suitable for testing the significance of a sample mean or for judging the significance of difference between the means of two samples when sample size is less than 30. For related samples, we have the paired t-test. It is also used for testing significance of simple and partial correlation coefficient. The t_{cal} value is compared with the t_{tab}.

The F-test: This test is used to compare variances of two independent samples. It is used in ANOVA for testing the significance of more than two sample means at a time. It is also applicable to judge signs of multiple correlation coefficients.

Analysis of Variance (ANOVA)

Analysis of variance (abbreviated as ANOVA) is an extremely useful technique concerning researches in the fields of economics, biology, education, psychology, sociology, business / industry and in researches of several other disciplines. The ANOVA technique enables us to perform this simultaneous test and as such is considered to be an important tool of analysis in the hands of a researcher. The ANOVA technique is important in the context of all those situations where we want to compare more than two populations such as in comparing the yield of crop from several varieties of seeds, the gasoline mileage of four automobiles, the smoking habits of five groups of university students and so on.

The essence of ANOVA is that the total amount of variation in a set of data is broken down into two types, that amount which can be attributed to chance and that amount which can be attributed to specified causes. There may be variation between samples and also within sample items. ANOVA consists in splitting the variance for analytical purposes.

The Basic Principle of ANOVA

While using ANOVA we assume that each of the samples is drawn from a normal population and that each of these populations has the same variance. We also assume that all factors other than the one or more being tested are effectively controlled. This, in other words, means that we assume the absence of many factors that might affect our conclusions concerning the factors(s) to be studied.

Illustration:

Set up an analysis of variance table for the following per acre production data for three varieties of wheat, each grown on 4 plots and state if the variety differences are significant.

Plot of land	Per acre production data		
	Variety of Wheat		
	A	B	C
1	6	5	5
2	7	5	4
3	3	3	3
4	8	7	4

Solution: First we calculate the mean of each of these samples.

$$\bar{X}_1 = \frac{6+7+3+8}{4} = 6$$

$$\bar{X}_2 = \frac{5+5+3+7}{4} = 5$$

$$\bar{X}_3 = \frac{5+4+3+4}{4} = 4$$

Mean of the sample means

$$\bar{X} = \frac{\bar{X}_1 + \bar{X}_2 + \bar{X}_3}{k}$$

$$= \frac{6+5+4}{3} = 5$$

Now we work out SS between and SS within samples:

$$\bar{X} = \frac{\bar{X}_1 + \bar{X}_2 + \bar{X}_3}{k}$$

$$= \frac{6+5+4}{3} = 5$$

Now we work out SS between and SS within samples:

$$\begin{aligned}
\text{SS between} &= n_1(\bar{X}_1 - \bar{X})^2 + n_2(\bar{X}_2 - X)^2 + n_3(\bar{X}_3 - X)^2 \\
&= 4(6-5)^2 + 4(5-5)^2 + 4(4-5)^2 \\
&= 4 + 0 + 4 \\
&= 8
\end{aligned}$$

$$\begin{aligned}
\text{SS within} &= \Sigma(X_{1i} - \bar{X}_1)^2 + \Sigma(X_{2i} - \bar{X}_1)^2 + \Sigma(X_{3i} - \bar{X}_1)^2, \ i = 1,2,3,4 \\
&= \{(6-6)^2 + (7-6)^2 + (3-6)^2 + (8-6)^2\} \\
&\quad + \{(5-5)^2 + (5-5)^2 + (3-5)^2 + (7-5)^2\} \\
&\quad + \{(5-4)^2 + (4-4)^2 + (3-4)^2 + (4-4)^2\} \\
&= \{0+1+9+4\} + \{0+0+4+4\} + \{1+0+1+0\} \\
&= 14+8+2 \\
&= 24
\end{aligned}$$

$$\begin{aligned}
\text{SS for total variance} &= \Sigma(X_{ij} - \bar{X})^2, \ i = 1,2,3... \\
& \qquad j = 1,2,3... \\
&= (6-5)^2 + (7-5)^2 + (3-5)^2 + (8-5)^2 \\
&\quad + (5-5)^2 + (5-5)^2 + (3-5)^2 \\
&\quad + (7-5)^2 + (5-5)^2 + (4-5)^2 \\
&\quad + (3-5)^2 + (4-5)^2 \\
&= 1+4+4+9+0+0+4+4+0+1+4+1 \\
&= 32
\end{aligned}$$

Alternatively, it (SS for total variance) can also be worked out the SS for total = SS between + SS within

$$= 8 + 24$$
$$= 32$$

We can now set up the ANOVA table for this problem:

Source of variation	SS	d.f.	MS	F-ratio	5% F-limit (from the F-table)
Between sample	8	(3-1) = 2	8/2 = 4.00	4.00 / 2.67 = 1.5	F(2,9) = 4.26
Within sample	24	(12-3) = 9	24/9 = 2.67		
Total	32	(12-1) = 11			

The above table shows that the calculated value of F is 1.5 which is less than the table value of 4.26 at 5% level with d.f. being $v_1 = 2$ and $v_2 = 9$ and hence could have arisen due to chance. This analysis supports the null hypothesis of no difference in sample means. We may, therefore, conclude that the difference in wheat output due to varieties is insignificant and is just a matter of chance.

5.18 Interpretation of Results

Mere analysis does not provide answers to research questions; interpretation is also necessary. Interpretation refers to the task of drawing inferences from the collected facts after an analytical and/or experimental study. It is the device through which the factors that seem to explain what has been observed by the researcher in the course of the study can be better understood.

Interpretation is essential due to the following reasons:
- Continuity in research can be maintained through interpretation by establishing links with similar studies having the same underlying principle.
- Interpretation leads to the establishment of explanatory concepts that can serve as a guide for future research studies.
- Researcher can explain to others the real significance of his research findings.

Precautions in Interpretation

The task of interpretation needs to be undertaken in an impartial manner and in correct perspective because even if the data are properly collected and analysed, wrong interpretations may lead to inaccurate conclusions. Hence the following precautions need to be taken while interpreting results:

- Researcher must assure himself that the data used are appropriate, trustworthy, adequate and homogenous and have been properly analysed.
- Researcher must be cautious about errors which may arise due to false generalisation while interpreting the results. He should be well equipped with the use of statistical measures. Broad generalisations must be avoided.
- Researcher must remember that interpretation is closely linked with the analysis.
- The researcher must remember that there should be constant interaction between theoretical orientation and empirical observation.

Need of Interpretation

The usefulness and utility of research findings depends upon the proper interpretation. It is a basic component of the research process. Interpretation is necessary in the research process due to the following reasons:

1. **Facilitates understanding of own research findings:** Only through interpretation, can the researcher think of what his findings are and why they are and then, he can make the others to understand the real significance of his research findings.
2. **Facilitates understanding of abstract principles behind findings:** Through interpretation, the researcher can well understand the abstract principle behind his own findings and can link his findings with those of other studies having the same abstract principle. Thus, he can predict about the concrete world of events and can maintain the continuity in research.
3. **Forms Hypothesis:** Interpretation is involved in the transition from explanatory to experimental research, because the interpretation of research findings of explanatory research study often results into hypothesis for experimental research.
4. **Guidance for future research:** Interpretation establishes the explanatory concepts that can serve as a guide for future research studies.
5. **Stimulates research:** Interpretation opens new avenues of intellectual adventure and stimulates the quest for more knowledge.

Importance of Interpretation

Interpretation is essential for the simple reason that the usefulness of research findings lies in proper interpretation. It is being considered a basic element of the research process because of the following reasons.

1. It is through interpretation that the researcher can well understand the abstract principles that work behind his findings.
2. It leads to the establishment of explanatory concepts that can serve as a guide for further research.

3. It makes others understand the real significance of his research findings.
4. In case of exploratory study, the interpretation helps to formulate a hypothesis or to develop a research problem.

Essentials of Interpretation of Data
1. **Accurate Data:** For the proper analysis and interpretation the data collected should be accurate.
2. **Sufficient Data:** The basic truth is that unless sufficient data is not available the researcher may never achieve the objectives of proper interpretation, analysis. Biased or unrepresentative results may be obtained if inferences are drawn based on unreliable or insufficient data.

Proper Type of Classification and Tabulation: To attain the objective of accurate interpretation, the investigators are required to base their calculations, estimations and judgments on data represented in a properly classified and tabulated form.

5.19 Research Reports

Once the researcher has collected information on the research problem, he also has to interpret the data and draw specific conclusions from it. The results of the research must be effectively communicated to the management. The work of a researcher does not end with analysis and interpretation. He now has to put down his findings. This is done through a research report. A Research report is a document that describes the research project, its findings, analysis of the findings, interpretations, conclusions and recommendations. The most important consideration in preparing any research report is the nature of the audience. The purpose is to communicate information, and therefore, the report should be prepared specifically for the readers of the report. Sometimes the format for the report will be defined for the researcher (e.g., a dissertation), while other times, the researcher will have complete latitude regarding the structure of the report. At a minimum, the report should contain an abstract, problem statement, methods section, results section, discussion of the results, and a list of references (Anderson, 1966).

Significance of Research Reports

Research reports form an integral part of the research process. Writing of a report is the last step in a research study and requires a set of skills and expertise. A very well conducted research study loses its importance if it is not well documented and presented for others to appreciate the efforts put in. Hence, the research report is considered a major component of the research study.

5.19.1 Structure of Research Report

Basic Ingredients of a Research Report

Five basic ingredients have been pointed out for the research report. These are:
1. A clear topic,
2. A review of literature,
3. A research design,
4. Analysed data, and
5. Conclusions and findings.

1. A Clear Topic

The topic of study should not be vague and unspecified. It should be posed in the form of research question(s), for example, merely writing the topic 'Political Elite' does not indicate anything. It could be 'Role of Political Elite in Social Change' or 'Factions among Political Elite', or 'Corruption among Political Elite', and so on.

2. A Review of Literature

The studies made by other scholars on the relevant topic under study may be referred. This literature could be used either for supporting one's owns findings or criticising their conclusions or developing a hypothesis or a theory and so on.

3. A Research Design

This is to clarify and explain the precise model the researcher worked from. It may describe the methodology used in the study, the conceptual model, the sample taken, the hypotheses prepared, methods by which data was collected, and so on.

4. Analysed Data and Findings

The findings of the study may be given in the report.

Steps in Report Writing

The various steps involved in writing a research report are:
1. Logical analysis of the subject matter
2. Preparation of final outline
3. Preparation of rough draft
4. Rewriting and polishing
5. Preparation of final bibliography
6. Writing the final draft

Layout of a Research Report

In order to convey the contents of the research study effectively, there is need for proper layout of the report. Layout of the research report refers to what the research report should contain and in which order.

The research report should comprise:

1. **Preliminary Pages:** Here, the report must carry a title and date, followed by acknowledgements in the form of Preface or Foreword. This should be followed by Table of contents, list of tables and illustrations so as to make the location of contents easy for the reader.
2. **Main Text:** Here, a complete outline of the research report in provided in detail. It contains:
   - **Introduction:** The researcher must introduce the research study to the readers. Objectives must be stated clearly and purpose of the study also highlighted. A brief summary of earlier relevant research, statement of hypothesis and definitions of major concepts should be stated explicitly. Methodology of conducting the study must be discussed in detail. Research design, sample design, statistical analysis tools and limitations under which the study is conducted must be described.
   - **Statement of findings and recommendations:** Statement of findings and recommendations in non- technical terms is expected here.
   - **The results:** Presentation of findings of the study supported by tables, charts, summarised data etc. should be included here.
   - **Implications drawn:** Inferences drawn, limitations in present study and further scope should be mentioned. Short conclusion summarising the main points of the study and related to the hypothesis should be included here.
   - **Summary:** The research problem, the methodology, major findings and major conclusions should be stated in brief here.
3. **End Matter:** Appendices, Questionnaires, sample information, etc., along with bibliography and index at the end must be included.

Types of Reports

Baker (1988: 421) has pointed out six types of research reports:
1. Dissemination in a book form,
2. Commissioned research reports,
3. Publication in professional journals,
4. Presentation before a professional audience,
5. Research papers for courses, and
6. Papers prepared for mass media.

Another classification says that the results of a research investigation can be presented in a number of ways namely, a technical report, a popular report, an article, a monograph or at times even in the form of oral presentation. The method(s) of presentation to be used in a particular study depends on the circumstances under which the study arose and the nature of the results.

Research reports vary greatly in length and type. In each individual case, both the length and the form are largely dictated by the problems at hand. For instance, business firms prefer reports in the letter form, just one or two pages in length. Banks, insurance organisations and financial institutions are generally fond of the short balance-sheet type of tabulation for their annual reports to their customers and shareholders. Mathematicians prefer to write the results of their investigations in the form of algebraic notations. Chemists report their results in symbols and formulate. Students of literature usually write long reports presenting the critical analysis of some writer or period or the like with a liberal use of quotations from the works of the author under discussion. In the field of education and psychology, the favourite form is the report on the results of experimentation accompanied by the detailed statistical tabulations. Clinical psychologists and social pathologists frequently find it necessary to make use of the case-history form.

Two types of Reports are discussed below:

(A) Technical Report

In the technical report the main emphasis is on (i) the methods employed, (ii) assumptions made in the course of the study, (iii) the detailed presentation of the findings including their limitations and supporting data.

A general outline of a technical report can be as follows:

1. **Summary of results:** A brief review of the main findings just in two or three pages.
2. **Nature of the study:** Description of the general objectives of study, formulation of the problem in operational terms, the working hypothesis, the type of analysis and data required, etc.
3. **Methods employed:** Specific methods used in the study and their limitations. For instance, in sampling studies the researcher should give details of sample design such as, sample size, sample selection, etc.
4. **Data:** Discussion of data collected, their sources, characteristics and limitations. If secondary data are used, their suitability to the problem at hand is fully assessed. In case of a survey, the manner in which data were collected should be fully described.
5. **Analysis of data and presentation of findings:** The analysis of data and presentation of the findings of the study with supporting data in the form of tables and charts be fully narrated. This, in fact, happens to be the main body of the report usually extending over several chapters.
6. **Conclusions:** A detailed summary of the findings and the policy implications drawn from the results to be explained.
7. **Bibliography:** Bibliography of various sources consulted to be prepared and attached.

8. **Technical appendices:** Appendices are given for all technical matters relating to questionnaires, mathematical derivations, elaboration on a particular technique of analysis and the like.

(B) Popular Report

The popular report is one which gives emphasis on simplicity and attractiveness. The simplification should be sought through clear writing, minimisation of technical, particularly mathematical, details and liberal use of charts and diagrams. Attractive layout along with large print, many subheadings, even an occasional cartoon now and then is another characteristic feature of the popular report. Besides, in such a report emphasis is given on practical aspects and policy implications.

A general outline of a popular report may be:

1. **The findings and their implications:** Emphasis in the report is given on the findings of most practical interest and on the implications on these findings.
2. **Recommendations for action:** Recommendations for action on the basis of the findings of the study is made in this section of the report.
3. **Objective of the study:** A general review of how the problems arise is presented along with the specific objectives of the project under study.
4. **Methods employed:** A brief and non-technical description of the methods and techniques used, including a short review of the data on which the study is based, is given in this part of the report.
5. **Results:** This section constitutes the main body of the report wherein the results of the study are presented in clear and non-technical terms with liberal use of all sorts of illustrations such as charts, diagrams and the like.
6. **Technical appendices:** More detailed information on methods used, forms, etc. and so on is presented in the form of appendices. But the appendices are often not detailed if the report is entirely meant for the general public.

Precautions for Writing Research Reports

A research report is a channel of communicating the research findings to the readers of the report. A good research report is one which does this task efficiently and effectively. As such it must be prepared keeping the following precautions in view:

1. The research report should be long enough to cover the subject but short enough to maintain interest. In fact, report-writing should not be a means of learning more and more about less and less.
2. A research report should not be dull; it should be such as to sustain the reader's interest.

3. Abstract terminology and technical jargon should be avoided in a research report. The report should be able to convey the matter as simply as possible. The layout of the report should be well thought out and must be appropriate and in accordance with the objective of the research problem.
4. The reports should be free from grammatical mistakes and must be prepared strictly in accordance with the techniques of composition of report-writing such as the use of quotations, footnotes, documentation, proper punctuation and use of abbreviations in footnotes and the like.
5. The report must present the logical analysis of the subject matter. It must reflect a structure wherein the different pieces of analysis relating to the research problem fit well.
6. A research report should show originally and should necessary be an attempt to solve some intellectual problem. It must contribute to the solution of a problem and must add to the store of knowledge.
7. Towards the end, the report must also state the policy implications relating to the problem under consideration.
8. Appendices should be enlisted in respect of all the technical data in the report.
9. Bibliography of sources consulted is a must for a good report and must necessarily be given.
10. Index is also considered an essential part of a good report and as such must be prepared and appended at the end.
11. Report must be attractive in appearance, neat and clean, whether typed or printed.
12. Objective of the study, the nature of the problem, the methods employed and the analysis techniques adopted must all be clearly stated in the beginning of the report in the form of introduction.

5.19.2 Report Writing and Presentation

Communicating Research Results Orally – PowerPoint Presentation

Sometimes, in addition to or instead of a written report, the researcher will be asked to provide direct, face-to-face reporting on the research. Again, the nature and organisation of these briefings will depend on the audience and their needs. Whatever the circumstance, here are some guidelines for presenting material orally so that it is effective and easily understood.

A report can be presented orally or through the use of some software programme like PowerPoint. The primary goal of an orally presented scientific report is to present a record of research work and to communicate ecological ideas inherent in that work in a short period of time. Usually oral presentations are created using PowerPoint and are around 15 minutes in length, so brevity and directness is essential.

The author should describe the procedures followed; the results obtained, and then place these results in perspective by relating them to existing knowledge and by interpreting their significance for future study.

Presenting Research Findings

The presentation of a research study will generally last up to 2 hours. They are almost always delivered using PowerPoint slides which may be supported by other materials such as sample products, video and audio clips. Audiences vary between one or two people up to 30 or more, though usually there will be around 10 people in attendance who have an interest in the study. As with reports, previous knowledge of the roles and responsibilities of those attending the presentation can help the researcher adapt the presentation to their different needs.

What makes a good presentation is a good presenter. In business research, the slides play a more important role than in other presentations as they are the source of the data.

The presentation is an opportunity for the researcher to emphasise the main points, explain details and generally add confidence to the results through a polished performance. A detailed preparation is the key to a good presentation. The audience want to hear the presenter talk around the slides, expand on the bullet points, pull out the vital data, draw their attention to the important words in a verbatim quote and to make links with previous slides (or even future slides, if appropriate). This makes a lively presentation and leaves the audience with a feeling of added value.

The researcher must think about what type of reporting style sits comfortably within the company? This means that it is vitally important that the researcher who is making the presentation is well versed with the data and knows it inside out. A researcher should thoroughly rehearse the presentation even if this is on their own, in front of the computer, or better still, in front of a known audience.

Tips for a Good Performance

The researcher should:
- Dress for the occasion.
- Use people's names (but making sure they are correct). Address their concerns and questions honestly.
- Control any unwanted body movements and habits, e.g., swaying, pacing, jangling keys etc. Try to avoid the constant repetition of words or phrases. He should not use "close up body language" of crossed arms and hand over mouth.

- Know the data and the presentation structure inside out.
- Memorise the slides and the background to the points on the slides.
- Practice the presentation.
- Sweep the room constantly to make eye contact with everyone in the audience.
- Smile and use encouraging gestures to engage with the audience.
- Speak clearly and use intonation of voice.

Format

One of the most challenging components of writing a PowerPoint presentation is the need to think modularly. Knowing what information goes where is essential.

The researcher can use the following structure for reports:

1. Title slide with author(s) name(s).
2. Introduction slides (3-4).
3. Materials and Methods slides (1-3).
4. Results slides (3-6).
5. Discussion and Conclusions including Error Analysis and Future Studies Slides (3-6).
6. Reference Slide (if any : only include if a specific paper or book is cited in the presentation).

The researcher should not overload each slide with too much information. It should be written in bulleted format. The researcher must include no more than 3 or 4 bullets on a single slide and try to make all the points on a single slide relevant to a single specific point.

As a researcher, you should do the following:

Introduction
- In this section state the nature of the problem, the aims and objectives of the study, and brief background information. The researcher should provide the context for the study he will be presenting - is what he is doing relevant to other work? How does it relate to this other work?
- The justification and relevance of the study should be included.
- Try to answer the following questions: why do the study? What is the existing state of knowledge of this topic? (Restrict background information to that which is pertinent to the research problem). What are the specific objectives?
- Clearly state the question that you sought to answer.

Materials and Methods
- State the hypotheses you tested.
- Include a description of the procedure you used that would enable a reader to duplicate the study to ensure repeatability.

- This will include data collection techniques, the equipment used, the experimental design, characterisation of the location of the study, and the methods used to record, summarise, and analyse data.
- Minimise descriptions of well known procedures and use references where appropriate.
- Use figures to explain experimental set-up where appropriate.

Results
- Start your results section with a text slide summarising what it is that you found - in subsequent slides, you will present graphs with the data to back up the points that you make on this slide.
- Summarise the data generated with tables, figures and descriptive text.
- Do not include raw data.
- Describe your data and the patterns, trends, and relationships observed.
- Proceed from most general features of the data to more specific results.
- Use graphics to display data in preference to tables whenever feasible.
- Use clear, concise, descriptive titles and explanatory legends for tables and figures.
- Ensure all axes of graphs are labelled and that units are identified in all tables and figures.
- The results section should be free of interpretation of data.

Discussion and Conclusions
- This section should include an interpretation and evaluation of the results.
- Compare with other studies and draw conclusions based on your findings - refer back to the review material you presented in your introduction in this section as well.
- Refer back to the original hypotheses you were testing.
- Draw positive conclusions wherever possible.
- Identify sources of error and any inadequacies of your techniques.
- Speculate on the broader meanings of the conclusions drawn.
- Address any future study that your research suggests.

References
- List all the references cited in the text and only the references cited in the text - if any references are not cited, then reference slide is not needed.
- Cite references in text by author(s) and date.
- If there are three or more authors of a reference abbreviate by the first author's surname followed by "et al." (e.g. "Smith et al. (1995) state that...").

- All references should be listed in full, alphabetically by first author in the Reference Cited section.
- Be consistent with format.
- Only the references pertinent to study and data should be used.

General Comments
- Use and evaluate all the data you report and do not be discouraged if your results differ from published studies or from what you expected - YOUR DATA DO NOT LIE, they may be inaccurate because of experimental design problems, but they do not lie.
- Justify all tables and figures by discussing their content and labelling them clearly.
- Be creative in your presentation of data, your analysis, and your interpretation of data - play around with different variations before completing your report.
- Do not force conclusions from your data or fudge data by omitting that which does not support pre-conceived conclusions.
- Make sure all calculations and analyses are relevant to the hypotheses you are testing and the overall objectives of the study.
- Justify your ideas and conclusions with data, facts, and background literature and with sound reasoning.
- Keep the different sections of the report discrete, i.e., methods in the methods section, results in the results section, and leave discussion and interpretation of those results for the discussion section.
- Plan your writing, organise your thoughts and data, and sketch the report before actually writing. This will help to maximise your time efficiency and lead to a concise, well structured report.

The Researcher thus needs to:
- Choose a single background for the entire presentation that is not too busy and distracting but visually engaging.
- PowerPoint is a fun programme with many bells and whistles (animations, backgrounds, ability to layer text and images, etc.).
- Be creative, but should not include so many of these that it distracts the audience from the content.
- Use large enough font so that the projected presentation could be easily visible in the back of a large room. Usually this requires something greater than 32 point font. Also, don't use a font that is too ornate and therefore distracting. Simplicity in presentation, while still being visually engaging is the key.

- Be certain that one logically leads into the next.
- Do not include slides that are self-contained, disconnected bits of information and images.
- Avoid footnotes.
- Write in the past tense.
- Use a heading for each slide.
- Underscore Latin genus and species names. The researcher should be certain to put the Genus name in upper case and the species name in lower case. For example, Homo sapiens.
- Avoid long, complex statements - breaking these down into several subcomponents, each with a separate bulleted entry.
- Check for excessive use of commas and conjunctions ("and", "but", "or") - he can often split these points into several.
- Avoid excessive use of nouns as adjectives.
- Use positive statements and avoid non-committal statements (For example, use "the data indicate..." rather than "the data could possibly suggest...").
- Avoid non-informative abbreviations such as "etc.", or "and so on".
- Reduce jargon to a minimum.
- Avoid repeating facts and thoughts.
- Be concise and succinct - don't pad out your report with irrelevant data or discussion or images.
- Above all, produce accurate, clear, and concise writing.

5.20 Use of Computers in Research

The word computer means "something which computes or a machine for performing calculations automatically".

Computers have now become an indispensable part of every profession and so is the case in research. A computer has three basic components. They are:
1. An input device (keyboard and mouse)
2. A Central Processing Unit (CPU) and
3. An output device (monitor and/or printer)

Important Characteristics of a Computer

1. **Speed:** Computers can perform calculations in just a few seconds that a human being would need weeks to do.
2. **Storage:** A lot of data can be stored in the computer and retrieved when needed. Whereas a human mind can remember limited information and unimportant data can be forgotten sometimes.

3. **Accuracy:** The computer's accuracy is consistently high. Almost without exception, the errors in computing are due to human rather than to technological weakness. i.e., due to imprecise thinking by the programmer or due to inaccurate data or due to poorly designed systems.
4. **Automation:** The computer programmes are automatic in nature. Individual instructions to perform which programme is needed sometimes.
5. **Diligence:** Being a machine, a computer does not suffer from human traits of tiredness and lack of concentration. A computer can perform a number of calculations continuously with the same accuracy and speed.

Computers in Research

Computers are indispensable throughout the research process. The role of computers becomes more important when the research is on a large sample. Data can be stored in computers for immediate use or can be stored in auxiliary memories like floppy discs, compact discs, universal serial buses (pen drives) or memory cards, so that the same can be retrieved later. Computers assist the researcher throughout different phases of the research process.

Phases of Research Process

There are five major phases of the research process. They are:
1. Conceptual phase
2. Design and planning phase
3. Empirical phase
4. Analytic phase
5. Dissemination phase

1. Role of Computers in Conceptual Phase: The conceptual phase consists of formulation of the research problem, review of literature, theoretical frame work and formulation of hypothesis.

Role of Computers in Literature Review: Computers help for searching the literatures (for review of literature) and bibliographic references stored in the electronic databases of the world wide web. It can thus be used for storing relevant published articles to be retrieved whenever needed. This has the advantage over searching the literatures in the form of books, journals and other newsletters at the libraries which consume considerable amount of time and effort.

2. Role of Computers in Design and Planning Phase: Design and planning phase consists of research design, population, research variables, sampling plan, reviewing research plan and pilot study.

Role of Computers for Sample Size Calculation: Several softwares are available to calculate the sample size required for a proposed study. NCSS PASS GESS is such software. The standard deviation of the data from the pilot study is required for the sample size calculation.

3. **Role of Computers in Empirical Phase:** Empirical phase consist of collecting and preparing the data for analysis.

Data Storage: The data obtained from the subjects are stored in computers as word files or excel spread sheets. This has the advantage of making necessary corrections or editing the whole layout of the tables if needed, which is impossible or time consuming in case of writing. Thus, computers help in data entry, data editing, data management including follow up actions etc. Computers also allow for greater flexibility in recording the data while they are collected as well as greater ease during the analysis of these data.

In research studies, the preparation and inputting of data is the most labour intensive and time consuming aspect of the work. Typically, the data will be initially recorded on a questionnaire or record form suitable for its acceptance by the computer. To do this the researcher in conjunction with the statistician and the programmer, will convert the data into Microsoft Word file or Excel Spreadsheet. These spreadsheets can be directly opened with statistical software for analysis.

4. **Role of Computers in Data Analysis:** This phase consists of statistical analysis of the data and interpretation of results.

Data Analysis: Many software are now available to perform the 'mathematical part' of the research process i.e. the calculations using various statistical methods. Softwares like SPSS, NCSS-PASS, STATA and Sysat are some of the widely used softwares in data analysis. They can be like calculating the sample size for a proposed study, hypothesis testing and calculating the power of the study. Familiarity with any one package will suffice to carry out the most intricate statistical analyses. Computers are useful not only for statistical analyses, but also to monitor the accuracy and completeness of the data as they are collected.

5. **Role of Computers in Research Dissemination:** This phase is the publication of the research study.

Research Publishing: The research article is typed in word format and converted to Portable Data Format (PDF) and stored and/or published on the World Wide Web.

The above description indicates clearly the usefulness of computers throughout the research process. Researchers using computers make their work faster with more accuracy and greater reliability. The developments taking place in technology will further enhance and facilitate the use of computers for researchers.

In spite of all these sophistications it is wise to remember that a computer is just a tool and a resource. It can only calculate or obey commands and cannot think. If the methods of handling the data are to be applied efficiently, adequate planning and suitable organisation is necessary. No facility can replace this aspect of planning. Further, it would be disastrous to replace the statistician by a computer, no matter how powerful, since statistical analyses are built on sound principles of design, implementation and handling of exigencies in data collection, all of which require the expertise of a qualified statistician. The human brain remains supreme and will continue to be so forever.

To conclude, computers are useful tools that make the research process easier and faster with accuracy and greater reliability and fewer errors. The programmer or the computer operator should have a thorough knowledge about the abilities and limitations of the software used for better use of computers.

Computers and Researchers

Performing calculations almost at the speed of light, the computer has become one of the most useful research tools in modern times. Computers are ideally suited for data analysis concerning large research projects. Researchers are essentially concerned with huge storage of data, their faster retrieval when required and processing of data with the aid of various techniques. In all these operations, computers are of great help. Their use, apart expediting the research work, has reduced human drudgery and added to the quality of research activity.

Researchers in economics and other social sciences have found, by now, computers to constitute an indispensable part of their research equipment. Computers can perform many statistical calculations easily and quickly.

Techniques involving trial and error process are quite frequently employed in research methodology. This involves lot of calculations and work of repetitive nature. Computers are best suited for such techniques, thus reducing the drudgery of researchers on the one hand producing the final result rapidly on the other. Thus, different scenarios are made available to researchers by computers.

Therefore, computers do facilitate the research work. Innumerable data can be processed and analysed with greater ease and speed. Moreover, the results obtained are generally correct and reliable. Not only this, even the design, pictorial graphing and report are being developed with the help of computers. Hence, researchers should be given computer education and be trained in the line so that they can use computers for their research work.

Internet Research

Internet research is the practice of using the Internet, especially the World Wide Web (www), for research. To the extent that the Internet is widely and readily accessible to hundreds of millions of people in many parts of the world, it can provide practically instant information on most topics, and is having a profound impact on the way in which ideas are formed and knowledge is created.

Research Information on the Internet
- Company reports and financial information
- Conference proceedings
- Contact details for other researchers
- Laws, government announcements and parliamentary debates
- News and current affairs
- Databases of reference material
- Places where one can discuss topics and ask for help.

However, in general, academic research that has been commercially published is not freely available on the internet.

Search Options

Search Engines: Enable you to search using keywords that describe the subject you are researching. Examples : AltaVista, Google, Excite.

Metasearch Engines: Enable you to search across many search engines at once. Examples : Dogpile, Search.com, Metacrawler.

Subject Gateways: Organised lists of web pages, divided into subject areas. Also known as Directories. Some gateways are general and cover material on as many subjects as possible. Examples : Yahoo, LookSmart. Others are specifically designed to cover a particular subject area in depth, or are specialised in providing academic information.

5.21 Importance of MS Excel and SPSS for Research Data Analysis

Once the data has been collected through questionnaires, MS Excel can be used for further preparation and analysis of data. SPSS is also a very efficient tool for the same, but it may not be easily available as MS Excel. Though, if available, it can be used very efficiently.

- The coding sheet for condensing the data can be easily made using MS-EXCEL or SPSS. The flexibility in adding the columns and rows makes it very easy to enter the data for all the respondents.
- Once data has been entered, frequency distribution can be prepared, queries can be formed, data sort techniques can be applied to classify and group the observations, and form suitable tables.
- Using functions available in MS-Excel/SPSS, Maximum, Minimum, Sum, Totals, Sub-totals, Standard Deviation, Averages, Correlation, Regression etc can be calculated. Data can be described more effectively through descriptive statistics.
- Data validation facility is also available along with facility to remove duplicate entries.
- What-if analysis can be carried out to view the situational results.
- Comparison can be down between the groups of observations.

- Arranging in ascending and descending order is also possible for sorting.
- Once data is ordered, and frequency tables prepared then charts and diagrams can be effectively drawn using the Insert - Charts tool. All the options are self explanatory and one needs to practice charts for effective presentation of data.
- For analysis purpose, add-ins are also available that can be additional accessed for use for drawing histograms, frequency polygons etc.
- Functions for statistical, mathematical, engineering, financial applications are available
- Testing of hypotheses can be carried out without having to make the complex calculations.
- Multiple worksheets make it possible to maintain large database efficiently.

Hence knowledge of MS Excel makes it very easy for the researcher to carry out complex data processing, analysis and presentation without hassles.

Points to Remember

- Data collection is a very important activity in the task of any research and the quality of data collected affects the results. Each research project uses a data collection technique appropriate to the particular research design.
- Quantitative data collection methods rely on random sampling and structured data collection instruments that fit diverse experiences into predetermined response categories. Qualitative data collection methods play an important role in impact evaluation by providing information useful to understand the processes behind observed results and assess changes in people's perceptions of their well-being.
- Secondary data is the data that have been already collected by and readily available from other sources. Such data are cheaper and more quickly obtainable than the primary data and also may be available when primary data cannot be obtained at all. Primary data are those which are collected for the first time by the researcher himself, and thus happen to be original in character.
- In observation method the data is collected by the researcher by observing or watching the units/respondents under study.
- Questionnaire is a data collection tool in which written questions are presented that are to be answered by the respondents in written form. This method of data collection is quite popular, particularly in case of big enquiries. This method is particularly useful to reach out to a large number of respondents in a short time.
- An interview is a data-collection technique that involves orally questioning respondents, either individually or as a group. It is primarily used to gain an understanding of the underlying reasons and motivations for people's attitudes, preferences or behaviour.

- When information required is very short and structured, with large number of respondents then telephonic interview may be used. Telephonic interview is an alternative form of interview to the personal, face-to-face interview and most useful in case of structured and minimal information required from respondents.
- Online surveys are a great option for companies to conduct their own research as online survey tools make it possible for these business owners to perform market research at a fraction of the usual cost. Surveys conducted over the email or internet are becoming more and more popular these days.
- In schedules through enumerators a schedule i.e. questionnaire containing questions is prepared and filled in by the investigator/researcher himself or by enumerators (persons appointed by the researcher) to contact each and every respondent and fill up by schedule.
- Sampling is the process of selecting a representative part of a population, studying it and thereby drawing conclusions about the population itself. Sampling is a very important aspect of research and due care has to be taken to arrive at the right sample to be studied.
- Sampling involves selecting a relatively small number of elements from a larger defined group of elements and expecting that the information gathered from the small group will allow judgements to be made about the larger group.
- Surveys are concerned with examining the nature of and relationships among demographic characteristics, social conditions and activities, opinions and attitudes of a group of people etc.
- Census refers to the complete enumeration of all the units in the population. Since each and every unit of the population is considered here, more accuracy is presumed in such survey data collected.
- Sampling may be defined as the process of selecting units (people, organisations etc.) from a population of interest so that by examining the sample units, results may be generalised about the population.
- Key terms in sampling are population, sample, need for sampling, sampling frame, sampling design. Factors determining size of sample are parameters of interest, budgetary constraints, sampling procedure, representative sample.
- Sampling frame or sample frame, survey frame is the actual set of units from which a sample would be drawn. It helps the researcher in identifying and locating the population elements and other related information necessary for clustering and stratifying. Hence, a sampling frame is a complete list of all the members of the population that we wish to study.

- Sampling error arises from the fact that samples differ from their populations as they are small sub-sets of the total population. Sampling error refers to differences between the sample and the population that exist only because of the observations that happened to be selected for the sample.
- Non-sampling errors are much serious and occur due to mistakes made while collecting the data or sample observations incorrectly. Non-sampling errors refer to the deviations from the true values which are not a function of the sample chosen.
- Probability sampling also known as random sampling or chance sampling is one in which every unit in the population has a non-zero chance of being selected in the sample, and this probability can be accurately determined.
- Non-probability sampling simply means sampling without using random selection methods. In this type of sampling, items for the sample are selected deliberately by the researcher and his choice concerning the items remains absolute.
- Probability sampling methods are Simple Random Sampling, Systematic Sampling, Stratified Sampling and Area and Cluster or Multistage Sampling.
- Random sampling is the simplest and purest form of probability sampling. It is a technique in which every unit in population has equal and known chance of being included in sample. A simple random sample is free from sampling bias.
- In stratified sampling heterogeneous population is divided into distinct, non-overlapping homogenous subgroups called strata; according to some important characteristics or variable like income, education, age, etc., and then a random sample is selected from within each subgroup.
- Systematic sampling is often used instead of random sampling. Systematic sampling is frequently used to select a specified number of records from a computer file. It is also called an nth name selection technique. A systematic random sample is obtained by selecting one unit on a random basis and choosing additional elementary units at evenly spaced intervals until the desired number of units is obtained.
- In cluster sampling the population is divided into heterogeneous groups called clusters. A cluster is then randomly selected from population and further sampling or complete enumeration of clusters done. This method divides the population into clusters at each stage and draws sample of required size at each stage. Sampling is done in multistage.
- Due to practical considerations, one often uses non-probability sampling even though it is technically inferior to probability sampling. It is useful when researchers do not need to generalise the results. Since cost and time-saving are high in non-probability sampling, it is a valuable tool in certain cases. This method is also useful when the entire population is not available for the study.

- Convenience sampling (or accidental sampling) is a method in which samples are drawn at the convenience of the researcher or interviewer. In judgement sampling or purposive sampling, participants are selected according to an experienced individual belief that they will meet the requirements of the study. Judgemental sampling is associated with a variety of biases.
- Purposive sampling is also known as judgemental, selective or subjective sampling. Selection of the sample is largely dependent on the judgement of the researcher (e.g., people, cases/organisations, events, pieces of data) that are to be studied.
- The quota sampling method involves the selection of prospective participants according to pre-specified quota regarding either demographic characteristics (e.g., age, race, gender, income), specific attitudes (e.g., satisfied/dissatisfied, liking/disliking, great/marginal/no quality), or specific behaviours (e.g., regular/occasional/ rare customer, product user/non user).
- Snowball Sampling involves the practice of identifying and qualifying a set of initial prospective respondents who can, in turn, help the researcher identify additional people to be included in the study. This method of sampling is also called referral sampling, because one respondent refers other potential respondents.
- The procedures used to select a sample require some prior knowledge of the target population, which allows a determination of the size of the sample needed to achieve a reasonable estimate (with accepted precision and accuracy) of the characteristics of the population.
- **Editing:** Is the process of examining the data collected through various methods to detect errors and omissions and correct them for further analysis.
- **Coding:** Coding refers to the process by which data are categorized into groups and numerals or other symbols or both are assigned to each item depending on the class it falls in.
- **Classification:** The process of dividing the data into different groups (viz. classes) which are homogeneous within but heterogeneous between them is called a classification.
- **Simple frequency** relates to the number of occurrences of the variable.
- **Relative frequency** refers to the frequency of the class divided by total frequency and percentage frequency refers to percentage of the proportion of occurrences.
- **Univariate** data analysis is applicable when the study concerns only single variable.
- **Data Analysis** consists of the following steps: 1. Editing 2. Coding 3. Classification 4. Tabulation
- **Types of Editing:** 1. Field editing, 2. In-house editing

- **Types of Classification:** 1. Qualitative Classification, 2. Simple Classification, 3. Manifold or Multiple Classifications, 4. Class intervals or variables classification
- **Tables:** A good statistical table must contain at least the following components: 1. Table Number, 2. Title of the table, 3. Caption, 4. Stubs, 5. Body, 6. Head note, 7. Foot note.
- **Graphing** is a way of visually presenting the data.
  The most commonly used graphic forms are: 1. Line graphs or charts, 2. Bar charts, 3. Pie Charts (Segmental representations), 4. Histogram, 5. Pictographs, 6. Leaf and Stem, 7. Candle Stick, 8. Box Plots.
- **Measures of Central Tendency** commonly used are mean, median and mode.
- **Arithmetic Mean:** The arithmetic mean refers to a unique number that represents the set of data.
- **Median:** The middlemost observation of a series of observations. It divides the series into two equal parts.
- **Mode:** The most frequently occurring observation in the data series.
- **Cross tabulation** is one of the most useful analytical tools. A typical frequency distribution is used to describe one variable at a time, whereas a cross tabulation describes two or more variables simultaneously.
  Each frequency in the cross tabulation table can be expressed as a percentage to facilitate comparisons with other data. Three types of percentages are commonly computed:
  (a) Column Percentages, (b) Row Percentages, (c) Total Percentages.
- **Correlation analysis** refers to the study of relationship between two or more than two variables.
  The correlation may be of different types: (a) Positive and negative correlation, (b) Simple, partial and multiple correlations, (c) Linear and non-linear correlation.
  The following are methods of studying correlation: (a) Scatter Diagram (Scatter Plots), (b) Karl Pearson's Coefficient of Correlation, (c) Spearman's Coefficient of Rank Correlation
- The chi-square test (denoted as ((χ^2) is an important test amongst the several tests of significance developed by statisticians. Chi-square, symbolically written as χ^2 (Pronounced as Ki-square), is a statistical measures used in the context of sampling analysis for comparing a variance to a theoretical variance. Chi-Square test is used to: (i) test the goodness of fit, (ii) test the significance of association between two attributes, and (iii) Test the homogeneity or the significance of population variance.

- **The formula to find the value of Chi-Square:**

  $\dfrac{(O_{ij} - E_{ij})^2}{E_{ij}} \Sigma$ This is the required χ^2 value.

  $$\chi^2 = \dfrac{\Sigma(F_o - F_e)^2}{F_e}$$

  where, F_o = Observed Frequency

  F_e = Expected frequency

- **Linear Regression Analysis** is a statistical tool to find relationships between independent and dependent variables.
- Regressions lines are the linear equations which are used to express the linear relationship between the variables. There are two regression lines:
  (i) Regression line Y on X
  (ii) Regression line Y on X
- **Parametric Tests:** These tests depend on the parameters of the population.
- **Non Parametric Tests:** These tests are also known as distribution-free tests as they are not based on the characteristics of the parent population.

  The three non parametric tests are Z-Test, t-test, F-test).
- **Analysis of variance** (abbreviated as ANOVA) is an extremely useful technique concerning researches in the fields of economics, biology, education, psychology, sociology, business / industry and in researches of several other disciplines. The ANOVA technique enables us to perform this simultaneous test and as such is considered to be an important tool of analysis in the hands of a researcher.
- **Interpretation** is essential due to the following reasons: (a) Continuity in research can be maintained through interpretation by establishing links with similar studies having the same underlying principle. (b) Interpretation leads to the establishment of explanatory concepts that can serve as a guide for future research studies. (c) Researcher can explain to others the real significance of his research findings.
- **Essentials of Interpretation of Data:** 1. Accurate data, 2. Sufficient data.
- A **Research report** is a document that describes the research project, its findings, analysis of the findings, interpretations, conclusions and recommendations.
- Five basic ingredients have been pointed out for the research report. These are:
  1. A clear topic,
  2. A review of literature,
  3. A research design,
  4. Analysed data, and
  5. Conclusions and findings.

- **Steps in Report Writing**
  The various steps involved in writing a research report are:
  1. Logical analysis of the subject matter.
  2. Preparation of final outline.
  3. Preparation of rough draft.
  4. Rewriting and polishing.
  5. Preparation of final bibliography.
  6. Writing the final draft.

  The research report should comprise:
  1. Preliminary Pages.
  2. Main Text.
  3. End Matter.
- **Types of Reports:** 1. Dissemination in a book form, 2. Commissioned research reports, 3. Publication in professional journals, 4. Presentation before a professional audience, 5. Research papers for courses, and 6. Papers prepared for mass media.
- Computers are indispensable throughout the research process. The role of computers becomes more important when the research is on a large sample. Data can be stored in computers for immediate use or can be stored in auxiliary memories like floppy discs, compact discs, universal serial buses (pen drives) or memory cards, so that the same can be retrieved later. Computers assist the researcher throughout different phases of the research process.
- Once the data has been collected through questionnaires, MS Excel can be used for further preparation and analysis of data. SPSS is also a very efficient tool for the same, but it may not be easily available as MS Excel. Though, if available, it can be used very efficiently.
- Knowledge of MS Excel makes it very easy for the researcher to carry out complex data processing, analysis and presentation without hassles.

Questions for Discussion

1. State the considerations for the preferences of the primary sources of data in comparison to secondary data.
2. Discuss briefly the methods of collecting primary data.
3. "Success of an interview depends on its success". Discuss.
4. Distinguish between primary and secondary data. Discuss the various methods of collecting primary data. Indicate the situation in which each of these methods may be used.
5. What safety measures should be taken while using data from a secondary source?
6. What are the advantages of using primary source of data over secondary sources?
7. Explain what precautions must be taken while drafting a questionnaire in order that it may be really useful?

8. Describe the various methods of collecting data indicating their merits and demerits.
9. *"Interviews introduce more bias than does the use of Questionnaire."* Discuss.
10. Define Sampling. State the advantages of sampling to a researcher.
11. Distinguish giving illustrations census survey and sample survey.
12. Discuss the advantages of sampling survey over census survey.
13. Discuss the need for sampling in research. What are the factors to be considered in determination of sample size?
14. What is a sampling frame? How is it determined?
15. What is non-probability sampling? How is it important in research?
16. Distinguish between Stratified Sampling and Cluster Sampling.
17. Discuss Judgement Sampling and its importance.
18. What are the factors that determine the size of the sample in research?
19. Discuss sampling and non-sampling errors. How can they be controlled?
20. Explain briefly the various steps involved in processing of data.
21. Discuss the various techniques for statistical analysis of data.
22. Discuss the ways in which percentages may be computed in a cross-tabulation table.
23. In a contingency table, what type of hypothesis is tested using chi-square test? What precautions may be taken while applying the test?
24. Why is tabulation considered essential in a research study? Give the characteristics of a good table?
25. Explain in brief the different forms of data presentation methods?
26. Discuss the meaning and need for interpretation of data.
27. What are the techniques for interpretation of data?
28. What precautions should be taken while interpreting data?
29. What is the significance of a research report?
30. What steps should be followed while drafting a research report?
31. Discuss the format of a research report.
32. What are the various types of research reports?
33. What precautions should be taken while writing a research report?
34. Discuss the role of computers in research.

Business Research Methods, Allan Bryman, Emma Bell, Oxford, 3e.
Business Research Methods, Donal Cooper, P. Schindler, Tata McGraw Hill
Research Methodology, C. R. Kothari. Vishwa Prakashan, 2002
Research Methodology in Management, P.P. Arya & Yesh Pal, Deep & Deep Publication, 2004

Multiple Choice Questions

1. A qualitative research question:
   (a) Asks a question about some process, or phenomenon to be explored
   (b) Is generally an open-ended question
   (c) Both a and b are correct
   (d) None of the above

2. Sources of researchable problems may include:
   (a) Researchers' own experiences as educators
   (b) Practical issues that require solutions
   (c) Theory and past research
   (d) All of the above

3. A review of the literature prior to formulating research questions allows the researcher to do which of the following?
   (a) To become familiar with prior research on the phenomenon of interest
   (b) To identify potential methodological problems in the research area
   (c) To develop a list of pertinent problems relative to the phenomenon of interest
   (d) All of the above

4. Which of the following ideas cannot be empirically researched?
   (a) Effectiveness of different methods of instruction
   (b) Description of educational practices
   (c) Issues of values and morality such as the correctness of having prayer in schools
   (d) Factors helpful in predicting future drug use

5. The feasibility of a research study should be considered in light of:
   (a) Cost and time required to conduct the study
   (b) Skills required of the researcher
   (c) Potential ethical concerns
   (d) All of the above

6. The research participants are described in detail in .... section of the research plan.
   (a) Introduction   (b) Method
   (c) Data analysis   (d) Discussion

7. Research hypotheses are _____.
   (a) Formulated prior to a review of the literature
   (b) Statements of predicted relationships between variables
   (c) Stated such that they can be confirmed or refuted
   (d) Both (b) and (c)

8. The Method section of the research plan typically specifies:
   (a) The research participants
   (b) The apparatus, instruments, and materials for the research study
   (c) The planned research procedures
   (d) All of the above
9. In order to begin research, one must:
   (a) start with a number of clear goals.
   (b) start with a number of predefined objectives.
   (c) have a well defined research method.
   (d) solve the research problem.
10. Conducting research requires drafting a working outline, which is:
    (a) having a predefined and clear-cut objective(s).
    (b) planning to get answers for what, why and where type of questions.
    (c) having a clear idea about the research problem solution.
    (d) none of the above.
11. Formulative research studies is a category of research that aims to:
    (A) achieve new insights of a concept.
    (B) analyse characteristics of something.
    (C) determine the frequency with which something occurs.
    (D) test the relationship between variables.
12. Descriptive research studies is a category of research that aims to:
    (a) achieve new insights of a concept.
    (b) analyze characteristics of something.
    (c) determine the frequency with which something occurs.
    (d) test the relationship between variables.
13. In order to make the research reliable, it requires that:
    (a) there is no deliberate attempt to either to conceal or highlight something.
    (b) quantitative and qualitative methods are to be used.
    (c) repeatability and accuracy are provided for the quality of measurement procedures used.
    (d) the solution to the research problem is known in advance.
14. Descriptive research is the type of research that:
    (a) is made for performing the basic or pure research; it's a theoretical research.
    (b) is intended for finding some solution to the problem considered.
    (c) includes fact-finding, enquires and surveys.
    (d) uses available information as the base to make the further critical evaluation.

15. Good research means the following except:
    (a) Purpose clearly defined
    (b) Research process detailed
    (c) Research design thoroughly planned
    (d) Findings presented ambiguously
16. Every research proposal, regardless of length should include two basic sections as:
    (a) Research question and research methodology
    (b) Research proposal and bibliography
    (c) Research method and schedule
    (d) Research question and bibliography
17. The purpose of _____ research is to help in the process of developing a clear and precise statement of the research problem rather than in providing a definitive answer.
    (a) Marketing
    (b) Causal
    (c) Exploratory
    (d) Descriptive
18. A researcher divides the populations into PG, graduates and 10 + 2 students and using the random digit table he selects some of them from each. This is technically called:
    (a) Simple random sampling
    (b) Stratified random sampling
    (c) Cluster sampling
    (d) none of these
19. A researcher divides his population into certain groups and fixes the size of the sample from each group. It is called:
    (a) cluster sample
    (b) Stratified sample
    (c) Quota sample
    (d) All of the above
20. Field study is related to:
    (a) Experiment situation
    (b) Real life situation
    (c) Laboratory situation
    (d) None of these
21. Hypothesis refers to:
    (a) The outcome of an experiment
    (b) A conclusion drawn from an experiment
    (c) A form of bias in which the subject tries to outguess the experimenter
    (d) A tentative statement about the relationship
22. Statistics is used by researchers to:
    (a) Analyse the empirical data collected in a study
    (b) Make their findings sound better
    (c) Operationally define their variables
    (d) Ensure the study comes out the way it was intended
23. A literature review requires:
    (a) Planning
    (b) Good and clear writing
    (c) Lot of rewriting
    (d) All of the above

24. A literature review is based on the assumption that:
    (a) Copy from the work of others
    (b) Knowledge accumulates and learns from the work of others
    (c) Knowledge dis-accumulates
    (d) None of the above option
25. Conducting surveys is the most common method of generating:
    (a) Primary data
    (b) Secondary data
    (c) Qualitative data
    (d) None of the above
26. After identifying the important variables and establishing the logical reasoning in theoretical framework, the next step in the research process is:
    (a) To conduct surveys
    (b) To generate the hypothesis
    (c) To focus group discussions
    (d) To use experiments in an investigation
27. The appropriate analytical technique is determined by:
    (a) The research design
    (b) Nature of the data collected
    (c) Nature of the hypothesis
    (d) Both (a) and (b)
28. A list of questions which is handed over to the respondent, who reads the questions and records the answers himself is known as the:
    (a) Interview schedule
    (b) Questionnaire
    (c) Interview guide
    (d) All of the given options
29. One of the most critical stages in the survey research process is:
    (a) Research design
    (b) Questionnaire design
    (c) Interview design
    (d) Survey design
30. The number of questionnaires returned or completed divided by the total number of eligible people who were contacted or asked to participate in the survey is called the:
    (a) Response rate
    (b) Participation rate
    (c) Inflation rate
    (d) None of the given options
31. Randomisation of test units is a part of ....
    (a) Pretest
    (b) Post-test
    (c) Matching
    (d) Experiment
32. All of the following are true statements about action research, except;
    (a) Data are systematically analysed
    (b) Data are collected systematically
    (c) Results are generalisable
    (d) Results are used to improve practice
33. Which of the following is characteristic of action research?
    (a) Variables are tightly controlled
    (b) Results are generalisable
    (c) Data are usually qualitative
    (d) Results demonstrate cause-and-effect relationships

34. Exploratory research addresses which of the following types of question?
    (a) If
    (b) How
    (c) Why
    (d) What
35. A variable that is presumed to cause a change in another variable is known as:
    (a) Discontinuous variable
    (b) Dependent variable
    (c) Independent variable
    (d) Intervening variable
36. Which of the following is the opposite of a variable?
    (a) An extraneous variable
    (b) A dependent variable
    (c) A data set
    (d) A constant
37. Which one of the following sets is the measure of central tendency?
    (a) Mean, standard deviation, mode
    (b) Mean, median, standard deviation
    (c) Arithmetic mean, median, mode
    (d) Standard deviation, internal validity, mode
38. A measure is reliable if it provides consistent _____.
    (a) Hypothesis
    (b) Results
    (c) Procedure
    (d) Sensitivity
39. The interview in which questions are already prepared is called _____.
    (a) Telephonic interview
    (b) Personal interview
    (c) Unstructured interview
    (d) Structured interview
40. The numerical description that describe sample may be expected to differ from those that describe population because of random fluctuations inherent in sampling process.
    (a) Sampling design
    (b) Non-probability sampling
    (c) Sampling error
    (d) Probability sampling
41. In _____ each population element has a known and equal chance of selection.
    (a) Purposive sampling
    (b) Quota sampling
    (c) Stratified sampling
    (d) Simple random sampling
42. _____ is the evidence that the instrument, techniques, or process used to measure concept does indeed measure the intended concepts.
    (a) Reliability
    (b) Replicability
    (c) Scaling
    (d) Validity
43. A review of the literature prior to formulating research questions allows the researcher to do which of the following?
    (a) To become familiar with prior research on the phenomenon of interest
    (b) To identify potential methodological problems in the research area
    (c) To develop a list of pertinent problems relative to the phenomenon of interest
    (d) All of the above

44. Which one of the following are types of research design?
    (a) Exploratory Research Design
    (b) Descriptive research design
    (c) Both (a) and (b)
    (d) None of the above
45. A measure is reliable if it provides consistent _____.
    (a) Hypothesis
    (b) Results
    (c) Procedure
    (d) Sensitivity
46. The researcher must be concerned about the following problems while using secondary data in research:
    (a) Validity
    (b) Reliability
    (c) Both of above
    (d) None of these
47. The sampling technique in which every element of the population has an equal, non-zero probability of being selected in a sample, is called:
    (a) Probability sampling
    (b) Convenience sampling
    (c) Purposive sampling
    (d) Quota sampling
48. A researcher wants to conduct a survey of the drug users. Which type of sampling technique will be most appropriate here?
    (a) Sequential sampling
    (b) Snowball sampling
    (c) Quota sampling
    (d) Convenience sampling
49. When there is a need to apply different data collection methods to different parts of the population, the best sampling method would be:
    (a) Double sampling
    (b) Cluster sampling
    (c) Stratified random sampling
    (d) Systematic random sampling
50. While terminating the interview, the fieldworker should not do one of the following:
    (a) record all the responses made by the interviewee before leaving
    (b) thank the interviewee
    (c) close the interview hastily
    (d) answer all the questions the respondent asks concerning the nature and purpose of the study

Answers

1. (c)	2. (d)	3. (d)	4. (c)	5. (d)	6. (b)	7. (d)	8. (d)
9. (b)	10. (b)	11. (a)	12. (b)	13. (c)	14. (c)	15. (d)	16. (a)
17. (c)	18. (b)	19. (c)	20. (b)	21. (d)	22. (a)	23. (d)	24. (b)
25. (a)	26. (b)	27. (d)	28. (b)	29. (b)	30. (a)	31. (d)	32. (c)
33. (c)	34. (d)	35. (c)	36. (d)	37. (c)	38. (b)	39. (d)	40. (c)
41. (d)	42. (d)	43. (d)	44. (c)	45. (b)	46. (c)	47. (a)	48. (b)
49. (c)	50. (c)						

Case Studies

Case Study 1

Gauri just gazed ahead as she saw Shreya leaving her cabin.

This was the fourth resignation in this fortnight. She tried to know from Shreya her reasons for resigning when everything seemed to be going on smoothly. Shreya just mentioned that she was finding it difficult to maintain healthy balance between her family and professional responsibilities. Earlier in the week, Jay had also put in his papers saying that he intended to join another organisation. Jay and Shreya were both good performers in the organization. She had heard of late that in general the employees were feeling very low on account of work pressures and related issues. Last month Akash had joined on a good rise in the competitor's firm.

She had also heard of many others exploring opportunities elsewhere. Meanwhile, a new entrant had joined the organisation recently on a very high grade than some of his present colleagues, reasons cited as being related to the top management. Something was amiss! Gauri was determined to go into depth about the entire issue and find a solution.

Give a detailed outline of how Gauri should go about?

Case Study 2

Ruby's New Responsibilities

Ruby is wondering whether this is the promotion she yearned for!

Ruby has been assistant manager with the department for the last five years and has been a good performer throughout. She is confident and also shares a good rapport with her subordinates who are capable and experienced. A couple of months back she got promoted as manager.

Today, Ruby is apprehensive whether she is really fit for the role? Her workday seems to be unending. She is busy assigning work and reviewing results. To add to it, there is a constant flow of visitors and phone calls to be answered. In the evening, she is tied up with administrative matters such as reading and answering mail, preparing budgets when earlier it was her time to relax.

Not able to take it any longer, she invited her friend Sania, to join her for Sunday lunch. Ruby told Sania she had something important to talk to her about. At lunch, she told Sania that she was thinking of giving up her manager's position as she just could not handle a career of working almost sixty hours a week. Sania listened and then said there might be another way. She suggested Ruby that the issue could be solved if they could review Ruby's time utilisation pattern. She asked Ruby to describe her typical weekly schedule and also asked some questions. Consider Ruby's situation and answer the following questions:

1. Why Ruby has to spend so much time in assigning work and reviewing results when her staff is supposed to be capable and experienced?
2. Who are the visitors and how can they be handled?
3. In what ways could Ruby gain more control over her time?
4. How can Ruby make best use of delegation here?

Case Study 3

Tata Nano - Marching Ahead

The Tata Group has set a benchmark in the world of automobiles by introducing the small ca with high technology – Tata Nano world's cheapest car of rupees 1 lakhs. The launch of the small car by Tata Motors has been a defining moment in the history of India's automotive industry.

Personal transport is an issue of concern in a fast developing country like India, and personal transport has become a big issue, especially since mass transport is often not available or is of poor quality. To answer the difficulties faced by the typical middle class Indian families commuting on a two wheeler with children in tow, the Tata Group came up with the idea of Tata Nano and the project to create a 1 lakh rupee car began in 2003, under the Chairman of Tata Motors, Ratan Tata. The strategy behind the project was the awareness of the number of Indian families who had two wheeled transport, but couldn't afford a four wheel car.

The company reinvented and minimised the manufacturing process, brought in innovative product design, and asked component manufacturers to look in a different perspective to produce logical and simple solutions. The attention to detail paid off: When the car rolled onto the dais at the Auto Show in New Delhi in January, and Ratan Tata stepped out of the driver's seat with ease, it made an immediate impact. What shook the automobile world most was the fact that the designers seem to have done the impossible: The sleek, sophisticated Nano did not look flimsy or inexpensive.

For the next three years, the Tata Group was applauded for innovation as the two wheeler owner could now upgrade to a comfortable four wheeler.

Customer Response

The customer expectations even at the bottom end are rising. According to the Four wheeler total Satisfaction Survey, the owners of Tata Nano expect more in terms of design and better servicing and has low rankings in terms of customer satisfaction.

Launching of NANO Diesel, CNG and Tata Nano 800: Continuing on with the trend setting, the Nano now marches forward with the vision of introducing a diesel version of the Tata Nano. The diesel powered small cars are expected to have good driveability and produce lesser CO_2 emissions than equivalent petrol motors. Also, plans are to roll out Tata Nano CNG and 800 in the near future.

Competitors on the Go: Observing the success of Tata Nano, player like the Renault - Nissan are planning to come up with similar low end, small cars in competition to Tata Nano.

Consider the given situation and answer the following questions:
1. What customer driven research would be important in this case?
2. Suggest the plan of research that the Tata group should follow to find the customers perceptions regarding the diesel version of the car.
3. Is customer satisfaction survey of Tata car owners is desired to be conducted in the city of Pune, suggest the details of how you would conduct it?

Case Study 4

Jones' Fast Food

Jones' Fast Food is a western style fast food outlet in Pune. Started eight years ago, the joint has seen a steady increase in the clientele and today it is a popular hangout in Pune. It has multiple branches spread out around the city and well patronised by the young and old alike.

The joint is famous for medium crusts with generous toppings that make for filling meals. They have offerings like Chicken Tikka, Mutton Mazza and Keema, Onion Blossom, Hot Pepper Passion which comes with three types of chilli pepper. Choice of fresh offerings like Garden Salad, Island Green Salad. Now they are considering introducing a variety of pastas and add-ons like Parmesan breadsticks and cheese sticks.

The owner of Jones' Fast Food wants to know the preferences of his customers regarding the new variety of pasta to be launched.

1. How should he go about?
2. Suggest the method of sampling and data collection to be used.

Case Study 5

Chaos at Suvidha

Suvidha hotel is located in a medium sized, tourism based town in the Gujarat. Rohan is the General Manager of Suvidha Hotel and has been in his current position for three month, rising from position of front desk Assistant to Assistant manager, and manager. He is good at screening potential employees for his front desk area of the hotel because he realizes the importance of that area of the hotel, especially in tourist areas. Recently the management has appointed Meena as HR Manager after she was facing some problems with the front of desk area staff. Meena being from a different department finds it difficult to coordinate and is busy trying to get hang of the things there. Also, it has come to the notice that customers are treated badly by some new and poorly trained employees, and the departments of the hotel do not communicate very effectively and therefore everyone blames everyone else when things go wrong. Rohan would like to find effective solution to Meena's problem.

1. What should Rohan do?
2. He wants to find detailed reasons for the customer's complaints,
3. Suggest a proper plan for above

Projects/Tasks/Activities

1. The owners of retails outlets in several shopping malls of Pune are facing a severe problem of shrinkages. Visit the different retail outlets and carry out a detailed study focusing on:
   (a) Nature of businesses/outlets
   (b) Sources of shrinkage
   (c) Measures for loss prevention
   (d) Research Plan of the study – sampling, data collection, questionnaire/interview/observation etc

2. 'Care and Cure' is a famous multi-speciality hospital in Kolhapur and has a panel of renowned specialist doctors giving the best of services to the patients. Recently the hospital administration is facing a lot of complaints from the patients and their relatives regarding different issues like the facilities, services, care etc. You as a researcher, are approached to conduct a detailed study of the patients and others concerned regarding the nature of the complaints, the problems faced, suggestions and desired facilities, of the concerned persons.
   (a) How would you approach the problem?
   (b) Discuss the different angles that you would probe into.

3. AMUL, a dairy cooperative from Gujarat is a brand managed by the Gujarat Co-operative Milk Marketing Federation Ltd. (GCMMF), which today is jointly owned by 3 million milk producers in Gujarat. Amul is attributed for India's White Revolution which made the country the world's largest producer of milk and milk products. Amul has established itself as the largest food brand in India and has also ventured into markets overseas. Recently, AMUL has forayed into direct retailing through "Amul Utterly Delicious" parlours in major cities of India. These parlours sell all the range of AMUL products. After the launch of these Amul Parlours, AMUL management is interested in finding out details like,
   (a) Customers experience with this new model of AMUL?
   (b) What are their preferred products when they shop here?
   You as a consultant are approached to carry out the project. Prepare the different steps that you would take to undertake this project.

4. A major university has launched its Executive MBA program which is designed in keeping with the current requirements of the industry. It has received a good response from the executives majorly. The university seeks to expand this offering of the program and wants to identify strategies for expansion of enrolment. Suggest the steps to be taken.

Research Methodology   Projects/Tasks/Activities

5. Mr. Shastri is a vendor of human resource management systems and supplies the software EXCELHR - which is HRIS - human resource information system i.e. software solution for small to mid-sized businesses to help automate and manage their HR, payroll, management and accounting activities. Mr. Shastri has over 5000 customers in the whole of Maharashtra. In order to improve the overall performance of the software, he has approached you for carrying out a survey on the implementation and feedback of this system. The information desired is from the users of this software regarding the implementation issues, the pattern of usage, the modules used, the problems faced, the price, the training needs etc. Prepare a research design on the following:
    (a) The key objectives of the study
    (b) The sampling plan
    (c) The tentative questionnaire
    (d) The operational design of the study.

6. A Credit Card company is interested in identifying the different dimensions of credit card usage by women executives in the city of Pune. Prepare a questionnaire both for the users and non-users to find the information regarding the nature of usage and also reasons for not using (from non-users) credit cards.

7. Over the past one year the Golden advertising agency has been experiencing a high turnover rate throughout the agency with regard to employees leaving the agency. This turnover rate affects retiring employees as well as those employees seeking other employment. Management's main question is why are the employees leaving and what can be done to decrease the number of employees leaving the agency? Prepare a suitable plan of study.

8. Prepare a suitable questionnaire to elicit information regarding the usage of Facebook among the youth in the age group of 16-22 years covering the different aspects involved. How would you approach the respondents? What measures can you suggest for maximum response to this questionnaire?

9. The owner of a well known gymnasium is interested in collecting the feedback of its customers regarding the gym equipments, facilities, schemes, ambience, trainers etc. The customer base at present is about 3000. How should the above study be planned? Prepare a research plan for the same and also draft a questionnaire covering the different questions.

10. The manufacturer of a car intends to introduce a new variant of cars targeted especially for the ladies. He needs to know the detailed inputs regarding the preferences regarding usage, suggestions on interiors, automatic transmission, etc.

Research Methodology   Projects/Tasks/Activities

   (a) How would you design the plan?
   (b) Give different details about the aspects to be covered.
   (c) What will be your population and sample?
   (d) How will you identify and approach the respondents?
11. Design a suitable questionnaire to collect information regarding customer satisfaction of Tata Nano car owners.
12. Mobile Number Portability (MNP) is a facility which allows a customer to move from one service provider to another while retaining existing mobile number. MNP is applicable for porting between mobile operators only, in the same telecom Circle. A telecom services provider is experiencing severe decline in the subscriber base of its customers. The management is desperate to know the reasons for subscriber switching to a different service provider. You are appointed to find the reasons and suggest suitable measures. How will you plan the task?

EXERCISES

Distinguish Between:
   (a) Census survey and sample survey
   (b) Exploratory studies and case study method
   (c) Deductive and Inductive Theory
   (d) Primary data and secondary data
   (e) Research Question and Investigation Question
   (f) Rating scales and ranking scales
   (g) Validity and Reliability
   (h) Probability sampling and non-probability sampling
   (i) Quota sampling and stratified sampling
   (j) Parametric tests and non-parametric tests
   (k) Type – I error and type – II error
   (l) Historical research and case study method
   (m) Schedule and Questionnaire method
   (n) Classification and tabulation of data
   (o) Qualitative and quantitative research design
   (p) Technical and popular reports
   (q) Parametric and non-parametric tests

Research Methodology — Projects/Tasks/Activities

Write Short Notes On:
1. Exploratory research (with examples)
2. Descriptive research (with examples)
3. Deductive theory
4. Experimental research
5. Requisites of a good questionnaire
6. Projective techniques
7. Sampling design
8. Sampling techniques
9. Report writing
10. Limitations of social research
11. Survey method and its limitations
12. Importance of hypothesis
13. Advantages and disadvantages of sampling
14. Merits and demerits of census method
15. Sampling and non-sampling errors
16. Factors determining the size of a sample
17. Precautions to be taken while using secondary data
18. Advantages of sampling over census method
19. Editing of data
20. Classification of data
21. Interpretation of data
22. Steps in report writing
23. Graphical Representation of Data
24. Chi-square test
25. Representative sample
26. Problems in measurement

Design Suitable Questionnaires:
1. To study the mode of commutation of employees of a factory.
2. To study the pattern of annual expenditure, saving and investment of 500 middle class persons.
3. To study the spending habits of students.
4. To study the relationship between browsing on the internet and sleeping hours of the students.
5. To know the causes for the decline in business of a fast food joint.

www.ingramcontent.com/pod-product-compliance
Lightning Source LLC
Chambersburg PA
CBHW081301170426
43198CB00017B/2869